CLEAR WORD AND THIRD SIGHT

NEW`AMERICANISTS

A Series Edited by Donald E. Pease

Catherine A. John

CLEAR
WORD
AND
THIRD
SIGHT

Folk Groundings and Diasporic Consciousness in

African Caribbean Writing

University of the West Indies Press

Jamaica · Barbados · Trinidad and Tabago

PR
9205.05
.J64
2003

Of the African slave trade,

some of the elders in Cuba say that

our being brought here was necessary

for the development of Western civilization.

Our music, our agriculture, our dance,

our language, and cultural expression.

May the blood of the ancestors

reclaim us.

Contents

Acknowledgments

This book grew out of my 1997 dissertation, entitled "The Haunting Past and the Production of Racial Subjects: Contemporary Afro-Caribbean Women's Writing." I would like to thank all those who helped to make both the original project and the current one possible. First and foremost I would like to thank my parents, for their emotional and financial support in graduate school and beyond, and to thank my sister, Julia "Spratty" John, for all the "groundings." Immense thanks to my Duke editor, Reynolds Smith, and Sharon Torian, editorial assistant. Thanks to my research assistant, Yaisa Guillory, who came through in the eleventh hour, making the impossible seem possible. Thanks also to my original dissertation faculty and graduate student colleagues back in Santa Cruz—Akasha Gloria Hull, Kristin Ross, James Clifford, Michael Cowan, Susan Gilman, Martha Bonilla, Carla Scott, Suran Thrift, Kamari Clarke, Jon Hunt, Judith Haas, Gordon Bigelow, and Clarence Robertson—and to some of the friends in California who helped to keep me sane by providing a haven outside of academia: Shawn Fong, Kelvin Burton, Howard, Millie and Lisa Francis, Fitima Morris, Melinda Palacio, and Steve Yao, as well as Warren and Sharon Bailey. I am grateful also to the Santa Barbara crew at the Department and Center for Black Studies for a year's worth of dissertation fellowship and intellectual engagement. Those folks include Charles Long, Marti Adams, Houston Roberson, Gerard Pigeon, Claudine Michel, Joanne Madison, Avery Gordon, Crystal Griffiths, Stephanie Han, and Francoise Cromer. I would like to thank various friends and scholars whose conversations helped to shape my ideas: Erna Brodber, Rupert Lewis, Paget Henry, Carole Boyce Davies, Michael West, Sylvia Wynter, Nadie Edwards, Belinda

Edmondson, Faith Smith, Lois Brown, and Katy Ryan. I would like especially to thank Greg Thomas, for conversations that laid the foundation for an entirely new way of approaching African diaspora culture and thought.

Of crucial importance in terms of shaping the shift in my ideas from the dissertation to this book was the dialogue I had with people in various communities, as well as the ideas inspired by students in various courses that I taught at the University of Oklahoma. I would like to thank specifically some of those students: Imani Johnson, Jeremy Johnson, Aaron Jackson, Patrice Williams, Samarla Dillon, Amber Jackson, Stephanie Brown, Walter Funches, Angie Nguyen, Jose Gonzalez, Aaron Carpenter, Stephen Butler, Andrew Haskins, David Harris, Rickey Bates, Bryan Pepper, Anne Cunningham, and Doug Rippy. My thanks also go out to University of Oklahoma faculty such as Betty Harris, Agymah Kamau, Robert Warrior, Vince Leitch, Catherine Hobbs, Susan Kates, Dan Cottom, and Rita Kerezstesi, not to mention Vinay Dharwadker at the University of Wisconsin, Madison, for his shrewd advice and extremely generous professional support early on.

Finally, to my Oklahoma family—Aunt Helen and Scotty, Donnette Brown, Dorscine Littles, Leslie Rankin-Hill, to Abimbola and Abiola Asojo, thanks for exposing me to Nigerian culture. To Amelia Marie Adams, and Briian Newhouse and family—big up! To the African Diaspora Links Crew for the cultural bashment nites, dancehall vibes, and for keeping the rudegirl spirit alive. To Changa Masomakali for being in the right place at the right time and helping me to develop third sight. To Akimi and Anurath Yessoufou for the Yoruba lessons, hair braiding, and exposure to the culture of Benin. Nuff respec' out to Baba Ifayomi and Ile Egbe Eegunjobi (the Ifa community in Dallas, Texas), as well as Egunwale Fagbenro and Omowale Si Ifa (the Ifa community in Tulsa, Oklahoma). Your spiritual support was immense and sustaining. To Dr. Erna Brodber, Ms. Pearl Crossman, Nya, Lennox "Melanik" Boyd, Tiffany Gillette and family, Shango and family, and all those from the Rastafari and grassroots community in Woodside, Jamaica, I thank you for bringing peace and a sense of home back into my life. To my aunts and uncles in Jamdown, as well as my extended family of brother- and sister-cousins throughout the diaspora, thanks for the sustaining positive energy. To Mr. Hercules and the Phills family, as well as my extended family in St. Vincent—thanks for re-introducing me to my father's land. To Glenroy Phills—may we

Acknowledgments

work together to restore my maternal great-grandmother's house in Chapelton, Jamaica, and my paternal grandmother's house in Brighton, St. Vincent. Thanks to Merle Hodge and the late Toni Cade Bambara, both of whom I was fortunate enough to meet briefly. Your fiction and critical essays shaped my consciousness as a scholar and more fundamentally as a Black woman. Jah bless!

Introduction

Rock speaks a rooster language
And the light is broken
Clear.

—AUDRE LORDE

The first chapter of Jamaican writer Erna Brodber's 1994 novel *Louisiana* is entitled "I Heard a Voice from Heaven Say." The chapter opens with these lines:

Anna do you remember? Can you still hear me singing it?

It is the voice I hear
The gentle voice I hear
That calls me home?
(9)

As the novel begins, the speaker, a spirit, recalls to her friend Anna the song that was sung at her funeral. The song called her home—to the other side, to heaven, to Zion, to Africa, to wherever the spirit travels after physical death. Describing the process to her friend, the spirit narrator continues, "And the singing. Vox populi. *I hear the voice, the gentle voice.* Is the voice of God. *That calls me home*" (10). The singing at the funeral serves a high spiritual purpose. It is not an empty ritual: it is nothing short of *the voice of God*, channeled through the singers to help the soul of the deceased transition to another place.

The last chapter of Brodber's novel, "Den Ah Who Seh Sammy Dead," is titled after the popular Jamaican folksong "Sammy Dead." Carrying the notion of spiritual survival to the novel's end, Brodber's resignification of the folksong coincides with the protagonist's own transition to a higher realm, while continuing to reinforce the connection between music and spiritual consciousness. What Brodber manages to do in this novel—by linking the spirit to the song, the voice, and the life-giving power of the word (*"I heard a voice from Heaven say"*)—is to tap into a profoundly felt but deeply unspeakable aspect of African diaspora consciousness.

Consider, for example, the close of Trinidadian writer Earl Lovelace's short story "Joebell and America," in which the gangsta-stylizing Joebell is arrested after a fraudulent attempt to impersonate an "American" and migrate to the United States. As he is being arrested after his unsuccessful performance of cultural mimicry, he says, "I might as well take my losses like a West Indian, like a Trinidadian. I decide to sing" (124). At the moment of struggle and deep tribulation, the song is invoked.

Song functions for the African diaspora subject in both the Brodber and Lovelace instances as the sign and substance of an alternate mode of consciousness. It is a literal strategy of survival, in which the exclusively rational mode of "modern" Western consciousness has reached its metaphysical limitations and something else must step in to save the individual from psychospiritual death. Within both continental African and African diaspora contexts, a strong oral tradition, characterized by folktales, folksongs, poems, and music, is almost always featured as a predominant trait of these cultures. Yet the questions of why and how these oral forms serve these communities on the deepest level is less frequently tackled. As the selections from these two African Caribbean writers, Brodber and Lovelace, demonstrate, these oral characteristics speak to a realm in which the strongest and most empowering aspects of who we are collectively as a people is maintained. The song, the folktale, and the poem function as an alternate register of consciousness, one that at its most profound seems to connect to ancestral knowledge in both conscious and unconscious ways.

One could also argue that "dance" represents another aspect of this alternate realm of consciousness, and maybe this is why we in the diaspora, no matter how many centuries removed from our origins in Africa, do not treat dancing or the rhythm of the drum lightly. It is almost as if, somewhere in the collective unconscious of even the most "modern" mind, there is the memory of a time when dancing was a sacred rather than simply secular activity.

In the last twenty years, within the context of academically produced intellectual discourse, increasingly heated exchanges have occurred concerning the notion of "authenticity" as it relates to definitions of culture and cultural identity. These debates have become most heated around two discursive practices related to Blackness, characterized as "Afrocentric" or "African-centered," on one hand, and "antiessentialist" or "hybrid," on the other. While "culture" in African-centered discourse is by and large exemplified by an imperative toward cultural cohesion, "hybrid" and "antiessentialist" discourses tend to emphasize the incomplete and unfinished nature of all identities; to imagine "wholeness," in this context, is seen as a fiction parading as truth. My hope in this book is to show that striving for a conception of wholeness and cohesion is a cultural characteristic that can be traced throughout some of the most profound aspects of African Caribbean and African diaspora writings. It appears to have been a sustaining feature of Black life in the diaspora, functioning hand in hand with the impulse to survive trauma and genocide.

In his 1988 book, *The Predicament of Culture,* James Clifford takes the title of his introduction, "The Pure Products Go Crazy," from the first lines of a celebrated poem by William Carlos Williams. Quoting the poem at length to demonstrate how Williams, a young white male physician, "finds himself off center among scattered traditions," Clifford argues that this short poem epitomizes "modernity[,] since the condition of rootlessness and mobility is an increasingly common fate" (3). The crucial lines read:

> Devil-may-care men who have taken
> to railroading
> out of sheer lust for adventure—
> and young slatterns, bathed
> in filth
> from Monday to Saturday
> to be tricked out that night
> with gauds
> *from imaginations which have no*
> *peasant traditions to give them*
> *character*
> but flutter and flaunt

sheer rags—succumbing without
emotion
save numbed terror.
(*Predicament of Culture,* 2, italics mine)

Clifford situates his analysis of Williams's poem within the context of a critique of Western anthropology's ethnographic practices and historical claims to know "the other." He juxtaposes the poem and the "modern" rootlessness of the speaker's perspective with the claims of cultural identity made by the descendants of Wampanoag Indians, described by Clifford as speaking a "New England–accented English" and living in Mashpee, Massachusetts. It is within this context that Clifford asks the questions "Who has the authority to speak for a group's identity or authenticity? What are the essential elements and boundaries of a culture?" (7–8).

Keeping his critique more or less focused on the collapse of Western, universalizing master narratives and the transgressive nature of the white gaze, which attempts to name and quantify the racialized "other," Clifford uses the poem to suggest that the Westerner can no longer speak for various "natives." The questions of who these "natives" culturally are, however, and who among them has the right to speak on behalf of the collective are seen by Clifford as still pending and pursuable. Clifford, at a reflective moment in his own narrative, honestly states, "We are not all together in Williams' car" (7). I would like to argue that, despite expanding the contours of the critique of Western anthropology's relationship to indigenous cultures, "the predicament of culture" described by Clifford is peculiar to the "postmodern" cultural situation of the European intellectual, still adrift in bankrupt master narratives tied to imperialist traditions. This "where to go from here" predicament, while not absent from non-European cultural contexts, is much more characteristic of the white Western subject than it is of peoples who have historically suffered aggressive racial and cultural oppression and who are the descendants of peoples who identify with non-Western stories of origins.

In William Carlos Williams's modernist piece, the crisis of identity and the unreliability of older narratives is made clear by phrases such as "imaginations which have no / peasant traditions to give them / character" and "succumbing without / emotion / save numbed terror" (*Predicament of Culture,* 2). This notion of "terror" that seems to increase as "white" things fall apart has long been depicted and documented by Black writers, and of late also by scholars in the up-and-coming arena of "whiteness studies." The Caribbean scholar Kenneth Ramchand, in an article titled "Terrified Consciousness," takes the concept from Frantz Fanon's chapter "On Violence" in *The Wretched of the Earth* to discuss how the terror of the white Creole slave-owning class increased as the Black population moved toward freedom. Representing the consciousness of the other side, and the existence of "peasant traditions that give a people character," Earl Lovelace states:

> The presentation of the history of African people in the Caribbean suggests that they were slaves—almost acquiescing in their enslavement—and then ex-slaves, as though, having ceased to be slaves, their ex-slavehood became their nationality; they weren't thought of as Africans. But when I look at history, I see the Africans not as slaves in a passive sense, but as *enslaved;* the central theme of their existence was a struggle against enslavement. (Jaggi, "Interview with Earl Lovelace," 25)

Earl Lovelace's portrait of the cultural psyche is quite different from Clifford's; it's an immediate reminder that "culture" means distinctly different things, depending on a group's experience of history. Lovelace's characterization implies and describes a people whose previous identities were systematically crushed and denied, but whose survival depended on their ability to both resist and remember. In this context, "culture" is, among other things, the thing that will help you to survive. Thus "culture" is an affirmative set of beliefs and practices, since —as Audre Lorde tells us in her poem "A Litany for Survival"—we were never meant to survive.

By contrast, in another interview, the Caribbean writer Jamaica Kincaid states:

> [T]here were Africans who had remained in Africa and there were Africans who were descended from slaves. I was descended from slaves. . . . It's not exactly the ancestral family you hope for, you know, the founding member of your family is a captured person. . . . This was very sobering. I came back and I thought, well, I'm just nobody. In this world I live in, I'm nobody, and its quite fine with me. I choose that. I'm not African, I'm not anything. In fact, I have the blood of quite a few different people running around inside me, but I don't claim them. This is dead. I'm now. (Dilger, "Jamaica Kincaid Talks to Gerhard Dilger," 24)

Jamaica Kincaid's and Lovelace's views represent the range of reactions that Black people in the diaspora may hold in relation to their historical experiences, but Kincaid's position is self-admittedly a defeated one, in which she claims to speak for herself rather than "the tribe." Her statements don't speak to the spirit of survival that has characterized African diaspora cultures as a whole. When Lovelace invokes the term "culture," it is implicitly overdetermined by positive characteristics: "the thing" that would destroy the spirit is not described as "culture" but as something else. When Clifford invokes the term "culture" it is seen as an ideologically neutral category, which may or may not have combinations of positive and negative historic associations. The term is also primarily used to describe the exterior form rather than the interior content of a thing. Thus in the post-Clifford cultural studies arena the surface loss of African languages, rituals, and practices are held as proof of the de-Africanization of the Black subject in the diaspora, while internal consciousness, patterns of thought, and the philosophical worldview are understudied and underestimated as powerfully determining transnational aspects of identity.

This struggle over how to talk about the formerly colonized, specifically Black subject is significantly raised in the self-described "anti-essentialist" discourses of Black British cultural studies critics Paul Gilroy and Stuart Hall. Gilroy situates his analyses of race first and foremost within the context of critiques of white nationalist, racially pure discourses of British cultural sensibility. Drawing on Clifford's theories of travel, toward demonstrating how "the pure products go crazy," in his article "Cultural Studies and Ethnic Absolutism," Gilroy explores British scholar Raymond Williams's analyses of "English cultural sensibility." He shows that this sensibility was "not produced spontaneously from [its] own internal and intrinsic dynamics but generated in a complex pattern of antagonistic relationships with the external, supra-national, and imperial world" (190). Similarly, Stuart Hall in his 1992 essay "What Is This 'Black' in Black Popular Culture?" begins by criticizing "European models of high culture" (21). The crux of Hall's argument in this piece centers on what he calls "the end of the innocent notion of an essential Black subject" (32). He speaks instead of "the production of new identities . . . the appearance of new subjects on the political and cultural stage" (25). Gilroy, in his introduction to the 1993 text *The Black Atlantic,* cites and echoes Hall's views and goes on to say: "The ontological essentialist view has often been characterized by a brute pan-Africanism. It has proved unable to specify precisely where the highly prized but doggedly evasive essence of Black artistic and political sensibility is currently located, but that is no obstacle to its popular circulation" (*The Black Atlantic,* 31).

In the work of both writers, a critique is made of aspects of contemporary Black cultural politics seen as the other side of white exclusivity and notions of purity. Gilroy's critique of "English cultural sensibility" as not produced solely by "its own internal and intrinsic dynamics" is clearly the mirror for his criticisms of what he calls "absolutist" aspects of Black U.S. cultural politics. He states as much when he says that "much of the precious intellectual legacy claimed by African-American intellectuals as the substance of their particularity is in fact only partly their absolute ethnic property" (*The Black Atlantic,* 15).

Yet the belief that "absolute" or even "essentialist" Black cultural politics are the other side of racist notions of conservative white culture is deeply flawed. If the historically different circumstances that produced both discourses are not to be elided, then great care has to be taken in discussing discursive practices that, even at their worst, are *reactions* to racist and imperialist violence as opposed to ideology formed from a spiritually bankrupt metaphysical order. In her 1987 keynote address at the "Journey across Three Continents Film Festival," Black U.S. scholar Toni Cade Bambara states:

> A classical people demand a classical art . . . classical in the sense [that] the people, the work, are informed by our origins, our precedents, our prospects, and are centered in the understanding that all great art is derived from the folk. For while we may feel compelled by circumstance to fashion new forms, new idioms, new modes, new genres, they are bound to be compatible with, centered in, and informed by the very old truth-speaking traditions from the ancient mother culture: the fables, the parables . . . as in mama say, "Don't let your mouth get you into what your backside can't stand." (8)

Rather than claiming a cultural sensibility that is produced solely by its own "internal and intrinsic dynamics," Bambara first and foremost shows that the old "ancient mother culture" always informs the best aspects of the new. Instead of calling for the "production of new identities" that will replace what Hall refers to as binary, "mutually opposed either/or's," Bambara is focused on the interiority of the Black culture she is describing, rather than its oppositional relationship to imperialist discourse. Within this context, unlike in Hall's analysis, the old is connected to the new in a cyclical, circular fashion, as opposed to being another linear departure announcing itself as progress.

Bambara continued her address with almost seamless exposure of the type of vulgar critique espoused by Gilroy when he speaks of "a brute pan-Africanism [that is] unable to specify precisely where the highly prized but doggedly evasive essence of Black artistic and political sensibility is currently located":

> [An art] classical in the sense that the people and the work are co-herent. That is to say, that the insights and impulses that give rise to our expression are made appropriable, apprehendable, usable, sensi-ble through metaphors and patterns that are familiar to us from every-day occurrence, rituals, ceremonies, tradition, spiritual practice. . . . And classical, too, in the sense that "it matters." That it's sustaining; that the work makes a difference between feeling disabled and en-abled, between feeling invisible and indelible. It is the difference be-tween feeling mute or being very much in voice. (8)

Here, Black artistic sensibility is explained in relation to the rituals of everyday life, while the functional nature of this art seems to be of the highest spiritual order when Bambara describes it as sustaining, enabling, and empowering. Once again, the differences between Clifford's and Kincaid's versus Lovelace's notions of culture are re-played in the differences between Gilroy's and Hall's versus Bam-bara's. This genealogy of culture and cultural expression, exemplified by Bambara and Lovelace, is at its best when it is providing the artist and his or her community with spiritually sustaining, functional forms of resistance art. The struggle between these competing eth-oses in the contemporary terrain can be intellectually contextualized in relation to the philosophical struggle, a generation earlier, over the racial and cultural history of ancient Egypt.

In January of 1974, UNESCO organized two consecutive sympo-siums in Cairo, as part of a larger attempt to document historical information about continental Africa. The research was eventually compiled into several volumes as a *General History of Africa*, the sec-ond volume of which was devoted to ancient Africa and included papers presented at the 1974 conferences, the "Symposium on the Peopling of Ancient Egypt" and the "The Deciphering of the Meroitic Script." Among the twenty international experts invited to speak on ancient Egypt and the Meroitic Script were Cheikh Anta Diop of Senegal and Theophile Obenga of the Congo. Laying the foundation for contemporary African-centered discourse and scholarship, Diop argued that ancient Egypt was settled by phenotypically Black people from southern regions of Africa who traveled north along the course of the Nile river. In this symposium, the positions of Diop and Obenga were, by and large, opposed by eighteen scholars from Europe as well as other parts of Africa, even though they were well documented. At the end of the symposium, the UNESCO officials in fact singled out these two historians for praise, stating that "although the preparatory working paper sent out by UNESCO gave particulars of what was desired, not all participants had prepared communications comparable with the painstakingly researched contributions of Professors Cheikh Anta Diop and Obenga. There was consequently a real lack of balance in the discussions" (Mokhtar, *Ancient Civilizations of Africa*, 77).

To substantiate his particular claims, Diop drew on evidence from several sources. These included: (1) physical anthropology, (2) reports from Greek and Latin authors describing the Egyptians physically, (3) artistic self-representations from various periods in Egyptian history, (4) biblical evidence, (5) information from Egyptian sources relating to how Egyptians saw themselves, and (6) comparative studies of the similarities between ancient Egyptian and modern African languages.

Diop argued that in their own representations of their history, the Egyptians referred to the Ethiopians as their ancestors. He also linked Leakey's research proving that the oldest human bones were found in Africa to Gloger's laws connecting the evolution of warm-blooded animals in tropical climates to the development of pigmentation. He argued that even after substantial time had passed, tests could be done on pieces of skin found on skeletons to prove the existence of melanin. Lively discussion ensued at the symposium about the genealogy of the term "kemit," meaning "Black" and/or "land of the Blacks." Obenga, in his contribution to the symposium, noted that linguistic similarities also existed among Egyptian, Wolof, and other indigenous African languages, as demonstrated by the similar variations on the meaning and form of the term "kemit" across linguistic contexts.

Since those conferences took place, the reaction to these theories has been strong and vociferous. On the one hand, one school of critics claim that the "race" of the Egyptians, then and now, should not be important. Other critics consistently describe any attempt to document and discuss this period of African history, before colonialism and transatlantic slavery, as recoursing to a mythic and imaginary past that has no significant or tangible bearing on the present. Yet for many continental Africans and their diaspora descendants, establishing historical truth is crucial to the creation of just societies in the present. Further, it is a well-established fact that the misrepresentation of Black history has been consistently used to maintain dominance and oppression over African peoples.

At both symposiums Obenga's analyses of language were hailed as innovative and significant. His argument was summarized by the editor of *Ancient Civilizations of Africa* in these words:

> Before making any comparison, one must be on one's guard against confusing typological linguistic relationship, which gave no clue to the predialectal ancestor common to the languages being compared, and genetic relationship. For example, modern English, considered from the typological point of view, had affinities with Chinese; but, from the genetic point of view, the two languages belonged to distinct language families. . . . Genetic relationship depended on establishing phonetic laws discovered by comparison between morphemes and phonemes of similar languages. On the basis of such morphological, lexicological and phonetic correspondences, one could arrive at common earlier forms. In this way, a theoretical 'Indo-European' language had been reconstructed in the abstract and had been used as an operational model. It was indicative of a common cultural macro-structure shared by languages which subsequently evolved along separate lines. (Mokhtar, *Ancient Civilizations of Africa*, 64)

Obenga's treatment of the issue of language seems of crucial relevance and significance to the philosophical questions of culture that have continued to hold sway. His emphasis on phonetic laws as crucial to establishing language history seems suggestive in terms of the relationship between ancient and contemporary African languages, on the one hand, and indigenous continental languages and the creolized languages that the descendants of enslaved Africans created, on the other. While these creolized "new world" languages have been primarily analyzed in relation to the colonial language groups that provided the outside structure, less attention has been paid to their relationship to indigenous African languages at both the phonetic and idiomatic levels. Whereas this research may be ongoing at the linguistic level, the question remains of not just how formative "old world" languages have been, but more importantly, whether or not the philosophies of culture associated with particular language families are still operative in diaspora contexts. Clearly, therefore, exploring the philosophical worldview of various diaspora peoples is another way to investigate the extent to which cultural identities have been maintained.

The treatment of this relationship is implicitly at stake in the philosophy and writings of the negritude poets explored in this book. Further, the work of the Nigerian female scholars Oyéronké Oyéwumi and Ifi Amadiume, also addressed in this book, directly addresses the importance of paying attention to the relationship between language and culture. Their work suggests that close attention to the worldview and world sense at stake in native African languages can shed light on the way in which gendered particularities on the African continent and in its diaspora differ from the worldview and world sense of mainstream Western societies. My study begins with a reexamination of what was philosophically at stake in the early negritude discourse of Léon Damas, Aimé Césaire, and Léopold Senghor. It ends attempting to assess how and in what ways the essential questions that emerged from those early discussions have continued to have a kind of implicit, unspoken power in African diaspora discourse and writing. A connection is therefore drawn between the questions implicitly raised about collective consciousness in the discourse of the three writers who are considered the fathers of negritude, and a discourse of collective "folk" consciousness implicitly at stake in the work of various Afro-Caribbean writers.

In her analysis of the negritude poetry of Léopold Sédar Senghor, Sylvia Washington Bâ describes the relationship between the notion of "life force," a kind of equivalent to the idea that power is internal, and the privileged position assigned to the word. She states that in the West African context "the word is both expression and creation, and, as such unites poetic creation and reinforcement of life forces" (*The Concept of Negritude*, 63). She describes the poet as someone who "possess[es] the gift of calling forth, or naming a force, an element, or a person and thereby ordering its realization. . . . The creative power of invocation enable[s] the spirit to transcend appearances and circumstances" (64). This description of the sensibility of the word and the philosophical worldview that informs Senghor's work creates an almost seamless theoretical rubric for understanding the later poetry of Audre Lorde and Simone Schwarz-Bart's writings, as well as Paule Marshall's *Praisesong for the Widow*. Senghor's theories and Bâ's explication of them also find a strong parallel in the critical essays of diaspora scholar, intellectual, and writer Zora Neale Hurston. Hurston's extraordinary essay "High John de Conquer," dealing with the folkloric figure of the same name, speaks more profoundly to this notion of 'inside consciousness' and creative power than many a text. In it, Hurston states:

> High John de Conquer came to be a man, and a mighty man at that. . . . [T]he sign of this man was a laugh, and his singing-symbol was a drum-beat. No parading drum-shout like soldiers out for show. It did not call to the feet of those who were fixed to hear it. *It was an inside thing to live by.* It was sure to be heard when and where the work was the hardest, and the lot the most cruel. It helped the slaves endure. They knew that something better was coming. So they laughed in the face of things and *sang*, "I'm so glad! Trouble don't last always." And the white people who heard them were struck dumb that they could laugh. In an outside way, this was Old Massa's fun, so what was Old Cuffy laughing for? . . . He had come from Africa. He came walking on the waves of sound. Then he took on flesh after he got here. . . . It is no accident that High John de Conquer has evaded the ears of white people. They were not supposed to know. You can't know what folks won't tell you. If they, the white people, heard some scraps, they could not understand because they had nothing to hear things like that with. (922–23, italics mine)

This then, this notion of internal knowledge, or inside consciousness, is a kind of third sight or spiritual way of knowing that substantially characterizes aspects of cultural expression on both the continent and in various parts of the Black world.

In the diaspora, once we break free of the Western imperative to think in linear, "progressive" fashion, precolonial and preenslavement ways of knowing become as important as postcolonial and postenslavement systems of knowledge, if not more so. The transcultural significance of the circle in precolonial Africa is suddenly endowed with new meaning. Functioning as a symbol of balance, while being the sign and substance of unity between seemingly disparate philosophical principles, the circle as a symbol is exceptionally important on the African continent and beyond. In the chapter "Slavery and the Circle of Culture," from his text *Slave Culture*, Sterling Stuckey argues:

> The circle is linked to the most important of all African ceremonies, the burial ceremony. From the movement of the sun, Kongo people

derive the circle and its counterclockwise direction in a variety of ways. . . . Coded as a cross . . . the sign of the four moments of the sun is the Kongo emblem of spiritual continuity. . . . In certain rites it is written on the earth, and a person stands upon it to take an oath, or to signify that he or she understands the meaning of life as a process shared with the dead below river or sea. The use of the circle for religious purposes in slavery was so consistent and profound that one could argue that it was what gave form and meaning to Black religion and art. It is understandable that the circle became the chief symbolism of heathenism for missionaries, Black and white, leading them to seek either to alter it or eradicate it altogether. That they failed to do so owes a great deal to Bakongo influence in particular, but values similar to those in Congo-Angola are found among Africans a thousand or more miles away. . . . Thus scholarship is likely to reveal more than we now know about the circle in Africa, drawing West and Central Africa closer together culturally than they were previously thought to be. Wherever in Africa the counterclockwise dance ceremony was performed—it is called the ring shout in North America—the dancing and singing were directed to the ancestors and gods. (12, notes omitted)

Stuckey's analysis of the power of the circle is significant for a variety of reasons. First, it reveals the cross-temporal and spatial impact of this symbol as something that has had a deeply felt impact on various parts of the continent and the diaspora. Second, it shows that respect for the ancestors was combined with respect for the natural environment, as is made clear by the central role of the primary elements of life: air, earth, fire, water. Third, it demonstrates that spiritual continuity encompasses physical life and physical death as part of a natural regenerative order, and in this way, scientific, rational, intuitive, and spiritual forms of knowledge are united. Fourth, the collective nature of this system of knowledge is emphasized, since these rituals require a range of participants to be considered successful. Fifth, and most important, it suggests that a particular kind of metaphysical logic is operative at conscious and unconscious levels for both African and African diaspora peoples. This gives substance to the notion that comparable traditions link Black people as much as, if not more so than, the oppressive experiences of colonialism and slavery.

Scholar Oba T'Shaka quantifies and classifies the kind of knowledge suggested by the significance of the circle, with recourse to aspects of ancient Egyptian philosophy. His analysis makes it clearer and clearer that research into precolonial African systems of knowledge provides a much richer framework for understanding diaspora cultures than systems of knowledge inherited exclusively from colonial and neocolonial institutions:

> African symbolic systems are . . . rich because they are the products of collective wisdom and genius. . . . The Kemetic Mystery System represented the greatest educational achievement known to humanity, during either the ancient or modern period. Under this great system, worthy candidates were initiated into a Sacred Science that encouraged each initiate to achieve self-knowledge, which was conceived as being the basis for all knowledge. Mystery education proceeded by degrees according to the candidate's ability to master his anger, resentment, greed, sexual appetite and other aspects of his lower nature. The mastery of the liberal arts, the social sciences, mathematics, logic, the sciences, astronomy, astrology and music were also designed to enable the candidate to place the lower nature under the control of the intuitive, higher mind. The one injunction repeated over and over again in mystery training was to think before you speak, and think before you act. Rational, intuitive thought and conduct was required of mystery students because intuitive reason was seen as a primary characteristic of the creator. . . . Reason was not to be separated from emotion and intuition; reason was to be synthesized with emotion and intuition, so each person could find her or his own unique path in life. This was very different from the exclusively rationalistic thought systems of the West. The great Kemetic (Egyptian) Mystery System grew out of the earlier Ta-Seti or Ethiopian Mystery System. (*Return to the African Mother Principle,* 95–96)

The notion that this particular system of knowledge is a product of collective rather than individual genius is suggestive. Among other things, this immediately calls to mind the plethora of proverbs from both continental and diaspora contexts which have no author but are referenced with regard to the ethnic community they originate from (e.g., Ashanti, Yoruba, or Jamaican proverbs). Further, the combination of rational and intuitive knowledge that T'Shaka describes provides a rich rubric for pondering the notion of "inside consciousness" referred to by Hurston and demonstrated in diaspora literatures.

T'Shaka moves from discussion of the ancient Egyptian mystery system to a brief but more specific focus on the comparable Dogon mystery system. The Dogon, an ethnic people living in Mali, are said to live by this knowledge system to the current day, having never converted to either Islam or Christianity. "The wisdom of the Dogon

Introduction

is contained in words that consist of four degrees of knowledge" (T'Shaka, *Return to the African Mother Principle*, 96). T'Shaka explicates these four degrees of knowledge in order to suggest the similarity between this system and the rich symbolic traditions that still exist in the diaspora. The four words represent different levels of knowledge. The first word, called *Giri So*, or *fore-word* knowledge. The fore-word represents knowledge that faces you: "It is more obvious and simple than the other levels of knowledge . . . [and] is learned through repeating over and over the symbolic events which gradually lead the initiate to gain a progressively deeper understanding of its meaning." This definition calls to mind the significance of repetition in old spirituals and folksongs, as well as the blues. The second level of knowledge is called *Benne So* or *side-word*. It is less obvious: it "contains more profound explanations of symbolic events . . . than those found in Giri So" (*Return to the African Mother Principle*, 96). *Bolo So* is the *back-word*. It "gives the initiate the opportunity to tie together the three degrees of knowledge. Synthesis is the characteristic of Bolo So." Finally, "the peak of this system of knowledge is the *So Dayi* or *clear-word*" (*Return to the African Mother Principle*, 97): "The clear-word is the highest word revealed to initiates who have spent years mastering the three lower degrees of knowledge—a process that requires the cleansing of the thought, words, and actions so that our words and insight will reflect the eternal wisdom of the soul like a clear word free of blemishes" (97).

In Simone Schwarz-Bart's novel *Pluie et vent sur Télumée Miracle*, several proverbial sayings, handed down to her by various mother figures in the text, function as her philosophical guide throughout her life. The four levels of knowledge in the Dogon mystery system could easily be applied to the process of transformation that Télumée goes through. She learns two key proverbs early on. One tells her to be like a drum with two faces, deflecting the bad energy and internalizing the good; and the other tells her to ride the horse rather than be ridden by the horse, that is, not to make a habit out of sorrow. As a child Télumée learns these proverbs, and her grandmother repeats the lessons of the proverbs in a variety of ways to reinforce their meaning. This seems similar to the Giri So, the first level of knowledge in the Dogon mystery system. At a later point, Télumée begins to synthesize and apply the knowledge of the proverbs, and this strategy allows her to survive the many hardships and tribulations she encounters. She appears then to have achieved the equivalent of the third level of knowledge referred to as Bolo So by the Dogon. At the end of her life, Télumée becomes a creator of proverbs, one who passes on this proverbial wisdom to others. It seems that at this point she is on the brink of a kind of So Dayi or *clear-word* level of knowledge. It is only after enduring and surviving significant tribulations that she arrives at this higher place. After making peace at the novel's close with an evil-minded wanderer who attempts to kill her, Télumée is given a new name by the village people. She is heralded not only for maintaining her spirit but also for having enough left over to help the same vagabond achieve peace before he dies. It is this ultimate act that makes the village people rename her Télumée Miracle, since, as they say, "Télumée, dear, Angel Medard lived like a dog and you made him die like a man" (*Bridge of Beyond*, 166). At the end of the novel Télumée and Simone Schwarz-Bart tell us:

> I shine my lamp into every dark corner, I go all over this strange market, and I see that heaven's gift to us is that we should have our head thrust into, held down in, the murky water of scorn, cruelty, pettiness, and treachery. But I also see that we are not drowned in it. We have struggled to be born and we have struggled to be born again and we have called the finest tree in our forests "resolute"—the strongest, the most sought after, the one that is cut down the most often. (*Bridge of Beyond*, 169–170)

I reexamine the significance of the negritude legacy of Aimé Césaire and Léopold Senghor within the context of the First International Conference of Negro Writers and Artists in chapter 1 of this book, "Paris in 1956: Negritude and Cultural Discourse." While this particular conference is of relatively minor significance in the large scheme of things, the questions raised and discussed among the Black writers who came together then are still part of the intellectual landscape of today. At the heart of their conversations were struggles over what philosophical and civilizational legacies most shape the cultural identities of Black people. If the exclusionary and oppressive nature of colonialism had told us who we were not, then these conversations were attempts to figure out who we were. Two questions emerged in the course of this conference: "How will we talk about who we are as a people?" and "Should 'one's people' be defined in national or transnational terms?"

If chapter 1 and the conference, in discussing negritude, ask, "Who are Black people?" then chapter 2, "Colonial Legacies, Gender Identity, and Black Female Writing in the Diaspora," asks "Who are Black women?" It goes on to consider what cultural theories and discursive practices guide how Black female writing is discussed and interpreted. Chapter 2 charts some of the post-1970 critical reactions to both Black women's identities in general and the themes at stake in Afro-Caribbean women's writing in particular. The discussions of identity that appeared after 1970 expose the extent to which slavery and colonialism bred Black women who both resist and imitate dominant European gender roles. Erna Brodber's study *Perceptions of Caribbean Women: Towards a Documentation of Stereotypes,* for example, and Sylvia Wynter's essay, "Beyond Miranda's Meanings," both theorize the extent to which colonialism, slavery, and European womanhood have historically shaped Black female identity and influenced the issues that surface in their writings. Yet strains within the early negritude debates and scholarship that have emerged since raise questions about alternate and complementary ways of theorizing this issue.

As early as 1970, Toni Cade Bambara in her anthology *The Black Woman* asked: "How relevant are the truths, the experiences, the findings of white women to Black women? Are women after all simply women? I don't know that our priorities are the same, that our concerns and methods are the same, or even similar enough so that we can afford to depend on this new field of experts (white, female)" (9). In her essay "On the Issue of Roles," from the same collection, she expands the question about how to discuss Black women's identity in the diaspora by going beyond the roles inherited from both the dominant society and the slave environment to ask what came before. The logical answer is to turn back to the continent and see to what extent pre- and postcolonial continental culture expands the framework for theorizing Black (female) cultural identity in the diaspora. I pick up Bambara's line of argument at the end of chapter 2, and in my analysis of the social theories of two Nigerian scholars, Oyèrónké Oyêwùmí and Ifi Amadiume, begin to expand the critical terrain within which this discussion can take place.

The third, fourth and fifth chapters of this book examine African Caribbean literature written from different locales. In these chapters I explore how both pre- and postcolonial cultural and civilizational legacies are represented in the work of various writers. The writers I study appear to use their characters as larger-than-life examples of the principles that actually do or should guide the societies they come from. Within African diaspora histories and cultural contexts, the impact of the colonial legacy has been substantially documented. On the other hand, ambivalence frequently overshadows any certainty about "what in us is African." This anxiety may be appeased by anthropological studies that document the retention of African words, phrases, dance steps, and ways of cooking in African diaspora culture. While these legacies are all valid, I suggest that the African cultural background is most evident in terms of four characteristics repeatedly demonstrated in the literature:

1. The notion of "power" as something experienced as internal rather than external.

2. The "word" and the rhythm of how the word is spoken as something endowed with the power to affect the spirit and influence spiritual transformation.

3. Art as produced by "the folk" or the "everyday people," while having definite aesthetic appeal, is frequently practical or functional. Hence songs and tales, although entertaining, often have a moral that is meant to guide or inspire.

4. A sense of time as cyclical rather than linear. The focus is on the effect of events on the individual's identity, rather than on a presumption of progress related to the abstract passage of time.

In short and long works of prose by Afro-Caribbean writers these characteristics appear again and again.

Chapter 3, "Negritude and Negativity: Alienation and 'Voice' in Eastern Caribbean Literature," juxtaposes writing by Merle Hodge, Jamaica Kincaid, and Earl Lovelace. In this chapter, "alienation" functions as the legacy of colonialism while Césaire's definition of negritude is used as a point of departure for exploring the existence of the African cultural traits delineated above. By the end chapter 3, Lovelace's character Joebell is shown to represent the principles of internal power and communal balance.

Chapters 4 and 5 are explorations of the transformative power of the word. Chapter 4, "Diaspora Philosophy, French Caribbean Literature, and Simone Schwarz-Bart's *Pluie et vent sur Télumée Miracle*," explores writing by three French Caribbean writers from French Guiana, Martinique, and Guadeloupe, respectively. Léon Damas's philosophy of negritude is explored through an examination of his poetry and is juxtaposed with Edouard Glissant's postnegritude theory of creolization. At the center of this chapter, however, is a lengthy analysis of Simone Schwarz-Bart's first novel. This work, more than any other, appears to move beyond both colonial alienation and negritude's basic questions to expose the African cultural mores and values at the heart of the folktale and proverb in the diaspora. In this chapter, I propose that Schwarz-Bart's character Télumée picks up where Lovelace's Joebell leaves off, expanding the complexity of how an individual's sense of internal power can function as a stabilizing force within a larger communal context. I also suggest that by the end of Schwarz-Bart's text, Black female identity is compatible with both communal theories about culture, on one hand, and the social gender theories of continental African scholars, on the other. In the final analysis, however, social relations and culture have taken primacy over any articulation of individual, gender identity at the end of Schwarz-Bart's novel.

Chapter 5, "The Spoken Word and Spirit Consciousness: Audre Lorde and Paule Marshall's Diasporic Voice," charts the poetics of loss in the early writings of Audre Lorde, showing the interconnections among Western notions of the individual, cultural alienation, and the breakdown in the connection between "vision" and "voice." In Lorde's later poetry and in Paule Marshall's groundbreaking work *Praisesong for the Widow*, a transformational transition occurs from individualism and spiritual numbness to a kind of ancestral knowledge and collective consciousness.

The complexity of what we know and have maintained as African peoples living in the diaspora has yet to be fully revealed to us. What is apparent, however, is that the rebirth of ancient forms in a variety of contemporary modes is still carried forth in our stories, songs, dances, proverbs, jokes, riddles, language, music, and literature. In her article " 'One of Dese Mornings, Bright and Fair, / Take My Wings and Cleave De Air': The Legend of the Flying Africans and Diasporic Consciousness," Wendy Walters argues that the Black female novel functions as one of the contemporary realms of folkloric transformation. Using analyses of Paule Marshall's *Praisesong for the Widow* and Toni Morrison's *Song of Solomon*, Walters begins her article by referring to the plethora of folktales and accounts across the diaspora about Africans during the period of slavery flying back home. What is most striking about her synthesis of these tales for the purposes of her article is not just how widespread they were, but how much "the old people" insisted on having been eyewitnesses to these events. From her quotation of Monica Schuler's essay "Alas, Alas, Kongo" we hear that in Jamaica in particular, the ability to fly was linked to avoiding salt; we also learn that fifteenth-century Portuguese missionaries to the Kongo kingdom put salt on the tongues of converts in place of a water baptism in order to signify their conversion to Christianity (Walters, "One of Dese Mornings," 9). We learn that research in the Sea Islands off the coast of Georgia revealed "twenty-seven variants of the Flying Africans legend" ("One of Dese Mornings," 7). We also learn that these reports surfaced not only in the United States and Jamaica; one of the most striking comes from Cuba, as reported by Esteban Montejo in *The Autobiography of a Runaway Slave*:

> Some people said that when a Negro died he went back to Africa, but this is a lie. How could a dead man go to Africa? . . . It was living men who flew there, from a tribe the Spanish stopped importing as slaves because so many of them flew away it was bad for business. [T]he Negroes [that] did not [commit suicide] . . . escaped by flying. . . . The Musundi Congolese were the ones that flew the most; they disappeared by means of witchcraft. . . . There are those who say the Negroes threw themselves into rivers. This is untrue. The truth is that they fastened a chain to their waists which was full of magic. That was where their power came from. I know all this intimately, and it is true beyond a doubt. (quoted in Walters, "One of Dese Mornings," 4, 9–10)

The suggestion that these accounts were not just myths and stories relayed for the worthy purpose of uplifting the spirit of an enslaved people is profound. It speaks, among other things, once again, to the complexity of who we have been and who we still are as a people. It certainly speaks profoundly to the existence of alternate forms of consciousness. This alternate consciousness is borne out in our songs, spirituals, creole and Black vernacular sayings, our music, and possession rituals. While the stories about flying Africans may seem fantastic, Christian belief takes literally the physical ascension of Jesus from the grave the third day after his death. The third day. Third sight. Three, and numbers that are multiples of three, have always been symbolic in African and African diaspora spiritual contexts:

> *I say fly away home to Zion*
> *(fly away home)*
> *I say fly away home to Zion*
> *(fly away home)*
> *One bright morning when my work is over I will fly away home*
> —BOB MARLEY, "Rastaman Chant"

Introduction

1

Paris in 1956

NEGRITUDE AND CULTURAL

DISCOURSE

Le chant n'était pas épuisé.—AIMÉ CÉSAIRE

Two earlier literary quarrels between Black French writers set the stage for the issues explored at the First International Conference of Negro Artists and Writers, held at the Sorbonne in Paris in 1956. The first was a 1930s dispute between two Black student journals, both published in Paris: *L'Étudiant Noir* (cofounded by Aimé Césaire, Léopold Senghor, and Léon Damas) and *Légitime Défense* (cofounded by René Ménil, Etienne Léro, and Jules Monnerot). The second was a 1955 disagreement between Aimé Césaire and René Depestre. These literary quarrels were, in effect, early struggles over what was later described as negritude.

In the years following the conference, the reactions to negritude as a discourse included some that were highly critical. An example is René Ménil's *Tracées* (1981), a relentless critique of negritude as a "political doctrine." Ménil claims that negritude exults in an "anti-intellectualisme . . . philosophique," is dominated by Sartre's existentialism, is ahistorical, and against "progress" (64). In a final moment of unchecked hysteria, Ménil argues that similarities exist between Joseph-Arthur de Gobineau's racist text, *Essai sur l'inégalité des races humaines* and Senghor's "The Spirit of Civilisation, or the Laws of African Negro Culture" (in Présence Africaine Conference Committee, *Présence Africaine*).

On the other hand, Aimé Césaire's views of negritude are quite different. In an interview of Césaire by René Depestre, included in Depestre's 1980 book *Bonjour et adieu à la négritude,* Césaire systematically articulated the position he had consistently held on the conception and purpose of negritude as he saw it. He described negritude as, first and foremost, a concrete coming-to-consciousness, premised on pride in a collective Black identity, and forged from the relationship between the individual and the community. This consciousness is initially a result of the experienced alienation caused by the *refoulements* (psychological repression) of a European colonial order that denied the humanity of the Black subject. Second, in a move that unites rather than separates him from Senghor, Césaire stressed that negritude takes the position that the African diaspora subject "n'était pas tombé de la dernière pluie" (did not drop from the sky with the last rainfall) but has a past that predates and survives slavery.[1] He argued that negritude asserts that there is an African civilizational legacy and that we see it alive in the diaspora; negritude is, in fact, the basis for the solidarity of all Blacks in their political struggles throughout the world (Depestre, *Bonjour et adieu,* 78–79):[2]

> I would say that négritude is, first in my opinion, a concrete rather than abstract coming-to-consciousness; it meant having a concrete consciousness of oneself, to first understand that one is "nègre," that we are "nègres," that we had a past and that this past brought with it cultural elements that have been very valuable, and "nègres," as you say, did not drop from the sky with the last rainfall. . . . At this particular era and historical moment, there are people who can take it upon themselves to write a universal history of civilization without consecrating a [single] chapter to Africa, as if Africa did not contribute anything to the world. . . . In the final instance, [negritude] was the idea that the "nègre" past was worthy of respect, it was the idea that this "nègre" past was not simply in the past; that "nègre" values still have something important to contribute to the world. It is also an affirmation of solidarity. I have always thought that what happens to blacks in Algeria and the United States has a [profound] effect on me. I thought that I was not able to be indifferent to Haiti. I could not be indifferent to Africa. So, to put it another way, we have almost arrived at the idea of a sort of black civilization dispersed throughout the entire world (78–79).[3]

It seems important to note that Césaire's final definition of negritude ("the idea of a sort of black civilization dispersed throughout the

Clear Word and Third Sight

entire world") is coterminous with the definition of "African dias-pora," addressing both cultural differences among Black populations around the world and civilizational similarities. With his description of negritude as political solidarity, a shared civilization, and a con-scious recognition of the past and present influences of Africa on the West, Césaire participates in the reconstitution of an intellectual de-bate involving himself, Depestre, and Ménil that had spanned fifty years.

Depestre had taken a different route to negritude. In 1955 in the pages of the journal *Présence Africaine,* we are told, "Depestre, then exiled in Brazil, had . . . rallied . . . to the French Communist party's emerging conservative line on poetic experimentation. In the wake of surrealism, Louis Aragon was pressing for a return to more tradi-tional prosody, to simpler forms and messages, linking these with the interests of revolutionary workers" (quoted in Clifford, *The Predica-ment of Culture,* 180).[4]

Césaire's poetic response, published in *Présence Africaine* in the same year, anticipated his own break with the Communist Party after Russia's invasion of Hungary. In a move that some critics interpret primarily at the level of its aesthetic and textual impact, Césaire en-couraged Depestre to withstand cooptation.[5] Yet at its base, Césaire's critique was a continuation of the 1930s dispute between his *L'Étu-diant Noir* and Ménil's *Légitime Défense* over what was referred to in Marxist circles as *la question nègre.* For *L'Étudiant Noir, désaliénation* (cultural decolonization) could not be achieved without a specific as-sertion of Black cultural identity. As Césaire recounted in his inter-view with Depestre, negritude was resistance to assimilation from both the French political Right and the Left. At the same time, Césaire emphasized *L'Étudiant Noir's* strategic investment in being aligned with the Left, since he never believed liberation would come from the Right (Depestre, *Bonjour et adieu,* 71).[6]

As Sylvia Washington Bâ notes in her book *The Concept of Negritude in the Poetry of Léopold Sédar Senghor,* "On June 1, 1932, appeared the first, and only, issue of *Légitime Défense,* a veritable manifesto voicing the discontent of the students from Martinique. By attacking the vapid imitations of Parnassian poetry then in vogue in the French West Indies, *Légitime Défense* condemned the entire system that had pro-duced the mulatto bourgeois mentality and the 'neither-nor' status of its culture" (11). Bâ then quotes Senghor's account, in a February 1960 letter to Lilyan Kesteloot, of the differences between this journal and *L'Étudiant Noir*: "If the two reviews had known the same influences, they differed nevertheless on several points. *L'Étudiant Noir* asserted the priority as well as the primacy of the cultural reality. For us . . . politics was only one aspect of culture, whereas *Légitime Défense* maintained . . . that political revolution had to precede cultural revolution, the latter becoming possible only in the wake of radical political change" (13).

Embracing Marxism but disagreeing with the stance that Aragon would take, *Légitime Défense* rejected the didactic social realism called for by Aragon in favor of a modernist surrealism, viewed as the only viable route to désaliénation for the Black colonial subject. What the *Légitime Défense* and *L'Étudiant Noir* dispute and the subsequent 1955 quarrel had in common was that Senghor and Césaire perceived as impossible that political struggle premised on (European) Marxist politics could ever seriously incorporate cultural perspectives specific to Black experience. Césaire's subsequent resignation from the Communist Party can be seen within the context of a historically consistent disenchantment with Marxism on the part of Black intellectuals. At the end of his text *The Wretched of the Earth*, Frantz Fanon remained avidly invested in third world decolonization. Yet when he states, "It is a question of the Third World starting a new history of Man," he explicitly renounces approaches to this struggle that view European aesthetic and political theory as the point of departure for these new solutions (*Wretched of the Earth*, 315). Harold Cruse makes a similar argument in his chapter "Marxism and the Negro" in his 1968 book *Rebellion or Revolution?* By the time of the 1956 conference the terms of this debate were less explicitly framed around European Marxist revolutionary theory and more specifically concerned with defining the nature of the third world struggle against colonialism. The negritude invoked by Césaire, while never actually named as such at the 1956 conference, lay at the heart of the controversial debates. While Senghor, Césaire, and Damas in various interviews describe negritude as a movement they founded as young students in Paris, theories about what factors influenced these three, as well as theories about where the foundational roots of negritude lie, differ from critic to critic.[7] Also controversial is whether negritude is viewed as an event with historically bounded dates or as a *consciousness-in-action* with systematic continuities and discontinuities over the course of time.[8]

Damas's contribution to the history of negritude should not be underestimated. In his introduction to the collection *Critical Perspec-*

tives: Léon Gontran Damas, Keith Q. Warner notes, "Most critics, in dealing with the movement, nearly always spoke of Césaire, Senghor *and* Damas, dealing at length with the first two and barely treating the third, to the extent that one had the distinct impression that Damas became quite sensitive to this perpetual relegation to the third spot in the négritude triumvirate" (5). Warner observes that Kesteloot's *Black Writers in French: A Literary History of Negritude* (originally presented as a doctoral thesis in 1961), despite receiving its share of criticism, has remained an important work on the literary aspects of the movement, being one of the first to examine negritude in detail and treat Damas on a par with Senghor and Césaire. Another testament to Damas's significance, as noted by Warner, is the Trinidadian writer Merle Hodge's unpublished master's thesis, "The Writings of Léon Damas and Their Connection with the Negritude Movement" (5). The influence of Damas on Hodge is significant since it helps to establish a climate of influence between Caribbean writers, intergenerationally and across linguistic and gendered lines. According to Warner, Hodge's thesis "had Damas's full support and approval" (5). This chain of influence seems significant in light of the substantial nature of the work that Merle Hodge was later to produce as both a writer and critic.

As Warner points out, Damas's *Pigments* (1937) predates Césaire's *Cahier d'un retour au pays natal* by two years. Damas himself cites *Pigments* as "the manifesto of the Négritude movement" (Warner, *Critical Perspectives,* 24). He talks about Césaire coming to his room early one morning to read him the as-yet unpublished *Cahier* and saying, "You'll tell me how much I have been influenced by you" (14). On the other hand, Damas describes Senghor as a great poet who always used "a very pure language" (since he was "an *agrégé* in Latin Grammar") and who saw an Africa that he and Césaire could only dream about (15). In terms of influences, Damas cites Etienne Léro's "Misère d'une poesie" in *Légitime Défense* and Claude McKay's *Banjo* (1929) as profound early influences on him (Warner, *Critical Perspectives,* 5, 16). Damas was also personally acquainted with Langston Hughes and Carter G. Woodson, founder of the *Journal of Negro History.* These various connections reveal the influence between these Black intellectuals from French colonies (seen as the initiators of the negritude movement) and Black intellectuals in the United States. After the publication of *Pigments,* Damas edited *Poètes d'expression française: 1900–1945* (1947), apparently the first of its kind. However it was Senghor's *Anthologie de la nouvelle poésie nègre et malgache* (1948), with Sartre's famous *Orphée noir* preface, that drew widespread recognition.

In more direct ways than the work of Senghor and Césaire, Damas's writing was a sort of manifestation of negritude-in-action. In 1939 the French government retroactively censored *Pigments* after its translation into Baoulé inspired the youth of the Ivory Coast to resist induction into the armed forces. In the early forties, the journal *Vu et Lu* commissioned Damas to write a story on French Guiana, eventually published under the title *Retour de Guyane*. Of the fifteen hundred published copies, the government of Guiana bought over one thousand and had them burnt (Warner, *Critical Perspectives*, 14).

Damas's legacy seems symbolic and important for any discussion of negritude, despite its critical marginalization and his seeming absence from the 1956 conference. In the preface to *Pigments*, French poet Robert Desnos calls attention to the fact that Damas in his celebrated first text draws attention to skin color in a way that the elite in his home country of French Guiana usually downplayed. He also embraced and appropriated the term *nègre* with all its connotations, as opposed to the more conservative and respectable *noir*. As I demonstrate in chapter 4, his embrace of this term is an embrace of the "native" Black culture at odds with the official French culture that dominated his childhood and the lives of the colored elite in French Guiana. It makes sense, therefore, that what Senghor would later positively describe as the unsophisticated, direct, and sometimes brutal nature of Damas's poetry was in fact a cultivated Black aesthetic or "negrification." His aim was to textually recuperate a Black cultural reality that had frequently been defined exclusively in terms of negation, and which was imagined by the hegemonic order as having no interiority of its own.

Another important figure in the history of negritude was Léopold Sédar Senghor. Like Damas he was substantially influenced by Black writers from the United States. As the Senegalese scholar Sylvia Washington Bâ writes, "In addition to the poets Countee Cullen, Langston Hughes, Jean Toomer, James Weldon Johnson, Sterling Brown and Frank Marshall Davis, he read regularly *Opportunity*, the publication of the National Urban League, *The Crisis*, the *Journal of Negro History*, and especially *The New Negro*, the anthology-manifesto edited by Alain Locke" (*The Concept of Negritude*, 11). However, the negritudinal legacy of Senghor is described by Bâ as first and foremost invested in establishing parallels between European and African civi-

Clear Word and Third Sight

lization. Far from being an antagonistic investment, Senghor's aim is for "a civilization of cultural coexistence and complementarity" (*The Concept of Negritude*, 13). This was also the explicit aim of the Association of West African Students, founded in the early thirties by Senghor and Ousmane Socé Diop (12).

Senghor's poetry, unlike Damas's, is not famous for its biting renunciation of European values since, as Damas himself observes, Senghor had a solid African cultural background that was under siege in quite a different way than that of his French Caribbean "frères." Consequently, his poetry was influenced by a world that, as Césaire notes, the other two could only dream about. Senghor was descended from the Serer tribe, "a north Sudanian ethnic group consisting primarily of farmers, fishermen and shepherds," so his childhood was a blend of Christian and animist traditions (Bâ, *The Concept of Negritude*, 4). "As is the custom in matrilineal societies where the child is entrusted to the maternal uncle, Senghor spent many hours with this uncle, a shepherd, who revealed to him the marvels of nature" (6). In Senghor's work, following the influences of his cultural background, the song and the poem are one and the same and (as he emphasized in his paper at the 1956 conference), art in this context is always functional; art for art's sake does not exist. Senghor translated the poetry of a famous sage and poetess from his region, Marône N'Diaye (c. 1890– 1950), and Bâ argues that the improvised song-poems of Marône echo in Senghor's verse and "attest to the profound influence of oral tradition on his poetic expression" (7). On the other hand, Bâ describes Senghor as "one who availed himself of the assimilationist policy to the fullest, mastering the French language and culture to an extent rarely attained by any but the most outstanding French minds. He analyzed the paradox of his situation with the most rigorous Cartesian logic and evolved a form of cultural militancy expressed through poetry and political action known the world over as négritude" (3). This then would appear to be a man who in certain respects was ready for the task of juxtaposing European and African civilizational legacies, having been both explicitly schooled and exposed to the traditions of his people while also reaching one of the highest levels of formal training within the French educational system.

Just as Damas endorsed Hodge's master's thesis, Senghor wrote the preface to Bâ's book (originally her dissertation), in which he states, "It is a curious sensation for a writer, especially a poet, to feel that he has been understood yet, at the same time, exposed and laid bare. He has been understood and he does not know whether to rejoice or to despair" (v). Between Senghor and Sylvia Washington Bâ there seems to have been a similar kind of intergenerational influence across gendered lines as there was between Damas and Hodge. With both Bâ and Hodge focusing their academic studies on the negritudinal legacies of male writers from their regions of the world, and having their theses read and approved by the writers themselves, a common cultural investment across gendered lines is clearly operative. Hodge's later work pays specific attention to gender difference within a Caribbean context, but her early thesis work drew the contours within which the later questions are articulated. These relationships establish the primacy of the cultural realities that circumscribe the lives of African and African diaspora subjects.

The first two chapters of Bâ's book detail the influences in Senghor's early life, particularly the path of his formal education. The next three chapters are rigorous analyses of his poetry and simultaneous explications of his philosophy of negritude. Here, Bâ divides negritude into three categories: Black African ontology (the basis of negritude), Black African psychophysiology (the expression of negritude), and rhythm and imagery (the fundamental traits of negritude). The final chapter is Bâ's interpretation of Senghor's "Civilization of the Universal." She concludes the study with her own translations of his poetry, including also an extensive glossary of African words that appear in his work. Throughout her study, Bâ focuses extensively on the manifestations of Senghor's cultural upbringing in his poetry. In this sense, her attention to rhythm and imagery, as well as the profound level at which his references to nature operate, are all relevant to a sophisticated comprehension of his poetic works. In order to do this, Bâ draws not only on her knowledge of Senghor's cultural background and influences but also on her extensive reading of Senghor's philosophical positions on culture, laid out in his numerous articles and essays.

In her chapter on Black African ontology, Bâ isolates certain key elements as forming the conceptual base of Senghor's philosophy of negritude. The two foundational elements are the concept of "life force" and the privileged position of the word. "At birth, the child receives a name which is in direct relation to a life force associated with his clan's frame of reference. This name is conceived of as designating a real ontological individuality and expresses the very nature of the person" (64). Senghor's middle name, Sédar, meaning "he who need never be ashamed before anyone," almost perfectly describes the public persona of the man (5). Quoting from the work of the Belgian missionary Placide Tempels, Bâ describes "life force" as the notion that "Being" possesses force. Occidental thought is described as conceiving of Being as static, the notion of force not being included within the concept of Being itself. Within the Black African context Being *is* force and every being is/has force. Thus "life force" is conceived of as extending beyond the "human" to include the natural environment (46).

Continuous with this notion of life force is the privileged position assigned to the word: "The word is both expression and creation and, as such, unites poetic creation and reinforcement of life forces" (63). Bâ, quoting Senghor, substantiates this conceptualization of the word with citations of Greek and Latin, French and English, in each instance comparing the notion of the word in the Black African context to the word or combination of words that do the same work in the context of these other languages. In each instance Bâ displays Senghor's rigor and thoroughness with regard to his comparisons of European and African civilizational legacies. Given this function of the word as both expression and creation, the role of the poet within such a societal context is extremely significant, since he or she "possesses the gift of calling forth or naming a force, an element, or a person and thereby ordering its realization. . . . The creative power of invocation enables the spirit to transcend appearances and circumstances" (64). This notion of the poet as "calling forth [and] naming a force, an element or a person" is amply demonstrated in Audre Lorde's poem "Call," which I analyze in chapter 5.

The role of the poet and the function of the word also determine the relationship to death. Bâ isolates two categories of death in Senghor's poetry: "complete death, physical and spiritual" and "cessation of existence without loss of vital influence." The difference between these two forms of death is the word and the will. As Bâ argues, "The extension of the chain of life into the realm of death depends upon the will of the living, so the degree of death depends upon the interpretation of the living" (57). So, like the role of the African mask within the context of ceremonial ritual, the poet's role moves beyond that of historian and observer in the coming together of the expressive and "creational" aspects of this word. Poetry moves beyond art and is functional, being integral to the very existence of the community and the relationship between the living and the dead. In this sense, the notion of time that is operative in this context is also structured differently: "Just as the philosophy of life forces conceives of interacting life forces above and beyond the divisions of life and death, it also conceives of time as synchronic and diachronic rather than historical" (53).

While Bâ's analysis of Senghor and Keith Warner's analysis of Damas are texts that attempt the work of explicating negritude as a literary and cultural phenomenon with political implications, more prevalent in the contemporary moment are the critical responses to negritude aimed at its deconstruction. These critical responses, however, reveal how the critics themselves envision the present political and cultural constitution of the African diaspora subject. The attempts to define, describe, and contain negritude, in the contemporary critical arena, directly parallel the struggles of the writers and artists over the cultural "body" of the Black subject at the 1956 International Conference of Negro Artists and Writers.

One of these critics, René Ménil, argues that negritude is, in its political philosophy (which he views as reactionary), fundamentally opposed to class struggle (*Tracées*, 75).[9] He goes on to link the ideology of the national bourgeoisie as described by Fanon with the political philosophy of negritude according to Césaire and Senghor.[10] Another critique comes from Renate Zahar, who sees Fanon's critique of negritude as similar to those that view it as antithetical to political struggle and bankrupt in its cultural legacy.

Ménil's analysis of negritude and Zahar's analysis of Fanon is emblematic of an often irreconcilable split between negritude critics who view the phenomenon in terms of politics versus culture.[11] Césaire, Senghor, and Damas, by contrast, systematically maintain that the political and cultural aspects of negritude are inseparable. Since negritude is primarily a response to an alienation particular to Black oppressed peoples generally, and peculiar to the Black educated elite especially, any substantial analysis of the phenomenon requires thorough treatment of issues of repression and alienation.[12] However, when the psychocultural alienation caused by colonial repression is treated by negritude critics, there is frequently an assumption that this is all in the past and not a phenomenon that has its parallel in the hegemonic continuity between colonial and neocolonial periods.

René Ménil in *Tracées* consistently makes a distinction between "Black poetry" and "la négritude," attributing all the qualities usually ascribed to negritude to "la poésie noire":

Clear Word and Third Sight

But this poetry is not narrowly and uniquely racial. Expressing the life of colonized blacks, it expresses at the same time the social and historic condition of "nègres" in modern civilization. Even more concretely, it tends to describe all the richness of the Black soul, as has been said, this is to say, the hates and joys, the resentments and hopes of the colonized Black man. This is, for example, essentially the content of *Notebook of a Return to My Native Land* by Césaire which will affect, evidently, the air of the new poetry. . . . Negritude is another thing. (63–64)[13]

Elsewhere, Depestre quotes Ménil as saying, "The culture of the Antilles passed through that coming-to-consciousness and racial feeling is a necessary part of it. . . . I said racial feeling. . . . [T]his is, more exactly, racial pride confronting the white racism of the colonials. . . . I did not say negritude" (*Bonjour et adieu,* 146).[14] Curiously, Ménil makes a distinction between racial sentiment, on one hand, and exploration of the historic and social condition of the Black subject "dans la civilisation moderne," on the other. He vehemently distinguishes both of these realities from negritude, implying that negritude represents some biological essentialism he wishes to avoid. Yet, in a passage from an interview by Lilyan Kesteloot, quoted by Depestre, Césaire states, "My conception of negritude is not biological, it is cultural and historical" (145).[15] The exploration of the very issues that Ménil situates under the rubric of "Black poetry" Césaire defines as the exploration of negritude. When Césaire refers to negritude as a historical and cultural versus biological phenomenon, he is referring to the civilizational similarities between Black cultures on the continent and in the diaspora, as well as the Black subject's political awakening to the collective predicament of his or her people. This is an awakening premised on the refusal of Black humanity by the European colonial order, a refusal that results in self-hatred on the part of the educated elite and misdirected violence on the part of the Black masses. This awakening is an explicit recognition that the cultural life of the African diaspora neither begins nor ends with the colonial order. Ultimately this negritudinal awakening is a commitment to both present and future collective political struggle in the name of one's people. Despite vehement opposition to the term "negritude," Ménil still employs the category "Black poetry," and under this rubric he refers to "the richness of the Black soul." There appears to be little difference, besides the categories they employ, between what Ménil sanctions and what Césaire does when it comes to recognizing the reality of psychological repression in the colonial situation as it relates to Black populations. But, it is precisely Césaire's assertion that the cultural realities of the African diaspora neither begin nor end with colonialism that Ménil refuses. Otherwise, there would be little difference between this position and that of Senghor—the notion that there is an African civilizational legacy that includes the diaspora.

Another critic of negritude is Renate Zahar. In her book *Frantz Fanon: Colonialism and Alienation,* she attempts first to distinguish the concept of "alienation" as defined by Marx from colonial alienation. Through an analysis of Marx's *Capital,* Zahar argues that "alienation" is in effect when the producer is ruled by the actions of the commodity. Less abstractly, alienation occurs when there ceases to be a connection between "man" and "nature" in capitalist society, since the process of creating a commodity is one in which the producer is separated from the means of production. Zahar states that alienation within the colonial context is doubled. She argues that the colonized are exploited by both the colonial overlord *and* exchange relations with the metropolis. Racial ideology, according to Zahar, is an indispensable coercive aspect of the colonial system. It is necessary since the colonized are not benefiting from the abstracted products of their labor, like the workers in the metropolis. Colonial alienation for Zahar encompasses all the subcategories of "alienation" that are possible within the colonial situation. This involves both economic and intellectual alienation, the former being experienced by all colonized peoples in some form, and the latter being experienced mostly by the most highly educated or the "evolués" (5–13). The assumption that the Marxist notion of alienation (the breakdown of connection between "man" and "nature") can transparently be applied to any postcolonial Black society with ease is, however, readily disrupted by the extensive work of Guyanese scholar Walter Rodney. Rodney's research makes it clear that capitalist production hardly ever touched the colonies in the same fashion as it did the metropole. Further, since most third world countries are still largely rural, without many of the amenities associated with urban, metropolitan environments, the sweeping nature of Marx's notion of alienation has to be cautiously analyzed in these contexts.[16]

In Zahar's analysis of the colonial situation there is also an uneasy relationship between racism and psychocultural alienation. In the chapter "Man's Alienation in Colonialism" she argues that "racial discrimination determines the individual and social conduct of the

Clear Word and Third Sight

colonized both in his living together with the other colonized and in his relations with the colonist" (35). Zahar states that the reason for this can be found in the bipartitioned nature of the colonial world, "characterized by domination and exploitation on the one hand, and ... the imposition of a foreign culture and civilization ... on the other" (35). The colonized adopts "the foreign norms suggested to him by the school, the press[,] ... books and ... Christian missions. This means at the same time that the racial stereotype of the colonized is interiorized by the victim himself. He reacts to this dilemma by mechanisms of compensation, over-adaptation and finally self-hatred" (36). In the very next chapter, "Negritude: An Antithesis of Colonial Racism," Zahar nevertheless states, "The growing awareness manifesting itself in négritude poetry is a reaction to colonial racism: since colonialism despises the colonized for belonging to another race, race and colour are now exalted and raised to the status of autonomous values" (61). Throughout this chapter, Zahar speaks of negritude as an understandable yet problematic reaction to colonial racism. The previous description of psychocultural alienation as characterized by the "imposition of a foreign culture" resulting in "over-adaptation and finally self-hatred" is underplayed and marginalized (35). In Zahar's account, the poetry of negritude is treated solely as an exaltation of race and color, isolated from a reclamation of *cultural* consciousness. Thus negritude can become "the antithesis of colonial racism," colonial racism's other side. Progressively, the racial violence at the heart of the colonial order is reduced in this analysis to simply economic exploitation (61). At this point negritude can become problematic, since colonial and "postcolonial" racism are no longer part of the focus. What Zahar's study makes clear is that substantial critical anxiety is awakened by any discursive marginalization of European paradigms. This is propelled by the implicit fear that nothing truly exists outside. Without substantial knowledge of alternate philosophical orders, discussions of Black culture are imagined to be two-dimensional discourses on race with no place to go but toward totalitarian ideology. Zahar criticizes negritude for being solely a reaction, yet it remains so within her analysis due to her inadequate treatment of psychocultural alienation and affirming cultural traditions. On the other hand, Ménil's analysis reduces negritude to biological determinism while artificially maintaining a separation between political resistance and cultural expression.

The 1956 Conference and
the Struggle over Black Cultural Identity

At the First International Conference of Negro Writers and Artists, Senghor's paper, "The Spirit of Civilization, or the Laws of African Negro Culture," instigated a heated discussion amongst the participants. In his presentation, Senghor, repeating many of the tenets explicated by Bâ, argued that "Negro African Culture" had to be understood predominantly in terms of synthetic rather than discursive modes of reasoning; "synthetic," in this context, implies the combination of separate elements into a complex whole. His attention to the relationship between "Being" and the natural environment, the power of the word, and imagery and rhythm as fundamental elements of style attempted to emphasize this synthesis-oriented approach to reality. In this reality functional and artistic values coincide and coexist and the disciplinary boundaries between science and history, philosophy and art, and politics and spirituality work together rather than separately. It is with this in mind, therefore, that Senghor describes the "Negro" as a "man of Nature . . . a being with open senses . . . himself at once the subject and the object [who] is, first of all, sounds, scents, rhythms, forms and colours" (Senghor, "The Spirit of Civilization," 52). His perspective here seems inflected by his identity as a poet, and by how his cultural background influences his view of the particular relationship between African peoples and the natural environment. Generalizing, as he states, for the purposes of brevity, he goes on to describe the whole aim of this societal aesthetic as one that has as its central focus "the increase and expression of vital power" (53). He says, "The Negro identifies being with life, or, more specifically, with vital force. . . . But his force, the sub-stratum of intellectual and moral life, and to that extent immortal, is not really living and cannot really grow except by co-existing in man with the body and the breath of life" (53). Here, "the tribe is a group of several families, the kingdom a group of several tribes. But what is the family? It is the clan, the totality of all those, living and dead, who recognize a common ancestor" (54). This description of a civilization that has the increase and expression of vital power ("life force," as explained by Bâ) as a goal substantiates Senghor's further claim that within this civilizational context "the distinction between sacred and profane, political and social, appears late and infrequently" (55).

Addressing the role of art specifically, Senghor writes that "works of

Clear Word and Third Sight

art are perishable. While their spirit and style are preserved, we hasten to replace the ancient work by modernizing it as soon as it becomes out of date or perishes. This means that in Negro Africa 'art for art's sake' does not exist; all art is social" (56–57). Moving on to describe image and rhythm as fundamental features of social art, which itself is part and parcel of everyday life, Senghor addresses first image, and then rhythm. First, he speaks about the image as integral to language expression: "the words are always pregnant with images; through their value as signs transpires their value as sense" (58). Additionally, the image "does not signify what it represents, but what it suggests, what it creates. The elephant is strength, the spider, prudence" (58). The image frequently tells a story. Senghor describes the complexity of the vocabulary and grammar in Fulah and Jolof, in which there are sometimes as many as ten and twenty words to describe an object, the words changing as the need to specify the weight, volume, and color of the object shifts. "In Jolof it is possible, by means of affixes, to construct from the same root more than twenty verbs with different shades of meaning, together with at least as many derivative nouns" (59). Senghor further argues that whereas Indo-European languages "lay emphasis on the abstract idea of time (past, present, future), the African Negro languages stress the aspect, the concrete fashion in which the verbal action unfolds" (59). In this context, "language is . . . power. . . . Spoken language, the word, is the supreme expression of vital force" (59). Rhythm, moreover, "is con-substantial with the image; it is the rhythm which perfects the image by uniting sign and sense, flesh and spirit into one whole" (60). It is rhythm that gives speech "its effective fulfillment, which changes it into the word" (60).

At the conference, the controversies that surfaced in response to Senghor's and Césaire's papers referred to the relationship between African continental and diaspora cultures (in response to Senghor's paper) and the nature of colonial violence (prompted by Césaire's). Senghor and Césaire both argued that there were similarities between continental and diaspora cultures under the rubric of civilization. Arguing that France, Spain, and Italy could all keep their distinct cultures while still being part of European civilization, both men maintained that the legacy of Africa and its diaspora could be discussed in comparable terms. The discussion following Senghor's paper opened with a question from Richard Wright on culture.[17] Wright (who later spoke on "Tradition and Industrialization") described himself as "an American Negro, conditioned by the harsh industrial, abstract force of the Western world" (Présence Africaine Conference Committee, *Présence Africaine*, 66). He asked where he stood in relation to the culture described by Senghor, stating that while he would like to lay claim to it he didn't see how he could. Wright also said that he remained deeply suspicious of the possible links between an oppressive missionary Christianity and the African spirituality defined by Senghor. He argued that this spirituality had not prevented the colonizers from physically taking over the land and wondered if there had not in fact been collusion between these two forces. Yet in the world Senghor describes, the highest value is the development of internal power—described as "vital force"—through synthetic knowledge systems linking science and history, philosophy and art, and politics and spirituality. It seems unlikely, therefore, that there would be collusion between this system and one premised purely on dominance, and more likely instead that one system would have underestimated the brutality of the other.

Wright was followed by the Haitian writer Jacques Stephen Alexis, who maintained that culture was national and that to speak of "Negro African Culture" was surely to speak of an abstraction, since the Black subject was produced in each instance by the competing forces native to the national environment as opposed to being informed by an ahistorical notion of the past. Asking for more specificity of time, dates, and geography, Alexis stated, "If it is a question . . . of turning culture into a vague conception, a purely spiritual conception, not linked to history, not linked to life, it seems to me that this would be committing a crime against these peoples who are suffering and struggling to achieve their individuality" (69). Alexis maintained that he was most comfortable thinking about the cultures of third world peoples "in the process of formation," being part and parcel of the nation-building process (70). For Alexis, the notion of spirituality informing every area of life was incomprehensible. When he spoke of this "vague conception of culture" as not linked to history and life, he was employing Western definitions of "history" and "life," making them universal.

Alexis and Wright, on the one hand, and Césaire and Senghor, on the other, generally represent the opposing ways that Black cultural reality was being imagined at the 1956 conference. Senghor and Césaire maintained that Alexis had confused a "cultural stock-taking" (an assessment of cultural similarities between African people on the continent and in the diaspora), which was the agenda for the first day,

Clear Word and Third Sight

with the "crisis of African Negro Culture" (the impact of colonialism and slavery on African people and the differences between them), the second day's topic. Senghor responded to Alexis by observing that if culture was not to be "art for art's sake" (a static and aestheticized object) then a cultural stock-taking was necessary to prevent this (71). Continuing to speak a language that was misunderstood by the other two, Senghor maintained that culture, like art, is functional and determining the similarities and differences between continental and diaspora societies meant observing, among other things, the *functionality* of their art.

Both Wright and Alexis, in their descriptions, conceptions, and language appeared confused by the very notions that were at the center of Senghor's thoughts. What they conceived of as a vague and problematic focus by Senghor on the spiritual elements of his own cultural background was in fact a difference of vision in terms of how culture was being conceptualized. But the differences ran deeper. The ideology of "man" at the center of the Western notion of culture was under siege, and it was here that the unarticulated yet more categorical differences lay. As Sylvia Washington Bâ, quoting Janheinz Jahn, describes the function of the Bantu word for man, *muntu,* it "serves to clarify the notion of the human being as life force. As this word designates not only 'human being' but also the life force of the dead, of the ancestors, and of God, it is obvious that the concept 'man–human being' is only one aspect of the concept expressed by the word *muntu*" (67). "Muntu," according to Bâ, combines the aspects of communal and cultural identity delineated by Senghor while refusing both the gendered specificity and individuality associated with the term "man" in the Western context. The difference between Wright's and Alexis's positions, and those of Césaire and Senghor, became sharply focused around European versus continental African notions of culture, communal relations, and individual identity.

Central to both Alexis's and Wright's comments is an implicit question. How could the culture Senghor described—with its focus on the "increase and expression of vital power"—assist in the fight against colonialism? Alexis stated that a purely spiritual conception of culture "not linked to history . . . would be committing a crime against these peoples . . . struggling to achieve their individuality" (69). Wright went further in his own conference paper, "Tradition and Industrialization," when he stated, "But I do say, *'Bravo!'* to the consequences of Western plundering, a plundering that created the conditions for the possible rise of rational societies for the greater majority of mankind" (365). For both Wright and Alexis the spiritually influenced societal order described by Senghor is the antithesis of the rational nation-state "in the process of formation." To embrace it is to commit a crime against "peoples . . . struggling to achieve their individuality." For Senghor, in the African context, political *collective* self-determination is inconceivable and inseparable from the vital force and power that informs all aspects of material everyday life and creative expression on the continent. If art for art's sake does not exist, then artistic expression (fused with the political role of the poet and the communal/historical significance of the poem) serves a spiritually empowering function, one that encompasses psychocultural resistance to colonial oppression. This form of functional artistic expression is abundantly in evidence in the creative, African diaspora work of Simone Schwarz-Bart and Audre Lorde, discussed later on. Both Wright and Alexis perceived Senghor's notion of culture as counterproductive to the birth of the postcolonial nation-state. In their eyes there was no perceivable connection between the cultural reality Senghor was attempting to represent and their own. This is exemplified by Wright's question about where he fit into it all as an "American Negro." Second, it was unclear to them what the relationship could possibly be between Senghor's culture and the mass struggle for liberation from oppression. The role of traditional customs, spirituality, and poetry was unclear to them. For his part, Senghor repeatedly stressed the overlap between the artistic and the political, the sacred and the secular, arguing that within the African communal context he was describing, these realities coexist in interactive ways rather than in separate and autonomous spheres. If in the course of transnational political struggle one hoped to reach the Black masses, then a complex understanding of the comparative cultural similarities and differences (a cultural stock-taking) was necessary in order to communicate in terms that would inspire and mobilize. Alexis's and Wright's critiques implied that the masses needed to be led by the intellectual elite and provided with an (implicitly Western) "education," which would presumably equip them to fight the oppressive realities they were faced with. A Western notion of progress and related ideology of "man" was apparent in their positions despite the fact that Alexis and Wright came from countries (Alexis from Haiti and Wright from the United States) in which the Black masses were culturally at odds with European values.

Clear Word and Third Sight

The work of scholar and critic Greg Thomas makes an important intervention here, in terms of the framework it provides to account for the colonial aspects of the trajectory of Black intellectual production. Situating the theoretical paradigms of E. Franklin Frazier's book *Black Bourgeoisie* in critical opposition to Carter G. Woodson's *The Mis-Education of the Negro*, Thomas sees these two works and figures as providing an explanatory framework that accounts for their opposing Black intellectual trajectories. While both Frazier's and Woodson's studies are critiques of the Black elite in the U.S. context, Thomas maintains that Frazier's is mobilized by his investment in "euro-erotic 'acculturation' [gender behavior modification in order to assimilate into white society] and in flight from the Africanist radicalism of Woodson," that is, Woodson's investment in Black cultural and political autonomy (21). While mobilizing a devastating critique against a "new" decadent Black bourgeoisie, Frazier idealizes an "older" Black bourgeoisie and is in favor of a "classical higher education" being open to the masses. "For if open to the masses of Black folk, the 'classical' discipline DuBois reserved for the elite . . . could in theory effect the Negro transformation Frazier so desired" (23). Thomas argues that "Frazier at once performs and promotes that historical activity theorized by Carter G. Woodson as *The Mis-Education of the Negro*" (19). What for Frazier, Wright, and Alexis functions as the desired, literal, and figurative "end" of Black mass subjectivity, and the beginning of "white mask" individuality with Western education as vehicle, was for Woodson the must successful example of miseducation. As Thomas states, "Woodson is therefore compelled to describe the ultra-westernized subject of Frazier's middle-class respectability . . . as a 'hopeless liability of the race' " (xiii). Importantly, this liability for Woodson is not the absence of a middle class old or new, but the presence of every "Negro thus educated," miseducation being "both sign and substance of class status" (20). Ironically, if not predictably, it is Frazier's (rather than Woodson's) model of survival through white education, minus his devastating class critique, that has survived into the "modern" era as part of the mainstream rhetoric of solutions to the Black problem.

Césaire, in his conference paper "Culture and Colonisation," set out to delineate the specific nature of this violence, arguing that colonial violence was as native to the experience of Blacks on the continent and in the diaspora as their civilizational similarities. He aimed, among other things, to aggressively demystify the notion that colonialism introduced "progress" of any sort, noting that this was counter to the nature of the beast. In order to argue this, he cites Margaret Mead's statement that "it should be possible by taking the necessary precautions 'to introduce into certain cultures, basic education, new agricultural and industrial methods, new rules of hospital administration, with a minimum of dislocation or at least to make use of the inevitable dislocation for constructive ends' " (198–99). Césaire observes that, despite Mead's good intentions, the logic of colonialism was such that the colonial power would not do for the colonies what it has refused to do at home.[18] Further, Césaire reveals the implicit assumption of "backwardness" in Mead's statement when he observes that the evolution of third world societies has to come from within and cannot be successfully provoked from without. In this sense, Mead's position coincides with that of Alexis and Wright and extremists like the American delegate John Davis, who stated that what Mead was concerned with was "how America could help *backward* countries by giving technical assistance and technical aid" (Présence Africaine Conference Committee, *Présence Africaine,* 217, emphasis mine).

The "enlightenment" trajectory of Wright's and Alexis's approach to the issue of Black cultural identity is situated in part by Thomas's analysis of the legacies of Woodson and Frazier, and the instructive nature of their work with regard to the competing paradigms constraining Black intellectual identity. Yet the question of a cultural stock-taking in order to determine civilizational similarities, raised by Senghor and Césaire in response to Wright and Alexis, deserves some final attention. Sylvia Washington Bâ, in her study of Senghor's work, maintains that far from having an antagonistic relationship to Europe, Senghor's main goal was a comparative investigation of European versus African civilizational legacies. It is to this end that Senghor compares the conception of the "word" in the Greek, Latin, French, and English contexts with the notion of the "word" in the Black African context.

Comparisons of Africa and Europe, which Senghor discussed in such depth, are also the subject of the work and scholarship of another Paris conference participant, Cheikh Anta Diop. In his paper, Diop discusses the cultural indebtedness of Europe to Africa, starting with the premises that Greece inherited its civilization from Egypt and that Egypt was in origin a Black civilization descended from older civilizations to the interior of the continent. Diop's 1967 book, *Antériorité des civilisations nègres: mythe ou vérité historique?* (The African Origin of

Clear Word and Third Sight

Civilization: Myth or Reality?) was a development of ideas in his 1955 work *Nation, nègres et culture,* published the year before the conference. At the conference Diop declared, "We have come to discover that the ancient Pharaonic Egyptian civilization was undoubtedly a Negro civilization. To defend this thesis, anthropological, ethnological, linguistic, historical, and cultural arguments have been provided. To judge their validity, it suffices to refer to *Nations, nègres et culture"* (Diop, 339).

Cheikh Anta Diop's analysis of the African contributions to civilization provide a context for viewing Europe's efforts to repress Africa's cultural legacies. While Césaire revealed the lies of "progress" that mystify colonial violence, it is worth noting that his analysis of the deliberate anti-"development" imperative of the colonial enterprise is substantially corroborated and expanded upon by the writings of Walter Rodney (who was assassinated in 1980). Rodney was just a boy of fourteen at the time of the Paris conference, but his highly influential 1972 book, *How Europe Underdeveloped Africa,* is of significance here for its discussion of Europe's economic indebtedness to Africa.

The notion of change from within for African and African diaspora societies implies the coming together of anticolonial strategies produced from the cultural experience native to the majority of the colonized; hence, therefore, the importance of understanding the cultural philosophies specific to this majority, as Senghor stressed.[19] This was the combined position of Césaire and Senghor. The struggle, therefore, at the 1956 conference could be described in terms of these differences: anticolonial strategies struggling to inform themselves by native cultural contexts versus anticolonial strategies informed by discourses of Western "progress" divorced from the cultural realities of the Black majority. These differing ideologies about resistance to colonial and imperialist oppression influenced the way the various Black cultural realities, at the heart of the matter, were imagined and understood.

Throughout this study I use the body of creative work of several African diaspora writers from the Caribbean and the United States to examine philosophical similarities across national boundaries and thereby to chart the contours of Damas's, Césaire's, and Senghor's negritudinal legacy. At the same time, although African diaspora literature from the United States is not the explicit focus of this study, the chain of relations between writers from various places requires that attention be paid to the significant influence of this body of writing on both continental and African Caribbean thought. In the next chapter, I examine the permutations of the Paris conference discourse on culture and identity with regard to post-1970 criticism and critical responses to Black women's writing from the Caribbean. How female gender identity figures in this discussion about cultural legacies is of central importance in chapter 2.

2

Colonial Legacies,
Gender Identity, and
Black Female Writing
in the Diaspora

While the First International Conference of Negro Writers and Artists may have no clear and direct relationship to post-1970s Black female writing, the ideological differences over culture and its manifestations articulated at the conference function, nevertheless, as part of the established terrain within which the later female writers necessarily negotiate. Trinidadian writer Merle Hodge's introduction to Erna Brodber's 1982 book *Perceptions of Caribbean Women: Towards a Documentation of Stereotypes* complements Aimé Césaire's 1956 conference essay "Culture and Colonisation" by pondering the relationship between the colonial legacy and literary production as it relates to the experience of the Black female subject. The pioneering essay "Characteristics of Negro Expression" by Zora Neale Hurston, which systematically argues for a "folksy" alternative to narratives of cultural imperialism under coloniality, is both a precursor of and parallel to the negritudinal legacy expressed in Léopold Senghor's contribution to the conference, "The Spirit of Civilization, or the Laws of African Negro Culture." This earlier male/female pairing of a different sort sheds light on the laws governing cultural expression emanating from the diaspora context. In this chapter, therefore, I will draw connections between the cultural debates engaged in at the 1956 conference and the questions raised by Black female writers and critics about the intersection of colonial legacies and gendered identities.

In 1934 Zora Neale Hurston published six short essays on the cultural characteristics of the "Negro" in southern rural Black life, in the anthology *Negro*, edited by Nancy Cunard, "of the Cunard shipping line family" (Hurston, *Sanctified Church*, 11; the essays were later reprinted in *Sanctified Church*). As Toni Cade Bambara said in the preface to the 1981 edition of *The Sanctified Church*, "Now there was a woman who worked. Waitress, manicurist, librettist, lecturer, secretary/companion, producer, scenarist, domestic, novelist, drama coach, file clerk, storyist, traveloguist, playwright, cook. Fun loving and bodacious, Zora was not playing" (9). Hurston came from a different cultural and class background than Senghor and used (among other things) the disciplines of literature and anthropology as a vehicle, but her similarities to Senghor lie in her investment in translating to a larger audience the cultural logic of the background that she came from.[1] Initially concerned with the aesthetic spirit and folklore of this population, Hurston's interest expanded to include the diaspora traditions of other "*African* Americans," such as African Jamaicans, Haitians, and eventually Hondurans. Published a year before her highly acclaimed collection of folklore, *Mules and Men*, her essays "Characteristics of Negro Expression" and "Spirituals and Neo-Spirituals" complement the cultural order described by Senghor, transplanted to a U.S. African diaspora context. While Senghor, in the early thirties, was just beginning to pose the question "What is negritude to me?"[2] Hurston, having already made her personal return to the source, was in the midst of waging a deliberate, if at times covert, war with the establishment position on the culture of the Black masses. As Senghor was preparing for the *agrégation*, the highest teaching diploma in France, Hurston struggled first through high school in Florida and then college at Howard, periodically working as a domestic to make ends meet. Yet despite the obvious differences of place and circumstance, Hurston and Senghor had one definitive similarity: they were both attempting to artistically represent and critically analyze the cultural realities of the largely oral communities they came from, alternately addressing a white public and a Black or "colored" elite. This elite was described by Alioune Diop in his opening address at the 1956 conference as alienated "from the populations which had remained attached to the soil and to their own traditions" (14). In "Spirituals and Neo-Spirituals" Hurston tells us:

> The real spirituals are not really just songs. They are unceasing variations around a theme. Contrary to popular belief their creation is not

Clear Word and Third Sight

confined to the slavery period. Like the folk-tales the spirituals are being made and forgotten every day. . . . These songs, even the printed ones do not remain long in their original form. Every congregation that takes it up alters it considerably. . . . To begin with, Negro spirituals are not solo or quartette material. The jagged harmony is what makes it, and it ceases to be what it was when this is absent. (*Sanctified Church,* 80)

Over twenty years later, at the 1956 conference, in his paper "The Spirit of Civilization, or the Laws of Negro African Culture," Senghor wrote:

Because they are functional and collective, African Negro Literature and art are committed. . . . They commit the person—and not only the individual. . . . That is why the African Negro works of art are not, as has often been said, copies of an archetype repeated a thousand times. Certainly there are subjects, each of which expresses a vital force. But what is striking is the variety of execution according to personal temperament and circumstances. . . . Because he is committed, the craftsman-poet is not concerned to create for eternity. Works of art are perishable. While their spirit and style are preserved, we hasten to replace the ancient work by modernising it. . . . This means that in Negro Africa "art for art's sake" does not exist; all art is social. (56–57)

In "Spirituals and Neo-spirituals" Hurston's aim was to contextualize the spirituals as sung within certain Black communal contexts while distinguishing this performance from what she describes as the no less valid and artistically interesting material performed by the Fisk, Hampton, and Tuskegee Glee Clubs. She argues, however, that the latter performances were not spirituals but rather "the works of Negro composers or adaptors *based* on the spirituals" (*Sanctified Church,* 80). What characterized the "real" spirituals were jagged harmony and a participatory Black church audience. The key distinction for Hurston was stylistic and contextual. Both Hurston's and Senghor's essays were short pieces in which they were called upon to generalize about large bodies of material. Hurston's essay focused on the specific characteristics of a particular art form, while the selection from Senghor's essay is devoted to the characteristics of "African Negro works of art." Yet the similarity of their descriptions approaches the uncanny. Hurston describes the spirituals as "made and forgotten everyday" and "not remain[ing] long in their original form" (*Hurston,* 869). Senghor states that "the craftsman-poet is not concerned to create for eternity"; works of art perish and, while the "spirit and style are preserved" (56), the ancient work is quickly modernized. Both essays describe art forms characterized by the element of communal participation. The commonality of their perspectives comes from the inseparable way in which they imagine the relationship between the individual and the community. Although Senghor is the one who explicitly describes the art in this context as social and never "art for art's sake," Hurston's entire essay is an attempt to force a distinction between a communal social art (spirituals in this case), and its static, even if beautiful, reproduction by the glee clubs. It is interesting to note at this point that the long rivalry and critical animosity between Zora Neale Hurston and Richard Wright is a product of the same difference in cultural vision that separated Wright and Senghor at the conference. While Hurston's work, like Senghor's, privileged the cultural identity of "the folk," Wright's work focused on the socioeconomic situation of the Black masses. Therefore, Hurston functions as the connection that Wright and the Haitian writer Jacques Stephen Alexis failed to make between the cultural reality represented by Senghor and their own.

In "Characteristics of Negro Expression," written after substantial folklore research but prior to the publication of *Mules and Men*, Hurston summarizes her observations on the rural Black communities she lived and worked among. The essay is divided under the subheadings "Drama," "Will to Adorn," "Angularity," "Asymmetry," "Dancing," "Negro Folklore," "Culture Heroes," "Originality," "Imitation," "Absence of the Concept of Privacy," "The Jook," and "Dialect." Here, Hurston not only expands the terrain of her analysis beyond the spirituals; she further allows this notion of communal social art to explode conventional ideas of what constitutes the artistic:

> Likewise love-making is a biological necessity the world over and an art among Negroes. So that a man or woman who is proficient sees no reason why the fact should not be moot. He swaggers. She struts hippily about. Songs are built on the power to charm beneath the bedclothes. Here again we have individuals striving to excel in what the community considers an art.
>
> It is all in a view-point. Love-making and fighting in all their branches are high arts, other things are arts among other groups where they brag about their proficiency just as brazenly as we do about these things that others consider matters for conversation behind closed doors. (*Sanctified Church*, 61)

Again, what is of significance is the overlap among the social, communal, and artistic arenas. Of further interest is Hurston's representation in this essay of female gender roles within this cultural context. While this issue is not explicitly the focus of any one subheading, the issue is inadvertently addressed throughout the entire essay.

> Oh de white gal rides in a Cadillac,
> De yaller gal rides de same,
> Black gal rides in a rusty Ford
> But she gits dere just de same.
> (*Sanctified Church*, 64)

Throughout the essay, the gendered behavior of Black females is described as oscillating between two poles of culturally inscribed actions. The first reference comes on the essay's second page, when Hurston describes the "Negro girl stroll[ing] past the corner. . . . Her whole body panging and posing" (*Sanctified Church*, 50). Here the sexuality of the behavior depicted is seen as part of a culturally inscribed ritual between young males and females on the various corners of locales within the United States. The second mention comes when Hurston uses a Langston Hughes poem as an example of the "asymmetry . . . of Negro art."

> I aint gonna mistreat ma good gal any more,
> I'm just gonna kill her next time she makes me sore.
> I treats her kind but she don't do me right,
> She fights and quarrels most ever' night.
> I can't have no woman's got such low-down ways
> Cause de blue gum woman aint de style now' days.
> I brought her from the South and she's goin on back,
> Else I'll use her head for a carpet tack.
> (Quoted in *Sanctified Church*, 54–55)

Despite the fact that the gender roles and sexual dynamics articulated are not Hurston's focus here, they are so forceful as to be inescapable. At first glance it seems mainly to be a description by an embittered mate seeking vengeance for his mistreatment. Upon closer observation, however, it becomes clear that despite the "generosity" of his choice of retribution ("I'll use her head for a carpet tack"), his actions are about equaling the score. The woman in this instance is not depicted as a passive party but as one who "fights and quarrels most ever' night." The embittered mate's anger is incited by "his woman's" lack of submissiveness. The violence of colonially inherited roles of submission coexist with models of resistant behavior, the historic legacy of Black survival through oppression.

Hurston's section on "The Jook" contains the most references to the gendered behavior of the Black female. It opens with her describing it as a place in which "men and women dance, drink, and gamble." And, she adds, "another interesting thing—Negro shows before being tampered with did not specialize in octoroon chorus girls. The girl who could hoist a Jook song from her belly and lam it against the front door of the theatre was the lead, even if she were as black as the hinges of hell" (*Sanctified Church*, 63–64). This is one of the first moments in which Hurston brings her analysis directly to bear on descriptions of female roles. Here she argues that the close-to-white octoroon chorus girls do not indicate consistently held beauty preferences on the part of the Black community: "the bleached chorus is the result of a white demand and not the Negro's" (64). Hurston's description of the kind of girl who used to appear in the Jook ("black as the hinges of hell" and able to "hoist a Jook song from her belly and lam it against the front door") captures not just the color difference between these imagined women, but also the aggressive yet culturally idealized behavior of the later ones.

Hurston briefly makes reference to color as it relates to women and marriage in the North and the South. In the North the "black woman is never the wife of the upper-class Negro" (64). In the South, on the other hand, she has observed on many occasions couples where the wife is dark-skinned and the upper-class husband has lighter skin. She then moves on to tell a key story, which she purports is indicative of the scorn periodically heaped on Black women despite their general idealization within a Black rural context:

> A man is lying beside his yaller wife and wakes her up. She says to him, "Darling, do you know what I was dreaming when you woke me up?" He says, "No honey, what was you dreaming?" She says, "I dreamt I had done cooked you a big, fine dinner and we was setting down to eat out de same plate and I was setting on yo' lap jus huggin you and kissin you and you was so sweet."
>
> Wake up a black woman and before you kin git any sense into her she be done up and lammed you over the head four or five times. When you git her quiet she'll say, "Nigger, know what I was dreamin when you woke me up?"
>
> You say, "No honey, what was you dreamin?" She says, "I dreamt

you shook yo' rusty fist under my nose and I split yo' head open wid a axe." (*Sanctified Church*, 65)

Hurston immediately follows this tale up with a counterrepresentation:

> Dat ole black gal, she keep on grumblin,
> New pair shoes, new pair shoes,
> I'm goint to buy her shoes and stockings
> Slippers too, slippers too.

Then adds aside: "Blacker de berry, sweeter de juice." To be sure the black gal is still in power, men are still cutting and shooting their way to her pillow. (*Sanctified Church*, 65)

Frequently, though not always, Hurston's descriptions of the differing culturally gendered behaviors of Black women establish a binary between lighter- and darker-skinned females, with the lighter-skinned ones represented as occupying the more Eurogendered position. In the tale of the two women, the bourgeois Western institution of marriage is only referenced in relation to the light-skinned female. The roles both women are represented as occupying differ substantially from there on out. The "yaller" wife is portrayed as imitating the behavior values of the nineteenth-century "cult of true womanhood," characterized by "piety, purity, submissiveness, and domesticity" within the context of marriage (Patton, *Women in Chains*, 29). The woman emulating these values would be perceived by the culturally Eurogendered listener/reader of the tale as more sympathetic. This "liberal" listener/reader would be self-righteously offended by the depiction of the Black woman (noticeably not described as a wife) as unable to imitate the behavior values premised on respectable notions of European womanhood. Such a reader/listener would be invested in arguing that a dark-skinned woman was equally capable of bourgeois gentility.

In the tale above, the Black woman's behavior falls emphatically outside the "cult of true womanhood." She is not submissive, and there is no cooked meal to suggest domesticity. Shaking her "rusty fist" under his nose and "splitting his head open with an axe" certainly suggest a lack of piety, while the notion of virginal purity is destabilized by the lack of any clear references to marriage despite the implied cohabitation. As in the Langston Hughes poem, in this second scenario, there is a consistent portrait of female aggression that "overbalances" the power in the Black male-female relationship. As Toni Cade Bambara says in her essay "On the Issue of Roles," "We are just as jammed in the rigid confines of those basically oppressive socially contrived roles. For if a woman is tough, she's a rough mamma, a strident bitch, a ballbreaker, a castrator" (*Black Woman*, 102). Bambara's assessment of this situation in her 1970 essay is consistent with Hurston's 1928 observations that "this scornful attitude towards Black women receives mouth sanction by the mud-sills. . . . They say that she is evil. That she sleeps with her fists doubled up and ready for action" (*Sanctified Church*, 64–65). Both Hurston's and Bambara's observations, recorded over a period of fifty years, document the stereotypes about Black female behavior that nevertheless reveal (in perverse fashion) that another set of cultural practices, beyond the dominant ones, inform the behavior of Black females. Hurston definitively affirms the cultural behavior of the Black female when she states thereafter, "To be sure the black gal is still in power, men are still cutting and shooting their way to her pillow" (*Sanctified Church*, 65). In this worldview, the pathological behavior is the one modeled on submissive domesticity that reinforces the colonially inherited gender roles.

In his essay "Emancipatory Perversions and the Sex of Slaves," Greg Thomas maintains that formulations and articulations of racial difference are inextricably intertwined with paradigms of gendered particularity. In this context, the terms "woman" and "man" are undergirded by the racial-cultural gender program of a European colonial order. Thomas maintains that if biology is not (simplistically and violently) read as destiny, then one has to take serious stock of how African diaspora race/gender disturbs heteronormative binary sex paradigms (1–4, 8). To make his argument Thomas turns his attention to contemporary critical analyses of gender roles as they relate to enslaved Black female bodies. Drawing on and quoting from Angela Davis's essay "Reflections on the Black Woman's Role in the Community of Slaves," Thomas states:

> In "Reflections" Davis writes that "the black woman had to be released from the chains of *the myth of femininity*"; indeed, that "[i]n order to function as slave, the black woman had to be *annulled as woman*." . . . Underscoring in "Legacy" the ineffably laborious activity of the majority of female slaves as field workers, Davis also upholds: "they might as well have been *genderless* as far as the slaveholders were

Clear Word and Third Sight

concerned" and "Black women were *practically anomalies.*" . . . In short, no dominating discourse of "feminine sex" functions to preclude the infliction and exploitation of colossal labors by the white slaver; she who is typologized as "breeder" and "not mother" is utterly exempted from the hegemonic discursive line of binarized sex. Consequently, this female slave oppression, construed as the chattelizing extraction of relentless toil, Davis delineates as "identical" to that of the male slaves. (6, original emphasis)

Using Davis to show how sexual exploitation and labor practices established that enslaved Black females fell categorically outside of the construction of "woman" through "femininity" and "domesticity," Thomas maintains that this resistance to a European colonial binary model of sex/gender has its roots not just in the institution of slavery but also in the varied African cultural backgrounds predating the Middle Passage (23). Thomas further destabilizes the category "woman" as it relates to the Black female body with reference to Hazel Carby's discussion of "the cult of true womanhood" in her *Reconstructing Womanhood* (Thomas, "Emancipatory Perversions," 27–29). "Despite the overwhelming discursive and institutional powers which unilaterally exclude the Black female slave from the construction of woman, Carby presumes the identarian unity of slave and mistress at the outset through this very category; . . . [and] perform[s] a feminization or womanization of the chattelized slave that is strictly refused by the society in question" (29). Through his analysis, therefore, Thomas attempts to historically situate the critical struggle over the gender identity of Black females. These critics are implicitly negotiating with definitions of womanhood most rooted in European female experience, or what I have heretofore been referring to as Eurogendered behavior.

It is this point of Erna Brodber's, the imitation of Eurogendered behavior, that Merle Hodge takes up in her introduction to Brodber's *Perceptions of Caribbean Women: Towards a Documentation of Stereotypes,* published in 1982. Hodge quotes a sentence of Brodber's: "These models [of true womanhood] . . . were internalized as 'right' if not as 'possible' and are seen today as part of [the Black] woman's psychic landscape" (xii). Hodge's introduction substantiates Césaire's analyses in "Culture and Colonisation" as they relate to the experiences of Caribbean women. Hodge examines how various women are represented in selected Caribbean novels, arguing that the representations have their parallel in Brodber's sociological research. She uses Brodber's conclusions as a point of departure for discussing how literary representations negotiate between official (European) culture, which contained particular prescriptions for what constituted "real" and "proper" female behavior, and the "mores of the tribe," with their own culturally specific gender role dictates.

The "stereotype," throughout Brodber's study as well as Hodge's introduction, refers to culturally Eurogendered notions of female roles. This is the behavior associated with "fair ladies in a fine castle" (viii). The "lady" is characterized by "pale and delicate" skin, a "pleasing, diffident, [and] unassuming" manner, marriage, and being primarily "devoted to comforting and serving the interests of one man in return for economic support" (xi and 55). This "fair lady in a fine castle" category appears to be the Hodge-Brodber Caribbean equivalent of the U.S.-based "cult of true womanhood." By contrast, Hodge describes the logic governing the behavior of Black "peasant" women when she states, "Where a stereotype belongs to a culture or to a stratum of society which is so 'remote' as to be inaccessible, then it does not determine *behaviour*, but it can affect self-image, the person's assessment of his/her own worth" (in Brodber, *Perceptions of Caribbean Women*, 55). By implication, Hodge suggests that another logic, what she otherwise refers to as "the mores of the tribe," primarily governs the gendered behavior of the Black masses in the Caribbean colonial context, a view similar to Hurston's on the cultural logic governing Black female roles and perceptions in the mass Black U.S. context. This is the case despite the discrepancy between the values of the "tribe" and the values officially sanctioned by the dominant culture. As Hodge adds later in her introduction, "The black woman operated outside of officially promulgated stereotypes of 'femininity.' Her behavior was determined by another set of prescriptions, chief of which was that the woman should stand up and fight on all fronts in order to ensure the best possible life for her children" (xi). Fighting and resisting as something that Black women are bred to do harkens back to Hurston's descriptions of Black female roles. Hodge observes, however, that this frequently goes hand in hand with the mother's investment in launching the child from the subculture to what she calls the image-making cultural context. The "image-making culture" refers to the norms originally shaped by European colonial values. These values shaped the official institutions of church, school, government, and the press.

It is significant that neither Hodge nor Brodber argues for drastic distinctions between the pre- and post-Independence Caribbean in terms of the effect on gender roles. Elsewhere, Hodge describes the situation in Trinidad after Independence as one in which one form of colonization replaced another.[3] In her introduction to Brodber's text she remarks that "today's image-makers have at their disposal more powerful instruments of persuasion than did those of the pre-Independence era. A crippling mystique of femininity today pervades our society through the agency of the mass media, affecting the self-image and the aspirations of hundreds of thousands of Caribbean women" (xiii). Despite Independence "the seat of power and of policy-making is not yet located in the Caribbean" (xiii). Brodber's study and Hodge's "intro" both view as significant the racial-cultural and class distinctions among Caribbean women. Hodge examines how Black, Indian, white, and biracial women are represented, further distinguishing between those who are poor working women and those who are "ladies in a fine castle." Hodge argues that this split between "Ideal Woman and Real Woman" is just one aspect of a tension that "is a permanent feature of Caribbean culture"—one that is constantly treated in the literature (viii). This is the discrepancy between official culture and the counter- or subcultures, "between school and home, between the culture of books, newspapers and religious instruction and the culture practiced by the adults" as is often seen through the eyes of the children in their care (viii).

Since Hodge's essay and Brodber's study, numerous anthologies of Caribbean women's writing have been published in the last fifteen years. More frequently collections of fiction rather than critical essays, these books, and their introductions in particular, exemplify the contemporary critical approaches to this body of writing. Significant among them are *Watchers and Seekers: Creative Writing by Black Women in Britain* (1987), *Her True-True Name: An Anthology of Women's Writing from the Caribbean* (1989), *Out of the Kumbla: Caribbean Women and Literature* (1990), *Caribbean Women Writers: Essays from the First International Conference* (1990), and *Green Cane and Juicy Flotsam: Short Stories by Caribbean Women* (1991).[4] Tying her literary analysis to tangible sociological research, Hodge argues that the dichotomies that are a permanent feature of Caribbean culture, and which produce the female subject in particular ways, are substantiated by the literary representations of generations of Caribbean writers. This is a departure from a more prevalent and utopian emphasis on Caribbean women writers as both self-inventing and controlling their image divorced from the historical realities influencing their actions. Further, Hodge's aim is not simply to observe that the literature, although fictionalized, is grounded in historical experience, but rather to use both as a way of further understanding the culturally gendered behavior of various Caribbean women.

Hodge concludes that gendered behavior is structured by one's racial and cultural background and the proximity between the cultural background and the image-making culture's notions of "femininity." As she states earlier, where the discrepancy between these two factors is large, as is the case for Black females, the "mores of the tribe" (the racial-cultural background emanating from the African context) still appears to dictate behavior although the image-making culture's notions of "femininity" may become part of the "psychic landscape" of the woman. Since historically, within the context of many Caribbean societies, the official societal institutions and the primary image-making culture has emanated from the white metropolis, the further removed one is from whiteness, racially and culturally, the less one will see one's racial-cultural reality reflected in the "national" institutions. This is the case even if the majority of the island population may be physically dark.[5] Within this context, the culturally gendered behavior of women who are Black, Indian, or white would differ based on the history of their community's arrival in the Caribbean, the size of these communities, and the position they occupy within the varying local hierarchies of culture and power. The specificity of these factors would dictate culturally gendered behavior despite the euphemism of the category "Caribbean woman."

Additionally, within the Caribbean, since the external colonial and imperialist nation's ability to control images is a manifestation of its economic power, it follows that economic mobility in the island context will necessarily mean aspiring toward the culture of the colonizer. This is the case even if, as Hodge and Brodber astutely observe, ultimate assimilation consistently proves impossible and the consequences of such a focus are increasingly devastating in almost all sectors of island life. This detrimental reality uneasily coexists with cultural transmission between African diaspora populations throughout the Americas. Increasingly, as imperialist technological developments have been appropriated by the everyday folk in small Black countries, cultural transmissions of folklore, fashion sensibilities, music, and film have traveled across geographic boundaries, continuing to fuel and shape an affirmative set of diaspora ideals and cultural

Clear Word and Third Sight

practices. These give identity and form to the mass Black populace while also continuously shaping what gets constituted as "national" culture within the various Caribbean contexts.

The First International Conference of Caribbean Women Writers, convened at Wellesley College in 1988, is a noteworthy event historically, but any straightforward link and comparison between this conference and the earlier 1956 conference is an uneasy one. Although the female focus in 1988 contrasts with the predominantly male presence in 1956, the later conference was more narrowly focused on the Caribbean populace, rather than extending to Black people from the continent and the diaspora. The collection that was produced in its wake (a combination of essays by critics summarizing the field of Caribbean women's writing and personal essays by the writers themselves) did not attempt to be the kind of Pan-African "cultural stock-taking" that arguably was at the center of the 1956 conference. Additionally, Selywn Cudjoe's introduction to the collection (the only male-authored introduction of all the texts examined here) is a clear departure from the discursive struggle between a universal feminist framework and a negritude-oriented "womanist" approach to the literature that other female scholars and writers engage in. While the Black female critics of both earlier and later collections wrestled to varying degrees with the theoretical relationship between cultural mores native to African diaspora communities and externally inherited models of female behavior, Cudjoe's introduction falls prey to a universalizing discourse of "Caribbean woman." Choosing to introduce the writing in conventional historical terms, Cudjoe begins with the earliest text in his chronological account and moves from region to region linguistically and geographically. Identifying the writers as "Caribbean women" he refuses any consistent reference to the race/class distinctions that Hodge and Brodber describe as foundational to any analysis of female cultural identity in the region.

The point of departure for the 1991 anthology *Green Cane and Juicy Flotsam* (which the editors, Carmen C. Esteves and Lizabeth Paravisini-Gebert, argue is one of the first collections exclusively devoted to short stories) is first and foremost a celebration of a collective Caribbean female identity, whose diversity is described primarily in terms of regional linguistic differences. In their introduction, Esteves and Paravisini-Gebert state, "The increasing popularity of Caribbean women writers has been sparked by a growing interest in voices from the Third World, where issues of gender and feminism are compounded by labyrinthine questions of race, power, colonialism, poverty, and the correlation between national and personal identities. Since their work often addresses some manifestation of gender, class, racial or colonial 'Otherness,' it has served as the catalyst for critical exchange on these issues" (xi–xii). In this anthology a universal feminist analysis is a frequently used lens, viewed more or less as encompassing and bespeaking the experience of Caribbean women. The "Caribbean woman's" taking up of the pen is seen as a clear and direct step toward the demise of colonial and patriarchal institutions.[6] Women's writing is constructed as a site of liberation, and the continuity between old culturally Eurogendered paradigms of womanhood pre- and post-Independence are not systematically traced in the "Caribbean woman's" representation of herself, despite the fact that the categories of race, class, and gender are constantly invoked. There is, at such a moment, a presumption that writing by Caribbean women will result in representations that are more realistic and that, because they emanate from a female center, will not be complicit in the perpetuation of the oppression of their "sisters" and "brothers." Yet Hodge's essay shows that Caribbean literature, rather than being an uncontaminated space of liberation, reflects the complexity of cultural realities in which both racial and socioeconomic factors shape the pull between officially prescribed and communal norms. Hodge's analysis makes it clear that female writers from the Caribbean context will necessarily be complicit in the structures they represent. It is precisely universal notions of "femininity" that are revealed to be deeply compromised by the culturally gendered differences between Black, Indian, and white women, based on their socioeconomic location and the communal norms of their people. This resistance to a universalizing Eurofeminism and, consequently, the implicit conflict between the Hodge-Brodber position and that of Esteves and Paravisini-Gebert over the discursive frameworks most relevant to an analysis of Black and other "third world" female writings, is the parallel to the earlier struggle between Euro-Marxist discourses and negritude at the 1956 Paris conference. While there is a clear investment in the Hodge-Brodber text in analyzing Black female-gendered behavior and societal power relations, feminism as a discourse is never explicitly invoked.

There is an implicit critique of feminism in the 1987 collection *Watchers and Seekers,* edited by Rhonda Cobham and Merle Collins. Cobham, in her introduction to the anthology of creative writing by Black women in Britain—without using the term "feminism"—de-

Clear Word and Third Sight

scribes the anthology as an attempt on the part of the young writers included to fashion and define the terms "Blackness and Woman-hood" through their art and for themselves. "Black," in the context of this anthology, includes women of African and South Asian descent. Cobham, referring to the writers in this collection, notes, "Listening to the way in which their 'Black British' speech rhythms were overlaid and complemented by Caribbean, Afro-American and, occasionally, African word patterns, I began to feel that the further the writers got from 'Home' the more responsive they seemed to become to the possibilities of interconnection between a range of Black voices that extended far beyond their immediate cultural experience" (9). While Cobham, like the editors in the introductions to the other anthologies, observes the prevalence in this writing of the focus on relations be-tween women of the "tribe" (mothers, daughters, and grandmothers), she is also most explicit in highlighting the significant influence of female writers from the Black U.S. context on the current generations of Black female writing in Britain. "The poetry and prose of Alice Walker and, to a lesser extent, the other Afro-American women writ-ers now published in Britain were mentioned recurrently as a source of inspiration by writers . . . as far flung as the Chinese/Guyanese Meiling Jin, living in London, and the Nigerian Rita Anyiam-St. John, working in Jos" (8).

In an uncanny way, Cobham, in her mention of the influence of Black U.S. writers on young, mostly second-generation, "Black" fe-males writing in Britain, highlights the negritudinal thrust that is produced by these young women's experience of alienation in Britain. The further away "Home" was, the more important Black intercon-nectedness became.[7] The experience forces a resort to two sources of inspiration: the mothers, grandmothers, and company of women who raised them *and* the writings of, not "women" generally, but Black U.S.-born females in particular, writing out of experiences of pro-found alienation on the one hand and a wealth of communal life on the other. Living in the center of British empire, without a "colored nation" to mystify their racial and cultural marginalization, it is no mystery that these women of color would gravitate toward the most experienced culturally resistant peoples living in the belly of imperial-ism: Africans in the "Americas," specifically in the United States. This attempt, therefore, at a coarticulation of the categories "Blackness and womanhood," far from being a self-evident liaison, constantly evokes a reconciliation of Black, specifically female, experience in the context of a larger Black communal existence. This, however, is done within the vexed context of rhetorical categories with a Eurogendered bias.[8]

It is this tension once again, over finding adequate rhetorical categories to theorize female experience and gendered behavior in the African Caribbean, that is at stake in the introductory "conversation" between the Black and white editors of the anthology *Out of the Kumbla: Caribbean Women and Literature*. In this conversation, they discuss their struggle with the difference between the terms "feminism" and "womanism." The Black editor, Carole Boyce Davies, describes "womanism" as a redefinition of "feminism" that qualifies the latter term's overdetermination by the experiences of Western white women. She states, "There is a consistent move to find new language to encompass our experience. This comes either in modifying the term by an adjective of some sort: 'Black' feminists . . . 'African' feminist[s] . . . radical or Marxist feminist[s] for some white or black women who find the term 'feminist' too contaminated with bourgeois experience" (xii). Davies goes on to describe further modification of the term "womanism" to "woman consciousness" by African women who want both men and women to have access to the discursive terrain.

The anthology's white editor, Elaine Savory Fido, states that what she appreciates about the term "womanism" is its emphasis, according to Alice Walker, on "the cultural aspects of African community in the United States" (xii). Yet she finds problematic what Chikwenye Ogunyemi (in a 1985 essay) argues is a "separation of black and white feminism along the terms of 'womanist' and 'feminist'" (xii).[9] Fido writes, "I found Ogunyemi's thesis too rejecting of feminism to be sensitive to the literature she used as examples. I simply cannot accept that all white feminists are x, y, z, or that all Black feminists are either. We are all complexly involved with various intersecting agendas" (xi–xii). Fido goes on to say that she sees feminism as referring to a "political agenda" and womanism as the "cultural manifestation—women's talk, customs, lore" (xii). What becomes apparent is that for Fido, the need to articulate a universal feminist agenda, which she can comfortably designate as the political one, blinds her to the very "complexly involved . . . intersecting agendas" that she herself critiques Ogunyemi for forgetting. In other words, she depoliticizes the "cultural manifestations" of womanism in her inability to acknowledge that a focus on "the cultural aspects of African community" is necessarily a war against racist and colonial institutions that would deny

Clear Word and Third Sight

this articulation of specificity. In this sense, then, her embrace of the term "feminism" and qualification of the term "womanism" is premised on a homogenization of the differences between women that Hodge and Ogunyemi cannot afford to forget.

The tension over the "womanist-feminist" conjunction is directly addressed in Sylvia Wynter's stunning "After/Word" to *Out of the Kumbla*, "Beyond Miranda's Meanings: Un/silencing the 'Demonic Ground' of Caliban's 'Woman.'" Getting to the heart of the issue immediately, Wynter opens her essay thus:

> The point of departure for this *After/Word* is to explore a central distinction that emerges as the dynamic linking sub-text of this, the first collection of critical essays written by Caribbean women. This distinction is that between Luce Irigaray's purely Western assumption of a universal category, "woman," whose "silenced" ground is the condition of what she defines as an equally universally applicable, "patriarchal discourse," and the dually Western and post-Western editorial position of a projected "woman/feminist" critical approach as the unifying definition of the essays that constitute the anthology. The term *"womanist/feminist,"* with the qualifying attribute "womanist" borrowed from the Afro-American feminist Alice Walker, reveals the presence of a contradiction, which whilst central to the situational frame of reference of both Afro-American and Caribbean women writers/critics, is necessarily absent from the situational frame of reference of both Western-European and Euroamerican women writers. (*Out of the Kumbla,* 355)

Among other things, Wynter's analysis makes it clear that the theoretical tension between the anthology's Black and white female editors, far from being unique and specific to them or this text, is instead a defining characteristic of Black and white female writers and critics' attempts to theorize gender. After Wynter, the fundamental question is not *whether* Black female critics and writers explicitly employ strictly feminist or womanist theories and themes in their writing; rather, the new question is *where* they ultimately locate themselves (or are located) on a preexisting, even if underemphasized, cultural continuum between the European and African philosophical worldviews. To substantiate her point, Wynter analyzes Shakespeare's *Tempest* as a way of further exposing the historical hierarchy of gendered desire in the Western imaginary. In this context, white femininity, as represented by Prospero's Miranda, occupies a central role, with Black female genders being nowhere on the landscape, as demonstrated by the absence of Caliban's mate or "woman."

Wynter's assessment of the womanist-feminist conjunction is in many ways a continuation of the explicit questions posed by 1970s Black feminists, such as Gloria T. Hull, Patricia Bell Scott, and Barbara Smith, whose anthology begged the question with its title, *All the Women Are White, All the Blacks Are Men, But Some of Us Are Brave.* More radical, even, than Hull, Bell Scott, and Smith, on the one hand, and Wynter, on the other, are the questions raised by the late Toni Cade Bambara. In her seminal introduction to *The Black Woman* (1970) she asks, "How relevant [are] . . . the truths, the experiences, [and] the findings of white women to Black women? Are women after all simply women?" While Wynter describes the differential theoretical ground separating the approaches of Black and white female writers and critics to texts and material, Toni Cade questions the formative foundations of their identities. With this move, she roots Wynter's statements about their different theoretical approaches back to the reality of historically lived experiences.[10]

An unusual and interesting move is made by the editors of the 1989 anthology *Her True-True Name.* The two Jamaican sisters who edited the volume, Pamela Mordecai and Betty Wilson, are at pains to emphasize the historical neglect of "women's" writing in the region while also addressing the differences within Caribbean female experience: differences that are operative within the fiction presented and that also cannot be separated from the experiences of the writers themselves. They state, "It is important to underline the fact that recent writing by anglophone Caribbean women is rigorously honest in its rendering of the societies. There is no ritual pursuing of psuedo-feminist agendas; rather there is sufficient detachment to allow for women to make the protagonists in their novels male (Velma Pollard, for example), not through any mimetic impulse but deliberately, as part of the creative statement" (xvii).

Mordecai and Wilson highlight three main themes as central to the body of writing in the collection. First among them is male-female relationships, which they state must find positive resolution before community can be restored and communal relationships rebuilt. Second is the mother-daughter relationship, which they argue is generally depicted with more ambivalence and complexity in the female writing than it is in the work of their male counterparts. Finally, there is "the issue of identity and the quest for wholeness" (xv). While it is

Clear Word and Third Sight

clear that the female experience in all its components is as much of a priority in Mordecai and Wilson's text as in their "sister" anthologies, the three themes they consistently isolate in the literature seem interestingly "womanist" in orientation. The male-female dynamic as represented in the literature is one in which "the man regards the woman as an object, [and] neglects, abuses, ill-treats and diminishes her"; for this reason, Mordecai argues that restoration of a notion of community among West Indians is impossible without reconciliation between men and women to overcome the history of violence in the male-female relationship (xiv).

In an essay published several years before her introduction to Brodber's study, Merle Hodge states, "The man-woman relationship is nowhere a straightforward, uncomplicated one—it is always perhaps the most vulnerable, the most brittle of human relationships. And in the Caribbean this relationship has been adversely affected by certain factors of our historical development, notably, I think, by the legacy of violence and disruption with which our society has never adequately come to terms" ("Shadow of the Whip," 111). Linking the male-female dynamic, like other facets of Caribbean culture, back to the violence of slavery, Hodge refers to the internalization of psychological violence (a by-product of the physical violence) by the survivors of slavery and their descendants. Her hypothesis is that, among other things, the violence and disrespect with which some Black Caribbean males treat Black females is due in part to the fact that they evaluate them by the (European) colonial societies' standards of femininity.[11] At the essay's close she writes, "When the black man no longer forcibly evaluates his women by the standards of a man who once held the whip over him [this will be] one stage of his liberation from the whip hand" (118). For Hodge, the advent of Black power ideology in the 1970s was a positive and influential step forward in the process of psychic decolonization necessary to the improvement of male/female relationships. This was the case because it "effectively set about revising our concepts of physical beauty" (118). So for Hodge, Mordecai, and Wilson, as for Toni Cade Bambara, the violence of the Black male-female relationship in the U.S. and Caribbean African diaspora is directly related to both slavery and the colonial situation as a whole.

Ultimately, however, it is the third theme that Mordecai and Wilson highlight, the issue of identity and wholeness, that most resonates with the questions of negritude central to womanist discourse. It is in their analysis of this thematic in Caribbean literature that they make their most definitive statements about the relationship between race, social location, and writing in *Her True-True Name*. Taking their anthology's title from a line in Merle Hodge's first novel, *Crick Crack Monkey*, Mordecai and Wilson argue that this text "begins the work of rescue" (xvii).[12] For these editors, the literary attempt to decolonize the self necessarily means recourse to folk narrative and a Creole voice. Attempting to textually represent orality is the biggest allegiance to the "tribe" that a writer can have. At this juncture, Mordecai and Wilson place emphasis on both accurate renditions of a Creole voice and sensibility as well as on textual representations that emphasize psychospiritual healing from "the shadow of the whip." Jean Rhys comes under attack despite her "valuing [of] island culture, black people and the creole language" for failing to offer a vision that restores the communal spirit (xvii). Similarly, Michele Cliff is critiqued for "a compromised authenticity in some aspects of her rendering of creole." This is attributed to both her social position, like Rhys, as a white Creole and her long absence from the actual Caribbean context despite the focus of her fiction (xvii). Like Rhys, they view Cliff as being more in "the alienated tradition of a 'francophone' than an anglophone consciousness" (xvii).[13]

If, in her *After/Word* to *Out of the Kumbla*, Sylvia Wynter points out the significance of the Black female's absence from the idealized hierarchy of gender and desire in the Western imaginary, *then* the question of the existence of another order of knowledge and desire still remains. Several significant single-authored texts by continental Black female writers have sought to critically redress historical misportrayals of continental cultural reality and female-centered experiences in these contexts. Nigerian scholar Ifi Amadiume's three-book trilogy, *Male Daughters, Female Husbands* (1987), *Reinventing Africa: Matriarchy, Religion and Culture* (1997), and *Daughters of the Goddess, Daughters of Imperialism* (2000), is worth mentioning here. Also of note is Oyeronké Oyewumi's 1999 study *The Invention of Women: Making an African Sense of Western Gender Discourses*. These texts all target the ethnocentric assumption that Western discursive frameworks rooted in cultural norms native to the European context are logical points of departure for any and all analyses of African and African diaspora reality.

Drawing on the traditions of the Oyo Yoruba peoples of southwestern Nigeria for both the theory and substance of her research,

Clear Word and Third Sight

Oyeronké Oyewumi maintains that "there were no *women*—defined in strictly gendered terms—in that society" (*The Invention of Women*, xiii). In her preface, Oyewumi states:

> When I started the research, I believed that it was possible for me to do a study on gender in a contemporary Yorùbá community that would primarily address the question from a local perspective. It soon became clear to me that because of the academic practice of relying on disciplinary theories and conceptual debates originating in and dominated by the West, many of the questions that informed the initial research project were not (and could not be) generated from local conditions. (ix)

While not citing his work as a precedent, Oyewumi comes to conclusions similar to those of Cheikh Anta Diop, who maintains that there has been a long history of what some Black scholars refer to as "scientific lying" on the part of Western and Western-educated historians of ancient texts.[14] Arguing that the "so-called woman question" is a "Western-derived issue—a legacy of the age-old somatocentricity in Western thought," Oyewumi roots her statements with three primary contentions (ix).

First, as stated above, is the contention that the Western conceptual categories that have been developed within related academic contexts are ideologically products of those self-same cultural realities. In the first chapter of her book, *The Invention of Women*, titled "Visualizing the Body: Western Theories and African Subjects," Oyewumi argues under the subhead "Western Hegemony in African Studies" that African studies by and large falls victim to Western conceptualizations. Stating that it doesn't matter "whether any particular scholar is reacting for or against the West," she argues, "the point is that the West is at the center of African knowledge-production" (18). Observing that one of the hottest debates in African studies at the close of the twentieth century is "whether Africans had philosophy before European contact or are . . . 'philosophyless' peoples," Oyewumi maintains that "African experiences rarely inform *theory* in any field of study" (18, italics mine). Although she goes on to draw a distinction between "nativist" and "antinativist" thought in African studies, she claims that both have "always focused not on *difference* from the West but on *sameness* with the West." This strong identification with the West has resulted in "African versions of Western things" (19). Situating Senghor on the "nativist" continuum, she criticizes his "acceptance of the European categories of essence, race, and reason" in order to claim that African versions of these same phenomena exist (20). On the other hand, her strongest criticism is reserved for "antinativists" such as Abiola Irele and Kwame Anthony Appiah, whom she describes as "unapologetic . . . Euro-nativist(s)" (19, 24).

Oyewumi's second contention elaborates on her reference to the "somatic" nature of Western thought. She argues that "the cultural logic of Western categories is based on an ideology of biological determinism: the conception that biology provides the rationale for the organization of the social world" (ix). Despite all arguments to the contrary, "this cultural logic is actually a 'bio-logic.' Social categories like 'woman' are based on body-type and are elaborated in relation to and in opposition to another category: man; the presence or absence of certain organs determines social position" (ix–x). Under the sub-head "Social Orders and Biology: Natural or Constructed?" Oyewumi describes the introduction of social constructivism into the discursive terrain of "second-wave feminist scholarship" as groundbreaking for Western feminists "since it was interpreted to mean that gender differences were not ordained by nature . . . [but] were mutable and therefore changeable." She notes that "this finding was understandably taken to be radical in a culture in which . . . gender difference, had always been articulated as natural and, therefore, biologically determined" (8). While she cites Judith Butler stating that "sex itself is a gendered category," Butler's very phraseology appears to further substantiate Oyewumi's claim. Whether or not Western feminist scholarship naturalizes "sex" and femininity or treats it as a social construction, there is an "inseparability of sex and gender in the West" with "the terms . . . essentially [functioning as] synonyms," since "gender" cannot really exist without "sex" in this context. She concludes, therefore, that by and large in the West, "sex has served as the base and gender as the superstructure" (9, 12). She goes on to argue that "the debate in [Western] feminism about what roles and which identities are natural and what aspects are constructed only has meaning in a culture where social categories are conceived as having no independent logic of their own" (9).

Oyewumi's third contention is that if African culture is to be unlinked from a debilitating dependence on Westernism (with regard to gender or any other issue), then native African languages have to be taken seriously. Starting with language, therefore, she says:

Clear Word and Third Sight

Gender as a dichotomous discourse is about two binarily opposed and hierarchical social categories—men and women. Given that, I should immediately point out that the usual gloss of the Yorùbá categories *obinrin* and *okùnrin* as "female/woman" and "male/man," respectively, is a mistranslation. This error occurs because many Western and Western-influenced Yorùbá thinkers fail to recognize that in Yorùbá practice and thought, these categories are neither binarily opposed nor hierarchical. The word *obinrin* does not derive etymologically from *okùnrin*, as "wo-man" does from "man." *Rin*, the common suffix . . . suggests a common humanity; the prefixes *obin* and *okun* specify which variety of anatomy. There is no conception here of an original human type against which the other variety had to be measured. *'niyàn* is the non-gender-specific word for humans. (32–33)

Oyewumi argues that *okùnrin* and *obinrin,* unlike English male/female categories, "are not normally used [to refer to] *omodé* (children) or *eranko* (animals)" (33). Yet, having stated this, Oyewumi acknowledges that, despite the absence of implicit connotation of either social privilege or disadvantage, the terms *okùnrin* and *obinrin* do refer to the anatomical differences between males and females specifically with regard to reproduction. She argues that in the Yoruba context, however, the "acceptance of distinctive reproductive roles for men and women" does not necessarily lead to the "creation of social hierarchies," since this society's logic is based on social relations rather than the body. Although obinrin bear the babies, the "essentializing of *obinrin*" is foreclosed because both obinrin and okùnrin "remain *èniyàn* . . . in an ungendered sense." Thus, Oyewumi maintains, "the distinction between *obinrin* and *okùnrin* is actually one of reproduction, not one of sexuality or gender" (36).

Oyeronké Oyewumi's position may appear contradictory, since she claims on the one hand that "there were no *women*" in Oyo Yoruba society and on the other, she is forced to resort to versions of the very sex/gender terminology she is criticizing in order to make her own argument. Yet three issues in particular make these apparent contradictions less substantial. First, if as Oyewumi argues, the Yoruba (and by extension other African cultures) operate from an entirely different "worldsense," then the translation of words and terms into English and other Western European languages is already a vexed issue. The dearth of serious studies privileging native languages, cultures, and an African "worldsense" negatively impacts the accuracy of attempts at cultural translation. Oyewumi's makes it immediately apparent that

Diop's 1950s assessment of the paucity of serious and systematic study of African cultures is still relevant. If the Oyo Yoruba world order is based on highly sophisticated social relations, then it would follow that there are terms for the numerous roles that various people occupy in society, roles that have no comparable equivalent in the West. The significance, therefore, of Oyewumi's critique of African studies' "Westernist" focus becomes apparent. Third, there is no denying the impact of colonialism on traditional African social and cultural institutions, as discussed with regard to the analysis of culture in the diaspora, earlier on in this chapter.

Oyewumi's claim that (Western) gender categories rely on a "bio-logic" (since social categories in the West have no independent logic of their own) is stated in contrast to an African Yoruba societal logic that is "based on social relations rather than the body" (36). This particular claim by Oyewumi is further addressed by another African diaspora scholar, Oba T'Shaka. In his most recent book, T'Shaka, in the chapter entitled "Male-Female Equality and Parallel Complementary Empowerment," gives a portrait of various traditional African societies that supports Oyewumi's claim. Here, T'Shaka enters into a textual dialogue with Cheikh Anta Diop, one in which he critiques Diop's "two cradle theory" about the origins of family structure and societal development.

Diop's "two cradle theory" rested on his own critiques of Western theoreticians such as Bachofen, Morgan, and Engels, who (universalizing Western European cultural reality) concluded that family structure had followed a linear pattern of development. This progression moved from sexual promiscuity outside of marriage to matriarchy and finally to patriarchy, defined as the highest level of social evolution (T'Shaka, *Return to the African Mother Principle*, 176). Turning to ancient history and juxtaposing the evolution of Greek social mores with those of Egypt and Ethiopia, Diop's "two cradle theory" maintained instead that matriarchy had never been a substantial part of the European civilizational past. Instead, the rugged, nomadic life on the Eurasian plains had instilled in the ancestors of the Greeks a view of "man" as the "conqueror of hostile Nature" (Diop, *African Origin of Civilization*, 230–31). The cold harsh climate not only favored a nomadic lifestyle and a "materialist instinct," but survival under these conditions required physical strength and the strength of the male was predictably favored over the strength of the female (T'Shaka, 177). In this worldview, the physical body is privileged and sets the terms for cultural mores and societal values. Extrapolating further from here, Diop attempts to make links between the privileging of the physical body, due to the natural environment, and the resulting Greek existential worldview.

> The horizons of the Greek were never to pass beyond material, visible man. . . . On the earth, everything gravitated around him; the supreme objective of art was to reproduce his exact likeness. In the "heavens," paradoxically, he alone was to be found, with his earthly faults and weaknesses, beneath the shell of gods distinguished from ordinary mortals only by physical strength. Thus, when the Greek borrowed the Egyptian god, a real god in the full sense of the word . . . he could understand that deity only by reducing him to the level of man. Consequently, the adoptive pantheon of the Greek was merely another humanity. Once they had borrowed Egyptian values, the worldly genius of the Greeks, emanating basically from the Eurasian plains and from their religious indifference, favored the existence of a secular, worldly science. Taught publicly by equally worldly philosophers, this science was no longer a monopoly of a priestly group to be jealously guarded and kept from the people, lest it be lost in social upheavals. (231)

Shifting to the southern cradle, Diop argues that where conditions were more favorable to a sedentary life, agricultural societies thrived and male and female roles were equally essential to survival, unlike the northern cradle where, due to her physical "weaker"-ness, the work of the (white) female was less essential. In many southern-cradle societies African women were the "discoverers of the food crops," with men being in charge of the hunt. While there was a clear interdependence, agricultural societies were centered around the woman. These conditions were therefore conducive to the rise of matrilineal and matriarchal family systems (T'Shaka, 178–79).

T'Shaka, in his critique of Diop's "two cradle theory," maintains that environmental factors alone do not explain the nomadic Eurasian's conquest-like approach to nature and cultural reality, since other peoples in equally barren climates did not respond in similar ways (229). On the other hand, what Diop describes as matriarchal or matrilineal, T'Shaka (in a study of fourteen randomly selected societies from north, south, east, west, and central Africa) maintains that the complex interweaving of male and female lineage in terms of inheritance and societal responsibilities evaded any neat classification as either matrilineal/matriarchal or patrilineal/patriarchal (188–96). Claiming that these terms need to be discarded, T'Shaka opts instead for the term "twinlineal" as a concept that more accurately reflects the balance more consistently maintained in African societies with regards to male/female dynamics (228). Yet on one particular point, T'Shaka's theories complement and expand upon Diop's. Building on Diop's notion of the deification of the physical, T'Shaka connects the alienation from nature, cosmos, and spirit, with the constant thematic alienation between man and woman that recurs in Greek history and philosophy (178).

Nigerian scholar Ifi Amadiume's three-text trilogy addresses different aspects of the culture/gender matrix in the continental African context. Her book *Male Daughters, Female Husbands: Gender and Sex in an African Society* is an expanded analysis of her study of the Igbo peoples in the town of Nnobi in eastern Nigeria—*African Matriarchal Foundations: The Case of Igbo Societies*. Like Oyewumi's work, *Male Daughters, Female Husbands* and the shorter *African Matriarchal Foundations* are both studies focused on the customs and people of a particular society. Amadiume describes Nnobi as a town "in the only Igbo area which has not been studied in detail by any social scientist or anthropologist, or written about from a lay point of view" (*Male Daughters,* 17). While Amadiume does not attempt to contest and destroy discursive sex/gender constructs as aggressively as Oyewumi does, her analysis of the male-daughter/female-husband phenomenon in Igbo society substantiates Oyewumi's claims and further destabilizes the applicability of Western gender discourse to African cultural realities.[15] Amadiume states:

> This system of few linguistic gender distinctions makes it possible to see certain social roles as separate from sex and gender, hence the possibility for either sex to fill in the roles. . . . Two examples of situations in which women played roles ideally or normally occupied by men, that is, what I have called male roles, in indigenous Nnobi society . . . were "male daughters," daughters who have been accorded the status of sons to enable them to continue their father's line of descent, and "female husbands," women who married other women. In either role, women acted as family heads. The Igbo word for family head is the genderless expression *di-bu-no*. The genderless *di* is a prefix word which means . . . master of something. . . . A woman in this position is referred to as *dibuno* in the same term as a man in this position would be called. . . . Whereas, in English, because of its rigid

Clear Word and Third Sight

gender construction, a female head would be referred to as mistress and a male head as master. (*African Matriarchal Foundations*, 28–29)

Just as Oyewumi analyzes *okùnrin* and *obinrin* as terms that do not imply the derivative hierarchy of man/woman and male/female, so Amadiume presents *dibuno* as gender-neutral, exemplifying a role for which there is no simple comparison in the Westernized context. In this regard Amadiume's analysis is complemented by Oba T'shaka:

> A most interesting dual or twin expression showing a belief in a philosophy of male-female complementary Twin-ness, and masculine-feminine synthesis within the same person is shown through the terms a child gives to the father's sister who is called "female father" and the mother's brother who is named "male mother." Swazi children behave the same way toward the father's sister (female father) as they do toward the father. Similarly, the mother's brother (male mother) is treated the same way the mother is treated. (*Return to the African Mother Principle*, 208)

In Amadiume, Oyewumi, and T'Shaka there is a dual investment in pointing out the relational rather than "bio-logical" nature of the cultural categories used, as well as the implied decrease in hierarchies of domination between people in relational societies. Their findings carry important implications for the relationships among power, hierarchy, and the social-historical conditions shaping cultures.

Amadiume's books *Reinventing Africa* and *Daughters of the Goddess, Daughters of Imperialism* are collections of essays that begin to draw connections diasporically among various continental African cultural realities. On one hand, at the heart of these two texts is a focus on matriarchal and matrilineal societal structures as a predominant legacy on the continent. On the other hand, Amadiume's larger mission and purpose seems to be to respond to Cheikh Anta Diop's call (she explicitly cites him as having a strong influence on her work) for historically accurate accounts of African history, from ancient to modern periods. While Oyewumi levels a devastating critique at the persistent Westernisms in African studies, Amadiume attacks social anthropology and the way in which its early racist assumptions influenced both colonial policy and European feminist thought.

In her preface to *Male Daughters, Female Husbands*, Amadiume states that her "primary incentive" to study this material was her "reaction, as an African woman, to both the interpretation and use of data on African women in the West." She observes that data collected within the discipline of social anthropology has been "used in wider political debates by all sectors of society in the Western world" (1). Arguing that colonial divisions of the world into "civilized" and "primitive" were "concretized by anthropology" Amadiume states that it is for this reason that "social anthropology has been called the child or handmaiden of colonialism" (2). With so-called "primitive women . . . at the lowest end of the scale" and "the Victorian lady . . . at the apex" it is no surprise therefore that female academics and Western feminists of the 1960s and 1970s were victims of this ideology themselves (3). The predominant assumption in these circles that "social and cultural inferiority of [all] women" was a universal reality was itself a direct result of their class- and culture-specific conclusions that "maternal and domestic roles were responsible for the supposed universal subordination of [all] women" (4). That "patriarchal cultures of Europe" had never accorded motherhood "the same status and reverence it . . . had in African cultures" and that matrilineal and matriarchal cultural realities linked economic wealth as well as domestic labor to female power was not consistently and seriously considered by Western feminists (3).[16]

Ifi Amadiume's substantial analysis of the oeuvre of Cheikh Anta Diop, as well as her attempts to make connections among African cultures cross-culturally, demonstrates an intellectual commitment to Pan-Africanist politics. This is consistent with the Césairean aspect of negritude (as explained in chapter 1) concerned with Black solidarity. While Oyeronké Oyewumi strongly criticizes Western gender frameworks as well as aspects of African studies, her neglect of any substantial mention of Diop seems indicative of a certain alienation from African-centered scholarship that is not as rooted in Westernisms as the texts and scholars she chooses to cite. Further, her brief critique of Léopold Senghor's negritude as rooted in acceptance of Western concepts of "essence," "race," and "reason" is at odds with Diop's claims that concepts such as "reason," rooted in Western philosophy, are themselves civilizational inheritances from Egypt and sub-Saharan Africa. On the other hand, her critique of Senghor as constructing an argument based on sameness with, rather than difference from, the West, as is the case with the other Africanists cited, is a superficial analysis that misses the substantial emphasis on difference at the heart of his work.[17] Of significance, in this omission, is the degree to which the cultural "worldsense" central to Senghor's logic, and uncannily comparable to the cultural "worldsense" described by Zora Neale Hurston, exposes substantial cultural continuities between the African continent and the diaspora.[18]

Several things seem apparent from this examination of selections from the work of Davies and Fido, Esteves and Paravisini-Gebert, Mordecai and Wilson, Cobham, Wynter, Hurston, Bambara, Hodge, and Brodber. First, despite the seeming embrace of a universal feminist lens, the universal feminist approach is continually if not systematically critiqued by the implicit and explicit questions raised by these predominantly Black female critics and writers about its appropriateness for defining and describing African diaspora female-centered realities. The coupling of dichotomous terms "goes a piece of the way," as Carole Boyce Davies states, "to find new language to encompass our experience" (*Out of the Kumbla,* xii).[19] Scholars of the continental African experience such as Oyewumi, Amadiume, Diop, and T'Shaka go further toward revealing what is similar, hidden, lost, or unexplored between the continent and the diaspora. The title of Amadiume's book *Daughters of the Goddess, Daughters of Imperialism* shows that the colonial dichotomy that is operative in the diaspora is also part of the schism of female identity on the continent due to the recent history of colonial violence. At the 1956 conference, the split between conceptions of cultural literacy rooted exclusively in national (imperialist geographical) paradigms versus formulations of literacy rooted in diasporic continuity parallels the splits between cultural individualism and negritude, feminist and womanist, and lady-in-the-fine-castle and mores of the tribe, as well as Amadiume's two categories, daughters of imperialism and daughters of the goddess.

As Amadiume and Oyewumi's work demonstrates, the study of language is key to the study of culture. The legacy of negritude is most apparent in the terminology and issues rooted in an African worldsense, struggling to be articulated, and in so doing, breaking the confines of limiting discursive practices. Oyewumi's conception of worldsense parallels the antidisciplinary synthesis that T'Shaka's concept "twinlineal" reaches for. What becomes clearer and clearer is that language and its poetics contains the cultural worldsense of a people. Translated into Hurstonian poetics, "folklore is the boiled down juice of human living" (*Go Gator,* 69). In the twenty-first century's Black vernacular folklore—rap music—Goodie Mob's T-Mo raps in the song "Thought Process":

Let me get a chop at this lumber
niggas from da down under
ground are hangin around
the A Town
lookin for a come up
working from 9 to 5
just to get some change
so T-Mo can stay alive.[20]

A Yoruba proverb states, "When the fool is told a proverb its meaning has to be explained to him" (Morris-Brown, viii); a Jamaican proverb addressing imperialist inequality states, "Jackass seh di worl nuh
level" (Morris-Brown, 139).[21] These examples show that language and
its poetics truly contain the "worldsense" of a people.

The concept "nation language" as bespeaking the nature of the
spoken creoles created by Africans transplanted to the Caribbean region is formulated and explored by Edward Kamau Brathwaite in his
short work *History of the Voice: The Development of Nation Language in
Anglophone Caribbean Poetry*. In this book Brathwaite explores the
relationship between sound and sense: "the actual rhythm and the
syllables [are] the very software, in a way, of the language" (9). In a
larger sense, Brathwaite attempts to trace the relationship between a
sense of cultural voice as it exists in the native languages of a people
and the constraints of the colonially inherited literary forms used by
Caribbean writers and poets as vehicles of self-expression. Brathwaite
argues that the closer the poet comes to merging his or her cultural
voice with the formative expressive registers of his or her people, the
more liberated he or she will become from the colonial experience.[22]
Hurston, in her essay "Characteristics of Negro Expression," brings
the theorization of language and sound to the African diaspora context of the United States when she writes, "It has often been stated by
etymologists that the Negro has introduced no African words to the
language. This is true, but it is equally true that he has made over a
great part of the tongue to his liking and has his revision accepted by
the ruling class. No one listening to a Southern white man talk could
deny this" (*Sanctified Church*, 52–53). Hurston states earlier that "[the
Negro's] very words are action words. His interpretation of the English language is in terms of pictures. One act described in terms of
another. Hence the rich metaphor and simile" (*Sanctified Church*, 51).
Here, Hurston adds a visual element to this conception of Black

Clear Word and Third Sight

speech as the merging of sound and sense. This theorization, by Hurston, of the intersection of imagery and rhythm is brought out in the short excerpt from T-Mo's rap quoted above; the reality of these intersections is brought vividly to life when one hears the song performed rather than reads the written lyrics. Hurston's analysis, once again, flawlessly complements Senghor's analysis of "the image as integral to language expression." He tells us, "The words are always pregnant with images; through their value as signs transpires their value as sense." The image "does not signify what it represents, but what it suggests, what it creates. The elephant is strength, the spider, prudence" (Présence Africaine Conference Committee, *Présence Africaine*, 58). The image frequently tells a story.

Hurston, Senghor, and Brathwaite, speaking and writing from the United States, Africa, and the Caribbean in the 1920s, 1950s, and 1980s respectively, theorize in different ways the confluence of language and worldsense. The creative expressivity that they cross-culturally articulate is useful in exploring the legacy of negritude at the level of form and cultural expression in the novels of various African Caribbean writers. If, as Mordecai and Wilson demonstrate and, as I argued earlier "the literary attempt to decolonize the self necessarily means recourse to folk narrative and a creole voice," then the textual representation of orality in various forms is indeed the biggest allegiance to the "tribe" that a writer can have. The challenge then, for the diaspora scholar and critic, is to build on these implicit conversations across space and time, with an eye to creating an alternate canon of literacy as root and foundation for new and evolving Pan-African diaspora identities.

3

Negritude and Negativity

ALIENATION AND "VOICE" IN EASTERN

CARIBBEAN LITERATURE

The presentation of the history of African people in the Caribbean suggests that they were slaves—almost acquiescing in their enslavement—and then ex-slaves, as though, having ceased to be slaves, their ex-slavehood became their nationality; they weren't thought of as Africans. But when I look at history, I see the Africans not as slaves in a passive sense, but as *enslaved*; the central theme of their existence was a struggle against enslavement, expressed in two centuries of war (of which the Haitian Revolution was perhaps the highpoint), revolts, maroonage, and abscondment, including the creation of independent communities, as happened in Surinam and Jamaica.—EARL LOVELACE, in an interview by Maya Jaggi

If negritude is defined politically as a "concrete coming-to-consciousness" about the collective condition of African and African diaspora people,[1] and culturally by the relationship of various writers to the oral traditions of their people, then this legacy is made manifest in terms of the thematic and aesthetic concerns expressed by various writers. The relevant thematic concerns necessarily involve an initial recognition of racial oppression. Of equal importance, however, is the way in which the relationship between racial oppression and cultural identity is theorized. Earl Lovelace's description of "slaves" as *enslaved Africans* brings to the fore the nexus of race and culture at stake in the negritude debates described in chapter 1. How a given writer historicizes cultural identity in relation to race determines the relationship to the legacy of negritude. To this end, texts that move in the direction of a transnational diaspora identity would seem to not only bespeak the negritude legacy but also improve upon and move beyond it in critical ways. On the other hand, at the aesthetic level, Kamau Brathwaite's seminal short text *History of the Voice: The Development of Nation Language in Anglophone Caribbean Poetry* sets the standard for the postnegritude discussion in terms of the relationships among literary form, cultural expression, and racial identity. With Brathwaite as guide, this legacy becomes aesthetically apparent by the extent to which the "voice" that is textually invoked by a Black writer locates itself within a poetic or prosaic trajectory that inscribes the orality of African diaspora culture within the writing of the novel or poem.

This chapter draws on the work of three Black writers from the eastern Caribbean who reflect three different approaches to how race and culture are connected and theorized in relation to Britain and, later, the United States's economic and cultural presence in the region. By exploring selected writings by the Trinidadian theorist and novelist Merle Hodge, Antiguan expatriate Jamaica Kincaid, and Trinidadian novelist Earl Lovelace, this chapter will examine the relationship of their work to the legacy of negritude at both the thematic and aesthetic levels.

To some extent the legacies of these writers reflect the sociopolitical realities of the islands they are from. Antigua, on one hand, characterized by Jamaica Kincaid as "a small place" in her book of the same name, is heir to a primarily British colonial past. Trinidad's mixture of predominantly British and Spanish colonization, on the other, is further complicated by the presence of almost equal numbers of formerly indentured and formerly enslaved Indians and Africans respectively. Additionally, being the southernmost island in the Caribbean Sea, Trinidad is less than an hour away from the shores of Venezuela and the South American continent. Its proximity to South America in conjunction with the substantial African presence and its varied cultural past has helped to lay the foundational framework for Trinidad's unique Carnival culture, the most developed and celebrated in the Caribbean region. Further, the U.S. military occupation of the island during World War II introduced another dynamic to the history of this particular "small place." After the military occupation of the island, Trinidad went through a period of struggle with the United States during the political tenure of Prime Minister Eric Williams to regain control of Chaguaramas, the portion of the island occupied during and after the war.[2] Trinidad, therefore, not only has a more varied cultural population and colonial past than Antigua; it was also more closely affected by events in the United States that sparked flames of cultural pride within African Trinidadians. The civil rights and Black Power movements in the United States made an impact in the region, with a small uprising against the establishment breaking out at one point in Trinidad. With regard to Trinidad Earl Lovelace states, "The Black Power movement was expressing . . . the demand for a better and more dignified life. The basis of the rebellion was the questioning of a black government under which black people still felt themselves disadvantaged in terms of opportunities for economic advancement; there was still racial prejudice" (Jaggi, interview, 26). Merle Hodge, influenced by negritude poet Léon Gontran Damas, had translated some of Damas's writings and made his work the subject of her master's thesis. Written in the early 1970s, Hodge's thesis on Damas's work coincides with the Black Power movement and the unrest in Trinidad referred to by Lovelace. What is clear is that various historical factors have influenced the degree of race consciousness of African Trinidadians. The sociopolitical and cultural histories of Trinidad and Antigua have to be seen as the backdrop influencing the writers born and raised on these islands.

Born Elaine Potter Richardson in St. John's, Antigua, in 1949, Jamaica Kincaid migrated to the United States in 1965. She worked as a servant in Scarsdale, New York, and took classes at the local community college. After a while she quit both job and school and answered a help wanted advertisement for an au pair job caring for four little girls in New York City. Eight years later, after several stints in and out of college and working odd jobs, she got her break interviewing Gloria Steinem, for *Ingenue* magazine.[3] As a young Black woman in her late teens living in New York City, she attracted a lot of attention with her bleached blond hair and shaved-off eyebrows. She met *New Yorker* writer George Trow and eventually the magazine's editor, William Shawn. In 1973 she changed her name to Jamaica Kincaid in order to avoid being ridiculed by her family for taking up writing and, as she put it, to "escape the thing [she] had been born into" (Bonetti, inter-

Clear Word and Third Sight

view; Garis, "Through West Indian Eyes," 44). While she has frequently claimed when interviewed that this particular choice of name has no greater signficance than camouflaging her identity, the irony and the significance of the name "Jamaica," given its status as one of the most recognized and familiar of the Caribbean islands to the American imaginary, cannot be overlooked.[4] In 1974 she began to write for *The New Yorker* magazine and continued to do so for the next twenty years. Her collection of short stories *At the Bottom of the River,* her early novels *Annie John* and *Lucy,* and portions of *The Autobiography of My Mother* were all first published as stories in this magazine. In 1979 she married the composer Allen Shawn, the son of William Shawn. In a 1991 interview for the American Audio Prose Library Series, interviewer Kay Bonetti told Jamaica Kincaid that she had a tendency, in her life and in her fiction, to reinvent herself, to "light out for the territory" in the style of Huckleberry Finn. Kincaid responded by saying:

> One of the things . . . I've come to know is what good luck it was that I did light out for American territory and not Britain. Because I do not think that I would have been allowed this act of self-invention which is very American and is sort of expected in America. I don't think I could have done that in . . . English-speaking Europe. I think I came to America and I came from a place where most of the people looked like me so I had a sense of solidarity. I wasn't concerned with the color of my skin, whereas in England I could only have been concerned with the color of my skin.

In a spring 1996 issue of *The New Yorker,* freelance writer Malcolm Gladwell published an article entitled "Black Like Them: Why West Indians and American Blacks Are Perceived Differently." In it he tells this West Indian immigrant story:

> My cousin Rosie and her husband, Noel, live in a two-bedroom bungalow on Argyle Avenue, in Uniondale, on the west end of Long Island. When they came to America, twelve years ago, they lived in a basement apartment a dozen or so blocks away, next to their church. At the time they were both taking classes at the New York Institute of Technology, which was right nearby. But after they graduated, and Rosie got a job managing a fast-food place and Noel got a job in asbestos removal, they managed to save a little money and bought the house on Argyle Avenue.
>
> To a West Indian, black is a literal description: you are black if your

skin is black. Noel's father, for example, is black. But his mother had a white father, and she herself was fair-skinned and could pass. As for Rosie, her mother and my mother, who are twins, thought of themselves while they were growing up as "middle-class brown," which is to say that they are about the same shade as Colin Powell. (74–76)

Kincaid's biographical journey could be described as entailing flight from the "tribe" for the purposes of anonymity and self-invention. On the other hand, Gladwell's story successfully stereotypes the differences and divisions that some imagine to universally characterize Black populations from the United States and the Caribbean. In Gladwell's Caribbean narrative, he claims that "black [is only] . . . a literal description," as opposed to a racial and cultural categorization that relates to both societal status and political identity. Yet he describes his mother as "middle-class brown," a description that links a skin tone lighter than Black to societal status, if not more. Further, the description of his relatives as arriving in America and immediately registering at the New York Institute of Technology bespeaks their level of educational achievement and privilege "back home." Kincaid's and Gladwell's worldviews are similar in a certain way. Kincaid describes America as the place where (for some unspecified reason) she need not be "concerned about the color of her skin" and England as the place where she "could only have been concerned about" it. Gladwell, on the other hand, describes a Caribbean context in which his people are highly conscious of the color of their skin yet removed from any sense of solidarity implied by the term "Black." Neither Kincaid nor Gladwell, however, identify the United States as a place in which they experience racial and cultural solidarity with others who self-identify as Black. Kincaid's reference to a "sense of solidarity" is expressly linked to her homeland and not the United States.

Although Gladwell comes to the conclusion that overcoming racism is not achieved simply by ignoring it, since "everybody needs a nigger," the rags-to-riches story of both his relatives and Jamaica Kincaid are paradigmatic of a particular narrative about West Indian immigration to the United States (Gladwell, "Black Like Them," 81). As these two examples show us, this narrative is typified by the Black Caribbean immigrant who arrives with seemingly little, yet manages to obtain a slice of the proverbial pie without viewing race as a factor that negatively influences his or her success.[5] In these migration stories, success and assimilation are always unquestioned goals, and

Clear Word and Third Sight

Black solidarity within the United States along African diaspora lines is treated as an undesirable curiosity.

To some extent Jamaica Kincaid's work addresses questions that have been long-standing ones for Caribbean writers. While she is celebrated in the United States and the Caribbean as a significant writer, Kincaid's exploration of both migration and what it means to come of age in the British West Indies is not new but has been a constant theme among male and female Caribbean writers alike.[6] In his introduction to the conference anthology *Caribbean Women Writers* (1991), Selwyn Cudjoe stated that when broached about the idea of a conference on Caribbean women's writings, Jamaican poet Lorna Goodison retorted, "It's about time that our critics began to take us seriously," and Jamaica Kincaid asked, "Are there many of us?" (5). "Sylvia Wynter and Beryl Gilroy . . . were delighted to see each other for the first time since they began writing and studying in England in the 1950's. Erna Brodber . . . who indicated an initial reluctance to attend . . . noted that she was happy that she had not missed this historic experience. Merle Hodge[,] . . . overwhelmed by the experience, vowed to continue writing about some of the things she felt she had lost the courage to write about because of her close involvement with the Grenada revolution" (6). Hodge's last novel, *For the Life of Laetitia,* published in 1994, was a response to this impulse.

While Paule Marshall's oeuvre is of substantial significance in terms of the African diaspora connections it establishes between the United States and the Caribbean, her first novel, the 1959 *Brown Girl, Brownstone* explores themes of migration and coming of age over twenty-five years before Jamaica Kincaid and over ten years before Merle Hodge. Merle Hodge's groundbreaking first novel *Crick Crack Monkey* (1970) is a Caribbean coming-of-age story that anticipates Kincaid's work by more than fifteen years.

British Colonialism and the Production of Sight

How success and assimilation are configured in relation to colonial authority, on one hand, and the Black masses, on the other, is of substantial significance in the work of Merle Hodge and Jamaica Kincaid. Merle Hodge's *Crick Crack Monkey* is a first-person narrative that describes the early life of a young Trinidadian girl, Cynthia Davis, nicknamed Tee. It charts what could be called the colonial production of young Tee's sight, the restructuring of how she interprets the knowledge she receives. The institutions of school and church figure prominently in this story. They are represented as the forces whose ideological tentacles entrap and transform Tee, with her two aunts (one situated outside the circles of church and school and the other firmly ensconced within them) waging a battle for her soul. Hodge's narrative captures the transformation of Tee from a pre–elementary school Trinidadian child, who is happy, psychologically well-adjusted, and an integral part of the community around her, to her symbolic "end" as an anxious scholarship-recipient high school student. By the text's close, Tee's shame-filled descriptions of herself and her environment parallel the progress of her colonial education and self-alienation. It is highly symbolic that Tee's success (her educational achievements and her increase in status in the eyes of her snobbish cousins as she prepares to emigrate to England) parallels her self-hatred and her desperate wish for some release from her claustrophobic psychological state.

Crick Crack Monkey opens with Tee's description of herself and her little brother Toddan awaiting their parents' return with a newborn baby. The narrative is such that the reader is both subject to young Tee's interpretation of the events as well as privy to a version that seems to elude her.[7] Apparently the mother and child die, and what ensues is a family quarrel over which of the children's two aunts— "Tantie" or "The Bitch"—will have custody over them.

> Ma Peters' wailing was disconcerting; the firm voice with high-heels and stockings was still saying "*We will take the children*" and Mr. Lucifer was declaiming in aggressive tones: "What the Lord give the Lord have every right to take-back." . . . Some quavery voices scraped themselves together into a slow singing, and then Toddan's shriek pierced the bedroom wall, and Papa, still carrying me, made a limping dash in that direction. . . . Then Papa went to sea. I concluded that what he had gone to see was whether he could find Mammy and the baby. (2–3)

In Tee's version, adult voices collide and Hodge's sentences run together, creating a nonlinear narrative in which the individual "I" seems always to be speaking from the space of a communal "we." After their father leaves for England, Tee and Toddan temporarily remain in the familiar environment of Tantie's household. The house is often filled with loud, hilarious company, and this, in addition to the presence of their older cousin Mikey, whom they adore, occupies their young lives.

> Sometimes to our delight the company spread over a whole weekend, like at Tantie's birthday. Then even Mikey was in a consistent good humor.
>
> The trouble was only with the Uncles; Tantie upbraided [Mikey] for slouching through the drawingroom without even Good-evening-dog and Mikey insisted that he always said good-evening and Tantie said yu call that good-evenin a grunt down in yu belly? and Mikey said yu want mih kiss them? and Tantie said who "them" is, Mr. George I talkin about, I don' know who you mean by "them" who is "them"? And [Mikey] took to slouching in through the back door instead. (4)

In the early part of *Crick Crack Monkey*, Tee and Toddan no longer have one main father figure after their father migrates to England; instead they have a multiplicity of male role models, key among them their cousin Mikey. Christine Barrow, in her article "Caribbean Masculinity and Family: Revisiting 'Marginality' and 'Reputation,'" argues that conventional sociological theory about the family has imposed European gender roles on Caribbean society. Close analysis of the dominant familial patterns in *Crick Crack Monkey*, however, reveals that serious caregiving and affection, if not economic support, are provided by fathers. Additionally, brothers and uncles function as father figures to sisters, nieces, and nephews, frequently providing both protection and affection. Mikey functions substantially in this capacity for Toddan and Tee in the first portion of the narrative, before he migrates to America.

Throughout *Crick Crack Monkey*, Tee's story is told in the first person. Yet, instead of revealing the isolated perspective of one individual, this narrative has the interiority of a third-person narration, one that has the capacity to give the reader insight into the psychological worldview of the people within the community.[8] In the passage quoted above, the proper diction of Tee the narrator collides with Tantie and Mikey's creole. Tee is not separate from her surroundings, and Hodge deftly uses Tee's narrative to bring to life, in a storytelling style and fashion, the oral, sensory-driven world of the everyday folk that are Tee's family and community. Tee imitates the sound of Tantie's voice and all of the other characters in the text in order to give the reader a sense of their worlds. Hodge as writer effectively manipulates this narrative strategy so that the imitation of various characters' voices on

Negritude and Negativity

Tee's part replaces the dialogue traditionally introduced in quotation marks by a third-person narrative.[9] There is no character introduction in the early portions of the novel. The reader therefore has a sense of tumbling into an environment in which social relations are privileged over social hierarchies. This is a characteristic that Oyeronké Oyewumi ascribes to the structure of the family in the West African Yoruba context. Additionally, for the first eight pages of the book, the narrative "I" is hardly separate from the "we" that Tee uses to refer to herself and her brother or her family in general. In later portions of the book, as indicated by the selection below, Tee's "I" not only appears more consistently but eventually becomes entirely separate from all communal identifications.

The day before school starts, Tee says:

> I looked forward to school. I looked forward to the day when I could pass my hand swiftly from side to side on a blank piece of paper leaving meaningful marks in its wake; to staring nonchalantly into a book until I turned over the page, a gesture pregnant with importance for it indicated that one had not merely been staring, but that that most esoteric of processes had been taking place whereby the paper had yielded up something or other as a result of having been stared at. (20)

Another aspect of Hodge's mastery over language is demonstrated by her manipulation of high English prose to portray Tee's fascination with the process of reading and writing that lies at the heart of Western literacy. As the text progresses, however, it becomes clear that the introduction into and the fascination with Western literacy competes with and displaces the previously developing but underarticulated "diaspora literacy" that she "is born into."[10] Diaspora literacy, in this context, refers to a knowledge of and comfort with everyday Black cultural practices and behavior. Tantie enrolls Tee at "Coriaca EC," an infant school run by a Mr. and Mrs. Hinds. Mr. Hinds's cultural affinities are aggressively emphasized by the huge picture of Winston Churchill on the classroom wall, and his constant references to fighting in the war and nearly becoming an English lawyer. Mrs. Hinds was only known to Tee through Tantie's references to her as "a mauvais'-langue horse-face maco with nothing to do but mind people business" (22). Tee describes her writing career as beginning with her learning that A was for apple, an "exotic fruit that made its brief and stingy appearance at Christmas-time"; and her reading career began with her following the trials of "two English children known as Jim and Jill, or it might have been Tim and Mary" (25). Every day at noon they sang grace, and anyone caught with so much as an eye open received a slap. In the afternoons they recited nursery rhymes, wondering what in all creation a haystack was, and why Miss Muffet sat eating her curls away. Songs like "God Save the King" and "Land of Hope and Glory," as well as recitations of "Children of the Empire Ye Are Brothers All," were standard fare. Mr. Hinds threw tantrums and made them start over if they were slouching or not standing at attention.

Tee's early formal education is one in which Christianity, discipline, and homage to England and Englishness are hopelessly intertwined. There is little distinction made between "God" and "Empire," so it comes as no surprise when Tee says, "It made perfect sense that the place where my mother had gone, Glory, should also be known as The Mother Country" (30). Yet what is most remarkable about this description of Tee's early schooling is not just the portrait of education as colonial indoctrination but rather the degree to which this process is unsuccessful. The systematic misrecognition by Tee and her classmates of both nursery rhymes and hymns indicates that they are not fully receptive to, or taken in by, the colonial worldview. This is the case because almost everything in their daily environment outside of church and school presents them with a decidedly different set of mores and cultural practices.

When Tee is promoted from infant school to "Big-school" (elementary school) she describes this environment as dominated by a whip, "a teacher who . . . kept a sharp eye on you all the time," and a blackboard motto that read "THE DISCIPLE IS NOT GREATER THAN THE MASTER" (54). At Big-school she and her schoolmates are subject to arbitrary discipline intended to expel their "niggery" ways. In a later essay, "The Shadow of the Whip," Hodge argues that the literal violence of the slave system had shaped relations between men and women as well as parents and children in the Black community. Tee's experience of Big-school as well as high school and, later, of her Aunt Beatrice's house make it clear that any environment modeled on the colonial system was ultimately a continuation of the violence of slavery. In third grade Tee conjures up Helen, an English schoolgirl who is her self-fashioned double. Helen is her age, spends her summer holidays at the seaside with her uncle and aunt, and as Tee puts it, "She was the Proper Me. And me, I was her shadow hovering about in incompleteness" (62).

The introduction of Helen seems to indicate a slight yet definitive shift in Tee's consciousness, subtly demonstrated at the level of the narrative voice. At the same time that Helen comes into existence, Tee's language as narrator shifts from its straightforward simplicity to a more obtuse and rambling prose. Although Tee describes Helen as a phase she quickly outgrows, Helen's birth and death is rivaled by a more concrete shift in Tee's way of seeing; this is symbolized by her increasing belief that there is a proper way to do things. As the narration progresses, Tee's voice shifts away from the interactive communal chorus that the earlier passages exemplify. Yet Hodge's mastery of narrative strategy is consistently effective in terms of its ability to depict the nuances of Tee's psychological deterioration while astutely maintaining substantial authenticity in the translation of the oral into the written. In the latter portions of the novel, although Tee's identity is changing, the orality of the text is maintained, since Tee as narrator continues to imitate the voices around her even though she is no longer experiencing communal solidarity with anyone. Tee takes to wearing shoes in the house, and Tantie's household is in a state of hilarity over Tee's pretensions. When socks begin to accompany Tee's shoes, however, Tantie sharply advises, "Look, Madam, when yu start to wash yu own clothes then yu could start to play the monkey" (62). This comment by Tantie is a fleeting yet significant reference within the text to not only the novel's title but also the devastating syndrome of European cultural imitation and loss of identity that is ultimately at the center of this literary work. In the opening pages of the novel, Tantie—who along with Tee's grandmother is the voice of cultural retention with the text—states, "Monkey can't see e' own tail." She says this in response to the citified Aunt Beatrice whose "high-heels and stockings" voice tell her she isn't fit for parenthood. The irony of this statement becomes apparent by the novel's end, when Beatrice's superficial and valueless upbringing of her own children exposes her own unfitness in relation to Tantie and Ma's "groundings" and culturally African mores.[11]

When Tee and her brother Toddan first visit their Aunt Beatrice, referred to by Tantie as "The Bitch," they are introduced into middle-class Trinidadian society, the portion of society in which respect for God, England, and manners are the rule and not the exception. But they soon discover that the rules of propriety in Beatrice's house are governed more by some mysterious internal logic than any real disciplinary measures. This being the case, these rules have no real power over them. Tee beats up her cousins constantly and objects to Aunt

Beatrice's calling Toddan by his proper name—Coddrington. Toddan, on the other hand, never learns anyone's names and views the sole advantage to being at The Bitch's house as his easy access to cakes and sweets. They put their energies into being sent back to Tantie's and self-consciously strategize toward this end. To their surprise and astonishment, however, acts that would have been rewarded with a whole day of punishment at Tantie's are mildly admonished or ignored at Aunt Beatrice's. While strict disciplinary measures for misbehavior are never carried out, what Tee notices is another form of policing. Aunt Beatrice always calls her "Cynthia," as if she were in school. Toddan is snatched away from the bedroom window when he is caught talking with the creole-speaking boy next door. Aunt Beatrice yells at Eudora the housekeeper for speaking in creole to her daughter Carol. When Aunt Beatrice's friends come over, Tee notes that their laughter and their talking is "clipped-off at the edge" (38). The kind of policing that takes place, then, involves speech and propriety. While Tee observes this, she doesn't yet have any anxiety about how she is seen by the people in this strange new environment. The policing of creole speech as one of the central themes in the text demonstrates that it is associated with the everyday (Black) context in opposition to the society of the "monkey"—the colonially imitating petty elite at whose expense the novel's title is "signifying."[12]

Another key term that is invoked to describe similar behavior is the one used in the novel's title, "crick crack." When Tee and Toddan spend time down by the bridge with their cousin Mikey, he and his young male friends mock one of their companions. The young man in question is nicknamed "Manhatt'n" by his peers, since he claims to have gone "stateside, fellers, up Amurraca-side—for he always spoke with his mouth screwed to one side and all the words coming out of his nose." Manhatt'n tells tall tales about his supposed exploits in the United States. One day, however, tired of his exaggerations, one of the members of the gang "maliciously murmured 'Crick-crack!' at the end of one of these accounts in perfect Western drawl." Manhatt'n, outraged, screams, "Crick-crack yu mother! Is true whe ah tell yu," and from then on the fellows referred to him instead as "Freshwater, the name they had formerly used only behind his back" (7). The name "Freshwater" of course, rudely implies that "Manhatt'n" has been nowhere. "Crick-crack" in this context is the mocking device used by his friends to suggest that all of his accounts of his experiences in America are pure fiction.

At the end of elementary school, Tee is the only person in her village to win a scholarship to St. Ann's high school. Aunt Beatrice insists that Tantie send Tee to live with her, but the Tee that arrives is a different person from the young girl who previously regarded the same environment with scorn. Intimidated and anxiety-ridden, she is reduced to tears by her cousins' giggles and she wonders, "How in the world had [she] ever thought to approach these two young ladies, far less beat them up, a few years before[?]" (70). In school she earnestly aspires to be the good student who maintains that there is no bad faith at work in the light-skinned girls consistently being selected for prominent positions. At home her situation is more complicated. The Bitch's house and The Bitch, in particular, are the forces that perpetuate the colonial mores in the home space outside of school. This is something new, since Tantie's house was an oasis from these forces, making school the peculiar exception. At one key point early on, Tantie, after stating how little respect she has for Tee's teacher, Mrs. Hinds, tells Tee, "Jus' you remember you going there to learn *book* do' let them put no blasted shit in yu head" (23, italics mine). Aunt Beatrice, on the other hand, picks up where the schoolmaster leaves off. She never lets Tee out of her sight, and her missionary zeal to haul Tee out of her "niggeryness" takes the form of a relentless assault on Tee's person. The result is a progressive deterioration in how Tee sees herself. She is mortified when she remembers the "common" nature of her life with Tantie. At Carnival time, sitting in the stadium stands with her snobbish cousins, she remembers previous Carnivals she spent with Tantie and Toddan. She says, "All this I was seeing through a kind of haze of shame; and I reflected that even now Tantie and Toddan must be packed into that ridiculous truck with all those common raucous niggery people and all those coolies" (86). As Tee becomes more and more vulnerable to Aunt Beatrice's stealthy attack on her psyche, Beatrice further destroys her defenses by breaking her promise to send her home for weekends and vacations.

In spite of Tee's weakening resistance, she never quite falls prey to the promise of Aunt Beatrice's unwearying smile; she never believes there is a place for her in Aunt Beatrice's household. Beatrice, on the other hand, neglected by her own badly raised daughters, desperately clings to Tee as a kind of surrogate. The relationship makes Tee uneasy, since it is quite apparent that Beatrice's attentions are less about fellowship and generosity than a selfish indulgence calculated to ease her bruised ego. A final moment of almost unconscious resistance to

Clear Word and Third Sight

her situation occurs when Beatrice asks Tee if she misses Tantie and her brother. Tee says, "This struck into the heart of my confusion. But I resolved that whatever my real thoughts, I owed it to Tantie to make a show of loyalty before Auntie Beatrice. So I replied, thankful of the dark, yes" (92). Being allowed a moment of privacy because her answer forces Beatrice to stop talking, Tee's resistance increases enough for her to savagely slap away the hand that Beatrice offers. Beatrice's mortification quickly turns to scorn, and her whole attitude toward Tee becomes one of anticipating her faults. What was previously the façade of a developing mother-daughter relationship quickly disintegrates, becoming instead the very thing that the unwearying smile was hiding all along—a relationship rooted in notions of superiority, inferiority, and charity. Henceforth everything is revealed. Tantie is now openly referred to as "that woman . . . with no culture, no breeding, no sense of right and wrong" (95). This is ironic and hypocritical, given that Beatrice, among other things, can barely get her daughters to eat together as a family or address her in a courteous manner. Tee is assaulted by her older cousin Bernadette for managing to look "so greasy all the time like a stevedore," and Aunt Beatrice announces her firm intention to haul Tee out of her "niggeryness" (95). Hodge's shrewd construction of the text exposes, to even the most unquestioning reader, the consistent way in which scorn and contempt for everyday (Black) social practices are the symbolic price of (white colonial) education. Tee says, "I wanted to shrink, to disappear. . . . At times I resented Tantie bitterly for not having let Aunt Beatrice get us in the first place and bring us up properly. What Aunt Beatrice said so often was quite true: how could a woman with no sense of right and wrong take it upon herself to bring up children[?]" (97). Predictably, therefore, Tee's new state is defined by a barely concealed self-hatred and an overwhelming desire to escape from herself.

The novel ends with Tee and Toddan's pending migration to England after their father has sent for them. The text strongly implies that Tantie is the catalyst for the children's emigration after she visits Beatrice's home, observes Tee, and probably concludes that her situation could not possibly get any worse. The night before the children leave, Tee is back at Tantie's for the first time since her negative transformation. She discovers that Ma, her beloved grandmother, has died and that no-one had bothered to call her. Tee notes, "Everything was changing, unrecognizable, pushing me out. This was as it should be, since I had moved up and no longer had any place here. But it was painful, and I longed all the more to be on my way" (110). Tee's description of herself as "moving up" shows her ideological acceptance of a world order in which social hierarchies are now privileged over social relations. The reader discovers almost as an aside at the end of the novel that Tee had come first in her class at school. Her academic success, however, is neither at the center of her psyche nor is it the novel's main concern. What we are left with instead is a picture of Tee's impending emigration representing a kind of psychological and cultural death. There is no place for her to escape to, not even in her head, since England had been previously conflated with "Glory," the place one goes after death.

It would be a mistake to interpret the psychological transformation traced in Hodge's text as simply a story about Tee's private deterioration from a state of pride to a state of shame. This is a narrative about the deterioration of what could be called Tee's cultural self-esteem. The text demonstrates the relationship between Tee's level of comfort with herself personally and her level of comfort with the collective Black culture she comes from. In a 1994 conversation, hip-hop artist KRS-One remarked, "Culture is self. There is no such thing as the individual. . . . The individual is part of the masses. The masses come first and the individual comes last. When the individual is last and culture is first you have self" (KRS-One, "Can the Teacher Be Taught?"). Tee's inauguration into a Western "modern" consciousness is at the cost of her Black communal "diaspora literacy" and identity; one is traded in for the other. In Hodge's second novel, *For the Life of Laetitia,* an attempt is made to create a narrative in which the young schoolgirl Laetitia more effectively negotiates between these two forms of literacy and consciousness. Here, rather than compromise her cultural self-esteem, she risks dropping out of school entirely, bringing to mind Carter G. Woodson's statements in his 1933 book, *The Mis-Education of the Negro*: "The thought of the inferiority of the Negro is drilled into him in almost every class he enters and in almost every book he studies. If he happens to leave school after he masters the fundamentals, before he finishes high school or reaches college, he will naturally escape some of this bias and may recover in time to be of service to his people" (Woodson, 2).

When Laetitia does give in to the pressures of school, she ends up having a nervous breakdown, and it is the Black, rural, communal environment that is eventually the force of psychological and cultural balance and restoration.[13] In a similar move, Jamaican writer Erna

Brodber describes her first novel, *Jane and Louisa Will Soon Come Home*, as delineating the psychological instability that can occur when the colonial educational track forces the individual to deidentify with his or her own cultural environment.[14]

Jamaica Kincaid and the Legacy of Cultural Loss

> There were Africans who had remained in Africa and there were Africans who were descended from slaves. I was descended from slaves. . . . It's not exactly the ancestral family you hope for, you know, the founding member of your family is a captured person. . . . This was very sobering. I came back and I thought, well, I'm just nobody. In this world I live in, I'm nobody, and it's quite fine with me. I choose that. I'm not African, I'm not anything. In fact, I have the blood of quite a few different people running around inside me, but I don't claim them. This is dead. I'm now.—JAMAICA KINCAID, in an interview by Gerhard Dilger

Jamaica Kincaid's attempt to come to terms with the relationship between slavery and ancestry is essentially the inverse of Lovelace's (see his statement in the epigraph to this chapter). Whereas Kincaid equates the fact of enslavement with a loss of cultural ancestry, Lovelace declares war on this position. He replaces the term "slave" with "enslaved African" and stresses that the centuries of Black resistance to oppression, a central theme within African diaspora cultures, are the expression of a surviving cultural legacy. He argues that Black people, by and large, have never collectively acquiesced and accepted slavery as defining their identity. If Lovelace's theory is correct, then the process of mental slavery (as exemplified by colonial education and the subsequent cultural mores that follow) rather than the brutality of physical enslavement is the point of departure for the loss of cultural identity.

Jamaica Kincaid's autobiographical essay "On Seeing England for the First Time" describes the extent to which English ideas permeated the Antigua of Kincaid's childhood. In a different way than Merle Hodge's *Crick Crack Monkey,* yet with moments of striking similarity, this essay tells a story about how young Kincaid came to see and understand the world around her. Opening with a description of her first geographic encounter with England on a map in school, Kincaid writes: "When my teacher had pinned this map up on the blackboard, she said, 'This is England'—and she said it with authority, seriousness and adoration, and we all sat up. It was as if she had said, 'This is Jerusalem, the place you will go to when you die but only if you have been good'" (32).

In both Hodge and Kincaid we are given explicit examples of how England functions as both literal and figurative salvation for the "West Indian" child in the British school system. When young Tee states, "At school I had come to learn that Glory and The Mother Country and Up-There and Over-There had all one and the same geographical location" (30), there is little difference between Tee's statement and Kincaid's conflation of Jerusalem and England as the place you go when you die if you've been good. But there are some subtle differences.

Throughout her essay Kincaid gives the reader a sense of how the English presence functioned in her life in ways that were both ordinary and awe-inspiring. Another example:

> At the time I saw this map—seeing England for the first time—I did not say to myself, "Ah, so that's what it looks like," because there was no longing in me to put a shape to those three words that ran through every part of my life no matter how small; for me to have had such a longing would have meant that I lived in a certain atmosphere, an atmosphere in which those three words were felt as a burden. But I did not live in such an atmosphere. (33)

The three words that Kincaid refers to here are "Made in England." She describes her breakfast, the hat her father wore, and even the way she was taught to eat her food with a knife and fork—all as "made in England." The idea of breakfast itself was English, and a "proper" breakfast was a big breakfast. The English presence in Kincaid's life is so pervasive as to be normalizing. It is not until much later, Kincaid says, that she realized that being ordered to draw a map of England in school "was something far worse than a declaration of war" (34). But she tells us that there was no need for war because she had already been conquered.

A quick revisiting of the early portions of *Crick Crack Monkey* reveals that young Tee had a very different relationship to England and En-

Clear Word and Third Sight

glishness than young Kincaid. When Mr. Hinds drags her classmates in front of the picture of Winston Churchill, referring to him as the greatest Englishman who ever lived, Tee states, "For us the personage on the wall was and remained simply Crapaud Face" (24). Far from responding with the adoration and reverence that Kincaid and her peers feel, Churchill's picture and the awe that Mr. Hinds has for it resonate for Tee and her classmates with absurdity. Another instance of this is what Tee describes as the intoning of sounds that they performed without a fault at the beginning and end of each day:

Our Father (which was plain enough)
witchartin
heavn
HALLE
owèdbethyname
THY
kingdumkum
THY
willbedunnunnert
azitizinevn. . . .
Ibelieveingoderfathalmitie.
(27)

While this may be humorously recognizable to the reader as the Lord's Prayer, it is significant that in Tee's narrative it is never explicitly identified as such. This implies that it was neither recognized nor understood by most of the children, so their identification with it and the immediacy of its power over them is questionable at best. Further, in Hodge's phoneticized rendition, the prayer is spelled in such a way that it resembles a foreign language. This spelling would make an interpretation incomprehensible to the reader who did not know what the prayer *sounded* like. The orality of the world that the children occupy is emphasized by Hodge's rendition of the prayer. It is a world controlled by sound. The prevalence of the oral culture is juxtaposed with the synonymous invasion of the colonial culture.

In her essay "On Seeing England for the First Time," Kincaid comes to realize at some point in her childhood that she was not and could never be English. She states, "The world was theirs, not mine; everything told me so" (35). She speaks of feeling as if her nose was pressed up against a glass window with an iron vise at the back of her neck forcing her head to stay in place. She tells us, "To avert my gaze was to fall back into something from which I had been rescued, a hole filled with nothing, and that was the word for everything about me, nothing" (36). Once again, there emerges a link in Kincaid's narrative between a lack of cultural identity and "nobodyness." The rescue of which she speaks is made manifest in her belief in England as her source of myth and meaning, her acceptance of there being a proper way to do certain things, and her speech as a sign of her educated/ civilized difference. In other words, this rescue is a physical event with certain psychological manifestations.

In Hodge's *Crick Crack Monkey* there are constant references made by Aunt Beatrice and school officials to the necessity of "dragging-Tee-up" and hauling her out of her "niggeryness." This is also a story about rescue, although here it is made explicit what Tee is being rescued from. Kincaid speaks about having been rescued from a hole that is filled with nothing but conquest, subjugation, humiliation, and enforced amnesia. By the end of Hodge's novel Tee also sees herself through the eyes of the colonizer. But what she has been rescued from is not "a hole filled with nothing" but rather, her "niggeryness," symbolized by Tantie, Toddan, Mikey, and Ma, her grandmother. Ma told Tee that she reminded her of her own grandmother, a woman whose name she had forgotten. At the end of *Crick Crack Monkey* Ma suddenly recalled her ancestor's name on her deathbed. Tee's biggest regret is that Tantie never bothered to write down her great-great-grandmother's "true-true [African] name" (19). It is highly symbolic that by the end of the text, Tee's great-great-grandmother's "true-true name" is something that she will never know. This is symbolic, because while the name may seem inconsequential, it is actually the "thing" that signifies a tradition that survived the realities of colonization. The inaccessibility of the name for Tee symbolizes the loss of culture at stake in her educational success. Despite the fact that this book ends with Tee in a state of psychological despair, the significance of the loss of the "true-true" name should not be lost on the reader.[15]

African diaspora traditions that have survived in the Caribbean are treated in Hodge's text as the roots that maintain a healthy sense of personal and collective identity. If we return to the legacy of negritude as embodied in how a given writer historicizes the relationship between racial oppression and cultural identity, then in Hodge's work the influence of the legacy is clear. Racial oppression is delineated by the scorn for Black culture at stake in the colonial enterprise, demonstrated in

Clear Word and Third Sight

the text. A healthy sense of cultural identity, however, is locatable in the text in the experiences of those that Langston Hughes would refer to as "the low-down folk" ("The Negro Artist and the Racial Mountain"). Tantie's belligerent spirit of resistance and even Tee's early resisting spirit demonstrate a consciousness and pride in cultural self.

In 1990 Jamaica Kincaid's second novel, *Lucy*, was published by Farrar, Straus and Giroux. While Annie in *Annie John* leaves for school in England at the end of that story, the young West Indian woman Lucy is a recent United States immigrant. Coming so close to being autobiography that it outraged some of Kincaid's friends and colleagues at *The New Yorker*, *Lucy* is a first-person narrative that maintains the ironic voice of *Annie John* but takes place in the United States of the 1960s rather than the Caribbean or England. The character Lucy begins her story by recalling, "It was my first day. I had come the night before, a gray-black and cold night before—as it was expected to be in the middle of January, though I didn't know that at the time—and I could not see anything clearly on the way in from the airport, even though there were lights everywhere" (3). With all of the air and drama of a nineteenth-century heroine of an English novel, Lucy narrates her arrival in "America." The prose is clear and proper, and the initial opening gives the reader no specific sense of the cultural identity of the character. She is a legal immigrant landing at an airport in the United States. She is alone: an isolated figure with a mysterious past arriving from an unidentified place that has a warmer climate.

Of interest in this text, however, is how Lucy (as immigrant) perceives and is perceived by others in two of the encounters related in this narrative. The first is with her white female employer, Mariah, and the second is with Mariah's Black female maid. What becomes clear in this, Kincaid's second novel, is that while Lucy the character is a subjective yet insightful critic of the imperialist enterprise, her resistance to America coexists with her isolation from *any* Black life within the text.

> One morning in early March, Mariah said to me, "You have never seen spring, have you?" And she did not have to await an answer, for she already knew. She said the word "spring" as if spring were a close friend, a friend who had dared to go away for a long time and soon would reappear for their passionate reunion. She said, "Have you ever seen daffodils pushing their way up out of the ground? And when they're in bloom and all massed together, a breeze comes along and

makes them do a curtsy to the lawn stretching out in front of them. Have you ever seen that? When I see that, I feel so glad to be alive." And I thought, So Mariah is made to feel alive by some flowers bending in the breeze. How does a person get to be that way? (17)

This seemingly simple phrase, "How does a person get to be that way?" is repeated throughout Kincaid's narrative at strategic points. Kincaid cleverly highlights socially and economically hierarchical dynamics masquerading as innocent interpersonal relations. In this way the text becomes a veritable ethnography of whiteness exposing the seeming innocence and good intentions of middle- and high-brow American society as steeped in thinly veiled notions of superiority and insincerity.

After Mariah shares her experience of daffodils, Lucy proceeds to share a childhood incident in which she had to memorize a poem about daffodils. The reference to daffodils, combined with the incident Kincaid narrates, is a trope within Caribbean literature that is highly symbolic of the dominant colonial presence within the Caribbean educational system. Lucy goes on to state that, after deciding to erase the poem from her memory, she has a dream in which she is pursued "by bunches and bunches of those same daffodils" and is eventually "buried deep underneath them" (18). A few days later, as if none of this had occurred, Mariah takes Lucy to a field of fresh daffodils, assuming that her pleasure upon seeing them will outweigh the trauma of her memories. Upon seeing the daffodils, however, Lucy noted to herself, "I did not know what these flowers were, and so it was a mystery to me why I wanted to kill them" (29). Unable to comprehend Lucy's reactions, Mariah's eyes "sank back in their head as if protecting themselves after some unexpected hard work" (30). Lucy feels sorry for having cast Mariah's beloved daffodils "in a scene of conquered and conquests; a scene of brutes masquerading as angels and angels portrayed as brutes." But, she comments to herself, "nothing could change the fact that where she saw beautiful flowers I saw sorrow and bitterness" (30).

Kincaid's *Lucy* is at its best when the ironic narrative voice exposes the imperialist worldview lurking behind the mundaneness of white middle-class existence in the United States. Mariah sees beautiful flowers and an angry young woman whose anger is incomprehensible to her. Therefore it is no surprise that the literal and symbolic significance of Lucy's relationship to the daffodils is also lost on her. It is

Clear Word and Third Sight

clear that Mariah wants to see Lucy as without a past—particularly, not an oppressive past that implicates the dynamics of their relationship in the present. Not only does she fail to understand that at ten years old Lucy had to memorize a poem about a flower that she would not see until she was nineteen, but the larger significance of Lucy's dream as the British colonization that she cannot escape is also lost on Mariah. At the end of the chapter, Mariah announces to Lucy, "I was looking forward to telling you that I have Indian blood, that the reason I'm so good at catching fish and hunting birds and roasting corn and doing all sorts of things is that I have Indian blood. But now, I don't know why, I feel I shouldn't tell you that. I feel you will take it the wrong way" (39). Desperate to escape her whiteness, which has become synonymous with her privilege and status as oppressor, Mariah tries to legitimate herself by recourse to a biological ancestry that bears no relationship to the cultural roles and behavior that structure her life on a daily basis. As Lucy says, "To look at her, there was nothing remotely like an Indian about her" (40).

On the other hand, of substantial interest here is Lucy's speech as a sign of her difference. In an October 1977 article entitled "Jamaica Kincaid's New York," published in *Rolling Stone* magazine, Kincaid describes aspects of her life at seventeen in New York City. While she was attending school there, she observes, "the strangest thing happened. All the white people liked me and thought me charming, particularly the way I spoke English. All the black people hated me and thought me ridiculous, particularly the way I spoke English. I didn't think twice about it. I became very good friends with the people who liked me" (72). In *Lucy*, as in all her work, there are no creole words and sayings, and no use of what Brathwaite refers to as "nation language." Whereas Hodge's novel employs "nation language" at the level of both character speech and narrative construction, the protagonists in Kincaid's texts seem to take pride in their ability to speak the king's English.

The exchange between Lucy and Mariah's maid can be interpreted as a confrontation between two Black women from different points in the diaspora who both have preconceived notions of the other. Shortly after her arrival, Lucy describes her second encounter with the maid:

> One day the maid who said she did not like me because of the way I talked told me that she was sure I could not dance. She said I spoke like a nun, I walked like one also, and that everything about me was so

pious it made her feel at once sick to her stomach and sick with pity just to look at me. And so, perhaps giving way to the latter feeling, she said that we should dance, even though she was quite sure I didn't know how. There was a little portable record-player in my room, the kind that when closed up looked like a ladies' vanity case, and she put on a record that she had bought earlier that day. It was a song that was very popular at the time—three girls, not older than I was, singing in harmony and in a very insincere and artificial way about love and so on. It was very beautiful all the same, and it was beautiful because it was so insincere and artificial. She enjoyed this song, singing at the top of her voice, and she was a wonderful dancer—it amazed me to see the way in which she moved. I could not join her and I told her why: the melodies of her song were shallow, and the words, to me, were meaningless. From her face, I could see she had only one feeling about me: how sick to her stomach I made her. And so I said that I knew songs, too, and burst into a calypso about a girl who ran away to Port-of-Spain, Trinidad, and had a good time, with no regrets. (11–12)

When Lucy hears the "three girls singing" she claims to feel scorn, but she also tells us she likes the song and is jealous of the maid's ability to dance to it.[16] This inconsistency is typical of the first-person narrator in Kincaid's texts in general: the scorn they express conceals their true feelings from the reader, and scorn and deception together are a consistent narrative device used to disguise genuine feelings of desire. Frequently Kincaud's narrators make statements which are the exact opposite of the emotions that are truly being felt. On the other hand, without having a name for it, Lucy understands what is at stake in the maid's not liking the way she acts and speaks. She recognizes it as a critique leveled against the authenticity of her cultural Blackness. Her response to the maid's critique is to burst into a calypso, a song form heavily associated with the cultural reality of the eastern Caribbean region. In this context, singing the calypso is a weak attempt on Lucy's part to demonstrate that she has a stronger link to Black cultural expression than the maid thinks.

On the other hand, Lucy's interaction with her employer, Mariah, requires her to perform a kind of "white imitation." With Mariah, Lucy is the good colonial subject gone wild. She consistently takes the moral high ground by exposing Mariah's complicity in systems of domination. Her colonial education serves her well as she points out to Mariah again and again the relationship between her privilege and the oppression of others. Mariah assumes she can relate to Lucy on

Clear Word and Third Sight

the basis of the universality of women's oppression. Assuming that whenever Lucy has problems they are a result of an experience of female disempowerment, Mariah tries to rescue her by speaking of "women in society, women in history, women in culture, women everywhere" (131). Lucy, overwhelmed, tells the reader that Mariah had completely misinterpreted her situation. While the maid perceives Lucy's alienation from Black everyday reality as a problem, it is precisely this alienation that leaves the door open for Mariah to imagine a commonality between herself and Lucy. Whereas Lucy's resentment of the maid's assumptions results in her singing a calypso, with Mariah she maintains her most perfect English. No calypso needed here.

The first time that the maid informs Lucy that she does not like her, giving as her reason the way Lucy speaks, Lucy observes to herself, "I thought it was because of something else, but I did not know what" (9). Ironically, in the exchange with the maid, Lucy seems to be positioned as Mariah was positioned in the encounters between them. She is confused by the maid's contempt for her, in the same way that Mariah was confused by Lucy's anger. The maid's response to Lucy is motivated by her critical perception of Lucy's speech and behavior. An intertextual reading of *Annie John* and *Lucy* makes it clear that these things are a product of her British colonial education. One of the things that close scrutiny of the maid's critique of Lucy exposes is Lucy's absolute isolation from Black life throughout the novel. It is significant, therefore, that the only character within the text whose presence reveals Lucy's duplicity is contained from the outset. Within Lucy's first-person narrative, the maid is effectively contained by her namelessness, her lack of explicit racial markings (she is the only character we get no physical description of), as well as her symbolic silencing by her absence from the rest of Lucy's story. With the worst threat neutralized, Lucy as narrator is free to control the reader's perceptions, since there are no other substantial Black characters in the novel. When Lucy becomes her own best literary critic, the most peculiar aspect of the text (this being the strangeness of Lucy's isolation) is normalized. While her isolation in a certain sense is always evident, her alienation from other Black people in her new home is not only invisible but vanishes without a trace. This flight from Blackness within the text remains credible (and invisible) in the context of paradigms that privilege self-invention and individuality.

Since Kincaid, the writer, makes no secret of the autobiographical nature of her early fiction, reading *Annie John* and *Lucy* as intertextual continuations of the world described in "On Seeing England for the First Time" makes sense. The isolation described at the beginning of *Lucy* is, therefore, the outcome we could expect when the worldview of a child like Annie (now Lucy) or Tee is transformed by her colonial education in school and certain societal contexts. The desire to be rescued from the "niggery" void that they perceive to be their past would necessarily result in a leaving behind of the communities that have been rewritten as spaces of alienation and savagery. In *Crick Crack Monkey,* Tee's education restructures how she sees herself as well as her community. And Kincaid has stated repeatedly in interviews that she changed her name and left Antigua in order to "escape the thing she had been born into."

In Paris in 1956, speaking to the delegates at the First International Congress of Negro Writers and Artists, Alioune Diop described the predicament of the "Negro" intellectual as one that was marked by the "crisis of conscience" that Hodge's and Kincaid's protagonists undergo. The Black intellectual, he said, could neither forget his or her difference vis-à-vis Europeans nor his or her alienation from the people who remained "attached to the soil and to their own traditions" (94). Diop goes further and describes assimilation as aiming "to make the individual (it is never concerned with anything but individuals) torn from the background natural to him, which brought out his personality, agree to replace his habits of thinking, feeling and acting by others which he could only share with an alien community" (94).

The question of Lucy's isolation with regard to other Black and Caribbean people is taken up by the Caribbean writer and scholar Opal Palmer Adisa. Adisa remarks, "Racism largely seems not to exist in Lucy's world—but it does" ("Island Daughter," 58). She reviews the section in the novel in which Lucy notices, while aboard a dining room car, that all the people being waited on look like Mariah's relatives, while all those doing the waiting look like hers. She decides that the waiters really aren't like her relatives since her relatives, "always gave backchat" (32). Adisa comments:

> I can't help but wonder why she feels so urgent a need to dissociate herself from blacks, since she and African-Americans share a common history and ancestry. This passage is snide. Lucy rejects the forging of links; she insists she has nothing in common with the black men who serve her, even though she too is beholden to the Mariahs of the world. She opts instead for *individualism,* being the anomaly, a

person immune to the ordinary needs of community and family. (6, italics mine)[17]

The fact that Kincaid is viewed by a mainstream literary public as a Caribbean writer with a strong sense of individualism is apparent in David Holmstorm's article "Jamaica Kincaid: Writing for Solace, for Herself." He states at the article's outset, "Her work gives voice to the lone, struggling individual" (14).

Moira Ferguson takes issue with Adisa's analysis, noting that "despite one reviewer's complaints that Jamaica Kincaid 'dissociates herself from blacks' in her fiction, Lucy's cultural awareness is abundantly evident. She employs a strategy of cultural reversal, revealing how the political legatees of residual colonial culture live their lives and think about their cultural positionality. In *Lucy* Kincaid thematizes hegemonic treatment of those regarded as native 'others'" ("Lucy and the Mark of the Colonizer," 239). Ironically, earlier in her own article, Ferguson concedes the point that she critiques Adisa for making when she states, "Unlike the protagonists of other texts, [Lucy] is surrounded almost exclusively by white people, not only in her immediate household but also within her circle of friends" (238). Further, while Ferguson identifies the maid in *Lucy* as "more candid, though no more empowered," she simplifies the complexity of their mutual critiques of each other (239). She boils it down to a situation in which the maid tries to make Lucy feel stupid and worthless, while Lucy's singing of a calypso is a display of pride in her heritage and a claiming of her history in the face of racist stereotypes. The disingenuousness of Lucy's singing and the ironic dishonesty of the narrative voice escapes Ferguson, along with Lucy's singing as a defensive reaction to the maid's criticism of her alienation from Black life.

Adisa and Ferguson's struggle over the absence of Blacks in *Lucy* emphasizes what is and is not imaginable in Kincaid's universe when her characters are analyzed in critical isolation from the rest of African Caribbean literature. Yet if the legacy of negritude is revealed by a writer's commitment to both exploring racial oppression and examining its relationship to collective cultural identity, then the isolation of Lucy and Annie John at the end of both novels seems significant. An alienated rather than transnational diaspora identity is exposed as at the heart of Kincaid's oeuvre. While England, due to the legacy of British colonialism in Antigua, can only function for Kincaid as a place in which racial oppression is omnipresent, "America" is the place of self-invention and opportunity. Of significant interest, therefore, is the representation of "America" on the part of other Caribbean writers.

Earl Lovelace's "Joebell" and the American Dream

> For the Africans who were brought to the Caribbean, the central theme was the struggle against enslavement. And because slavery was essentially a process that denied personhood, the central struggle after the wars and the marronage was for self-affirmation: they struggled to declare the self, rather than utilizing property to gain a self, so they cultivated the business of non-possession.— EARL LOVELACE, in an interview with Maya Jaggi

Earl Lovelace's "Joebell and America" is a story about a failed migration attempt to the United States. Joebell's relationship to the United States and his home community differs substantially from Lucy's. The story is a snapshot in the life of Joebell, variously referred to as "vagabond," "hero," and "of bad character" by his girlfriend's mother, his friends, and the police. The story opens with Joebell's dreams about "America": "Joebell find that he seeing too much hell in Trinidad so he make up his mind to leave and go away. The place he find he should go is America, where everybody have a motor car and you could ski on snow and where it have seventy-five channels of colour television . . . and you could sit down and watch . . . all the boxing and wrestling and basketball right there as it happening" (111). Unlike Lucy, or Tee, Joebell speaks in the "nation language" of Trinidadian creole. Like Merle Hodge, Lovelace is extremely skilled at narrativizing oral consciousness, and his capacity to capture the cultural logic of Trinidadian creole is by and large unparalleled.

In her 1928 essay "Characteristics of Negro Expression," Zora Neale Hurston, generalizing about the cultural behavior of rural Black people in the southern United States, anticipates some of the characteristics of Lovelace's style. She examines cultures under such rubrics as "drama," "dialect," and what she calls "the will to adorn." While speaking about the characteristics of dialect, she states, "In storytelling 'so' is universally the connective. It is used even as an introductory

Clear Word and Third Sight

word at the beginning of a story. The trend in stories is to state conclusions" (*Hurston*, 846). Lovelace was writing some sixty years later than Hurston and from the geographical space of the Caribbean, but Hurston's early insights nevertheless apply to his work in the wider diaspora. Not only is the transitional "so" apparent in Lovelace's first sentence, but the main event is stated: "so he make up his mind to leave and go away." We know it will be a story about a migration attempt. Linear time is of no consequence; instead, the narrative is organized around the events that precede and immediately follow the attempted migration.

In Hurston's essay, "the will to adorn" is characterized as the "second most notable characteristic" of Black culture, and she describes adornment in terms of language (831). In Lovelace's story, this same will to adorn verbally is found in—to take just one example—the passage recounting Joebell's anger with his mother for consulting with the spirit-world-dabbling *obeah* woman behind his back. Rather than simply stating, "Joebell was angry," Lovelace writes, "Joebell fly up in one big vexation with his mother for enticing him to go to the *obeah* woman" (114). Lovelace's use of language is in this sense exemplary. In reference to Lovelace's novel *Salt,* Jamaican scholar and writer Velma Pollard states:

> Critics concerned with theory will eventually hail Earl Lovelace as the post colonial writer par excellence, not only because he includes in his text phenomena from all the strands that make the culture-history of his island but because he takes a summary leap in the manipulation of language. In this more than in any other of his novels, Lovelace moves beyond the traditional boundaries of the genre. The writing seems to be unselfconscious and disarming. Close scrutiny, however, reveals a complexity of style which runs parallel to the complexity of the society whose social, cultural and political problems the novel tries to resolve. ("Mixing Codes and Mixing Voices," 94)

Stylistically, Lovelace's narrative is divided into two segments. The first part, titled "One," is Joebell's migration story, told from the perspective of a close male friend, most probably one of his gambling partners. Here, Lovelace brings to life, in writing, the oral storytelling tradition practice that is at the heart of African diaspora cultural expression. He does this in two ways: first, by his use of a conversational, everyday Trinidadian creole as the official language of the story; and second, like Hodge, with her use of Tee as a first-person narrator who tells a story about her community while describing her personal life, Lovelace uses "the friend" to give the reader an intimate sense of who Joebell is and how he thinks. The telling is so personal that the reader has a sense of Joebell's every motivation. Lovelace also exemplifies Hurston's ninth characteristic of "Negro" expression, "the absence of the concept of privacy." We see it in his short story in the figure of the other member of the community who knows so much about Joebell's life.

The second part of Lovelace's narrative begins after Joebell is detained and held under suspicion in a Puerto Rican airport, having been denied entry into the United States. From this point until the story's end, Lovelace shifts to a first-person narrative and Joebell tells his own story to the reader. His every utterance resonates with his communal ties. The contrast with Kincaid's Lucy could not be more stark. The United States as a site of fantasy for Joebell, who never arrives, and for Lucy, who arrives but without a past, are quite different.

In his home society of Trinidad, Joebell emanates from what Langston Hughes describes as the "low-down folks":

> But then there are the low-down folks, the so-called common element, and they are in the majority—may the Lord be praised! The people who have their hip of gin on Saturday nights and are not too important to themselves or the community, or too well fed, or too learned to watch the lazy world go round . . . Their joy runs, bang! into ecstasy. Their religion soars to a shout. Work maybe a little today, rest a little tomorrow. They furnish a wealth of colorful, distinctive material for any artist because they still hold their own individuality in the face of American standardizations. (Hughes, "The Negro Artist," 1268)

Joebell, like Hughes's "folk," is more concerned with getting from day to day, making some quick money, being comfortable, and enjoying life than he is with how to succeed based on status and imitation of elite behavior. Unlike Lucy, who enters America without a clearly described connection to her past or her people, Joebell sees himself through the eyes of his community. His most intimate community, those to whom he is the most loyal, comprises other Black men who are his gambling partners in the context of the story. Those striving for respectability in the larger society see him only in terms of his so-called low-down qualities. To them he is a gambler and a criminal, someone without a steady job who is a bad influence on those striving to fit in.

When Joebell wins money gambling he decides that if he doesn't go to "America" now he never will. From the first paragraph, "America" is established as the place that produces an endless stream of entertainment and luxuries. It is a place that has the power to *rescue* Joebell from his "hellish-Trini-life." The whole notion of self-invention and creating a new identity plays its role in Lovelace's short story. In fact, this was to be his ticket into the United States, his ability to pass himself off as an American. However, it becomes clear that the rescue imagined is not a genuine attempt to escape the Black Caribbean cultural identity that, despite all performance, is clearly at the heart of who Joebell is and how he sees himself. The American presence in Joebell's world is typified by the names of his gambling partner friends, who are fashioned after cowboy/western movie stars, as well as by the constant reference to various icons of the American music and sports industry. Joebell tells us, "Really, in truth, I know America so much I feel American. Is just that I aint born there" (123). America has acquired the status once held by Britain. As Merle Hodge writes in her essay "Challenges of the Struggle for Sovereignty: Changing the World versus Writing Stories": "The colonial era came to an end and we moved into independence. Theoretically, we could now begin to build up a sense of our cultural identity. But we immediately found ourselves in a new and more vicious era of cultural penetration. Television, which is basically American television, came to Trinidad and Tobago in 1962, the year the British flag was pulled down" (205). The United States as a culturally dominant commercial presence that replaces Britain is contextualized by Hodge's statement and Joebell's desires.

Joebell is a gambler. He wins close to two thousand dollars at wappie, a card game won almost entirely by luck. He could have taken his money and left, but "Joebell have himself down as a hero, and to win and run away is not classy. Joebell have himself down as classy" (112). He stays and plays poker, which involves more skill than outright luck and loses five hundred dollars. Returning to the familiarity of wappie, he wins again and leaves the club with fifteen hundred dollars—being hailed by his friends as "the Gambler of Natchez." He buys an American passport, and (the narrator tells us), "not for one moment it don't strike Joebell that he doing anything wrong. . . . Joebell believe the whole world is a hustle. He believe everybody running some game, putting on some show and the only thing that separate people is that *some have power* and others *don't have none*" (119, italics mine).

Because of his prison record for wounding, resisting arrest, and using obscene language, Joebell is refused the letter of good character that he needs to legally obtain a passport. It is his gambler instinct that makes him buy a passport and try to pass himself off as a (Black) American to the immigration authorities in Puerto Rico. He stops in Venezuela to see his brother and goes through Puerto Rico to avoid arousing suspicion. His brother tries to convince him to stay in Venezuela, but Joebell says by the time he learns Spanish he will be an old man. "*Caramba! Caramba! Habla! Habla!* No. I done pay my thousand dollars. I have my American passport. I is an American citizen" (118). His friend who sells him the passport tells him, "Listen, in America, every black face is the same to white people" (118). Joebell reflects and sees the point, since he isn't sure he could tell the difference between two Chinese. But then he asks, "Suppose I meet up a black immigration" (119)? The friend responds, "Ah! You thinking. Anyhow, it aint have that many of them, but, if you see one stay far from him" (119). The exchange between Joebell and his friend takes the fact of racial discrimination against Black people internationally as both a given and the point of departure from which they must offensively strategize. In the second part of Lovelace's narrative, after Joebell is detained, he has another encounter that reveals his sense of race consciousness as something that crosses national lines. As Joebell waits to be questioned, he tells us:

> I sit down there by myself alone and I know they watching me. Everybody else in the room white. This black fellar come in the room, with beads of perspiration running down his face and his eyes wild and he looking round like he escape. As soon as I see him I say "Oh god!" because I know with all the empty seats all about the place is me he coming to. He don't know my troubles. He believe I want friends. I want to tell him "Listen, man, I love you. I really dig my people, but now is not the time to come and talk to me." . . . But I can't tell him that 'cause I don't want to offend him. . . . He shake my hand in the Black Power sign. And we sit down there side by side, two crooks, he and me. (121–122)

Here, despite his plight, Joebell still expresses feelings of solidarity with his Black American brother. The Black Power handshake is a recognizable sign that situates Joebell's politics within a Pan-African context. The collective coming-to-consciousness that Césaire cites as a foundational principle of negritude is presumed in the Black world of Lovelace's short story.

Donning both the attire and mannerisms that he learns from American films, Joebell gambles on the fact that he won't get caught since "he grew up in America right there in Trinidad" (121). His overplaying of the role, however, arouses suspicion, and he is subsequently detained for further questioning. He describes the whole encounter as if it were a game that depended on his ability to control the forces of luck—like the power he banks on when he is playing cards. This attitude toward life that is perceived by others as his craziness is something that charms his girlfriend, Alicia, but frightens both of their mothers. When he leaves Trinidad, his mother, Miss Myrtle, says, "Joebell gone away, Praise God!" (114) Alicia's mother says, "Thank you, Master Jesus, for helping to deliver this child from the clutches of that vagabond" (114).

Joebell gets caught when he is asked to recite the alphabet and pronounces the last letter as "zed" instead of "zee." As he recites, the images that float through his head are of Alicia, his community, the fact that he still "has himself down as a hero," and a hero has to lose with class. At the same time, it is specifically *Black* U.S. popular figures that he remembers (Paul Robeson, Sammy Davis Jr., Nina Simone, Aretha, Belafonte) as he approaches the end of the alphabet, realizing he's been caught. This is significant, since it demonstrates that despite being influenced by white American cinema growing up in Trinidad, not only is Joebell aware of the representations of Black life in the United States, but this is what he turns to when he needs a strategy for survival.

In his 1996 interview with Jamaica Kincaid, Charlie Rose asked her if she felt she was the tribune of Caribbean women and whether she felt a responsibility to define, share, and reflect their experiences. Kincaid responded by saying that she didn't feel a particular responsibility to any group but felt instead a responsibility to be a good citizen. Joebell, on the other hand, is the essence of the bad citizen; yet he sees himself as a hero and a substantial part of his home community. Further, whether he wins or loses, at the heart of Joebell's praxis is an attempt to devise a strategy of psychological preparedness to face any circumstance:

> The thing is that Joebell really don't be betting on the card, Joebell does be betting on himself. He don't be trying to guess about which card is the right one, he is trying to find that power in himself that will make him call correct. And that power is what Joebell searching for as

he queue up in the line leading to the immigration entering Puerto Rico. Is that power that he calling up in himself as he stand there, because if he can feel that power, if that power come inside him, then, nothing could stop him. And now this was it. (120)

In his text *From Trickster to Badman: The Black Folk Hero in Slavery and Freedom,* sociologist John Roberts concerns himself with what he describes as culture building within the Black community in the United States. He describes this as "a recursive, rather than linear process of endlessly devising solutions to both old and new problems of how to live under ever-changing social, political and economic conditions" (11). His purpose is to talk about Black folk heroes and Black folk heroic tradition as serving the culture-building needs of a Black population in the United States. He states that (white) folklorists have generally been incapable of conceding that Black folk heroes served as models for the Black community, since they were perceived as trickster figures invested in private revenge. This marginalization of the significance of the Black folk hero is a result of heroic action being defined "within a so-called normative model" (1). But, "actions dubbed heroic in one context or by one group of people may be viewed as ordinary or even criminal in another context/by other groups . . . at different times" (2).[18]

In the chapter " 'You Done Me Wrong': The Badman as Outlaw Hero," Roberts describes how Black singers and storytellers combined conceptions of the trickster and the conjurer to create the badman. His book devotes a chapter each to the trickster and the conjurer, citing their appearance in stories and ballads as evidence of their significance. The "black characterization of badmen as 'bad' derived from their association with a kind of secular anarchy peculiar to the experience of free black people" (193). Roberts examines a ballad about Railroad Bill, who was considered a conjurer by Black folks but a desperate criminal by the law. After his capture, Railroad Bill was talked about within the community as having successfully evaded the law for so long because of his ability to change out of human form. He was also believed to live on in other forms after his execution. What is significant about what Roberts attempts to do in his analysis of the badman is the way in which what some would consider to be the pariah of society—the criminalized Black subject—gets reconfigured, not just as the model for the Black folk hero who invigorates the community but also as symbolic of a tradition of heroic creation that

Clear Word and Third Sight

can be traced back to slavery. The trickster figure was seen as one who, among other things, *avoided work and other forms of exploitation to which Blacks were subject during slavery*. The trickster, however, was also capable of aggression and violence when cornered. Roberts states at one point that "in freedom and under the law, African Americans discovered that many of the behaviors associated with the trickster of folklore and adaptable under the conditions of slavery had become, after emancipation, *behaviors associated with the criminal*" (186, italics mine). Of significance in his chapter is the description of "badmen" as those individuals whose acts of lawlessness functioned as a kind of communal exoneration within a system in which their communities were never meant to survive. By the end of Lovelace's short story, this description of the "badman" smoothly typifies Joebell.

High up on the list of what constituted secular anarchy was the activity of gambling. Roberts describes the world of gambling that the badman occupies as paralleling the practice of conjuration in the Black community. During and after slavery, conjurers were seen as individuals whose behavior protected the values of harmony and communality. He speaks of the idealized worldview in which gambling functions as a socioeconomic system. In other words, the extent to which there are similarities between conjuration and a belief in "luck" is the extent to which the parallel is viable. Roberts writes,

> As in conjuration, participants in gambling games do so willingly and stake the outcome on their ability to buy into a mysterious supernatural power called "luck." Gamblers ideally do not play against each other but rather contest their abilities to control the whims of chance. . . . Ideally in black folk heroic tradition, the tricked or duped individual in *an act of conjuration looks within himself or to a conjurer for a superior source of power to realign social relationships* or bring equilibrium to the situation. (206, italics mine)

The parallels between this account and how Joebell both sees himself and functions within his community are so similar as to appear uncanny. Lovelace's story has two narrators: an anonymous friend of Joebell's and Joebell himself. From the outset Joebell is both part of the community as well as a heroic figure of sorts. The first narrator tells us, "Joebell really don't be betting on the card, Joebell does be betting on himself. He don't be trying to guess about which card is the right one, he is trying *to find that power in himself that will make him call correct*" (120, italics mine). Not only does Roberts's description of the purest gambling games as those that involve that mysterious super-natural power called "luck" parallel the description of wappie but his statement about the tricked or duped individual in Black folk heroic tradition looking within him- or herself for a superior source of power to realign social relationships is an almost verbatim description of Joebell's process when he loses at both gambling and immigration. In addition, Joebell's investment in having no hard feelings when he gets caught seems to function as a way of realigning his social relation-ships after loss.

> And just so I know I get catch. The question too easy. Too easy like a calm blue sea. And, pardner, I look at that sea and I think about Alicia and the warm soft curving sadness of her lips and her eyes full with crying, make me feel to cry for me and Alicia and Trinidad and Amer-ica and I know like when you make a bet you see a certain card play and it will be a miracle if the card you bet on play. I lose, I know. But I is still a hero. I can't bluff forever. I have myself down as classy. And, really, I wasn't frighten for nothing, not for nothing, wasn't afraid of jail or of poverty or of Puerto Rico or America and I wasn't vex with the fellar who sell me the passport for the thousand dollars with Iron Jaw and Squirrel Eyes. . . . They catch me. God! And now, how to go? I think about getting on like an American, but I never see an American lose. I think about making a performance like the British, steady, stiff upper lip like Alec Guiness in *The Bridge over the River Kwai,* but with my hat and my boots and my piece of cigar, that didn't match, so I say I might as well take my losses like a West Indian, like a Trinidadian. I decide to sing. (123–24)

There is a communal sentiment at the heart of Joebell's thoughts and utterances as the story closes. He references Trinidad and Amer-ica and, strangely, he has compassion for them both. Further, despite his own criminalized situation, he does not see himself as a victim. He states, "I lose I know. But I is still a hero . . . and really I wasn't frighten for nothing [not] jail or . . . poverty" (123).

In Merle Hodge's *Crick Crack Monkey* and in Jamaica Kincaid's "On Seeing England for the First Time," England becomes (for Tee) and is (for the young Kincaid) the thing that they desire as well as the thing that restructures how they see themselves. England is transmitted to them through the institutions of church and school. When they start to see their worlds through English eyes, a whole moral order comes with their new sight, one in which there is a proper way to do things. Kincaid tells us that a proper breakfast is a big breakfast, and Tee describes "Helen," her imaginary English double, as "the proper me." In this universe, Tee tells us, "the whole of life was like a piece of cloth, with a rightside and a wrongside" (62). Joebell's desire for "America" and "Americanness" does not require a reconfiguration of the world into a moral order marking his way of life as wrong, and another way as innately right. While "America" with its endless stream of pleasures is a site of substantial fantasy, it still functions primarily as part of the costume of the hustler in a world which is all about hustling. But there is more. How "America" functions for Joebell is quite different from how it functions for Lucy. His desire for "America" does not require him to distance himself from his community.

Prior to young Tee's rise up the educational ranks, Hodge's narrative (like Lovelace's) emphasizes Tee's proximity to her community. There is no distance from her community in her gaze. Lucy and Joebell, however, are far apart. Ironically, even in spite of this difference, neither Lucy nor Joebell is representative of the kind of immigrant narrative described by Malcolm Gladwell in his *New Yorker* piece, "Black Like Them." Lovelace's short story ends with Joebell's arrest in Puerto Rico, one in which he goes out singing. As he puts it, he takes his losses like a West Indian. *Lucy* on the other hand ends with the main character's complete isolation. She is totally alone in a shrinking and unreliable circle of companions, and with no plans to return home.

While Gladwell's narrative tells a story of the Caribbean in which the racialized past is either misremembered or unaccounted for, the stories of Joebell, Tee, and even Lucy in her isolation collectively represent a kind of counternarrative. The young Tee who goes to visit Aunt Beatrice and views the pretensions of that household with scorn is similar to the Joebell whose spirit remains unbowed during his arrest. This depiction, however, is radically different from the older Tee, who is defenseless once she is "well-educated," and different too from the "well-educated" Annie John transformed into Lucy, who is isolated at the novel's end with no recourse. Young Tee's and Joebell's location within "Black space" in their home societies functions as a refutation of the view that Black solidarity across national lines is unimaginable for Black Caribbean populations. It is within the context of these home communities that sites of culture exist that resonate with a sense of tradition that survived both slavery and colonization.

To close, it makes sense to return to the original premises of the argument in this chapter and summarize how selections from the work of these eastern Caribbean writers are situated in relation to the concepts of negritude and negativity or "voice" and alienation. Césaire defined negritude as "a concrete rather than abstract coming-to-consciousness" about the collective racial and cultural condition of African peoples across the world. The connections among Césaire (born in Martinique), Léon Damas (born in French Guiana), and Léopold Senghor (born in Senegal) and the association of all three bespeak the attempt to make the concept of negritude transnational. The focus on the "concrete" rather than the "abstract" in Césaire's definition makes it clear that at the heart of this conceptual formulation is an active rather than an ambivalent or passive stance in relation to the question of Black identity. In other words, as long as racial oppression exists, abstract critiques of the social construction of race that are not equally grounded in critiques of racism are not viable strategies for survival.[19] Lovelace's opening statement describing "Africans not as slaves *in a passive sense*, but as *enslaved*" speaks directly to the philosophical tradition within negritude geared toward concrete, active conceptualizations. By contrast, Kincaid states, "There were Africans who remained in Africa and there were Africans who were descended from slaves. . . . It's not exactly the ancestral family you hope for [that] . . . the founding member of your family is a captured person. . . . I came back and I thought, well, I'm just nobody." Here, a passive stance is assumed both in relation to the history of oppression as well as the subsequent formulation of cultural identity.

The notion of being conquered is evident in how the history of Britain functions in Kincaid's essay "On Seeing England for the First Time." Both *Annie John* and *Lucy* end with the main characters leaving their home communities for a foreign land, and crying in that foreign land, isolated from home, family, and community. What appears to be self-invention, in both texts, is revealed to be a clever manipulation of a variety of emotions. As I noted earlier, the first-person narrator in Kincaid's stories in general uses scorn as an emotional response to deflect the reader's attention from the character's self-deception, and those responses of scorn and self-deception are narrative devices consistently used to disguise genuine feelings of desire. The endings, however, reveal the extent to which this strategy is a failure.

The concern about the collective racial and cultural condition of African peoples at the heart of negritude is therefore more apparent in Hodge and Lovelace than in Kincaid, in the way that Hodge and Lovelace thematically and aesthetically represent the relationship between

Clear Word and Third Sight

the individual and the community. In their work, the development of an individual identity separated from a sense of community consistently leads to the no-man's-land of cultural alienation. Ironically, however, it is precisely the inventive, transformative aesthetic at the heart of African diaspora cultural praxis that, in the final instance, bequeaths the most developed notions of individuality. In the first part of Hodge's *Crick Crack Monkey*, before the deterioration in young Tee's self-esteem, the literary "I" is always spoken from the context of a communal "we." Young Tee has a multiplicity of male role models, a strong mother figure in Tantie, and a substantial sense of cultural ancestry produced by her relationship with her grandmother, who tells Tee she is her own great-great-grandmother reincarnate. At this point in young Tee's life, her individual identity and sense of cultural self-esteem are at their most developed. When Tee moves to Aunt Beatrice's house and becomes ashamed of her humble beginnings, ironically she loses both cultural self-esteem and individual identity. The "society of the monkey" that the novel's title speaks to becomes Tee's standard for identity. Yet this society is premised on what Hurston calls "slavish imitation" rather than what she describes as mimicry for the sheer love of it (838).[20] Tee's shame at the end of *Crick Crack Monkey* and "the society of the monkey" described in the text are at the extreme end of Hurston's "slavish imitation" continuum. Hodge's text, as I noted earlier, "demonstrates the relationship between Tee's level of comfort with the collective Black culture she comes from and her level of comfort with herself personally." On the other hand, mimicry for the sheer love of it is most personified by Joebell and is demonstrated by his attempt to impersonate an American.

Of the three writers, Lovelace carries the thematic and aesthetic concerns of negritude furthest. If Brathwaite's theories are correct about the aesthetics of Caribbean writing being most reconciled to the cultural environment when Caribbean writers bring to life in their texts the sound and sensibility of the oral tongue, then Lovelace exceeds both Kincaid and Hodge in this regard. At the end of "Joebell and America," unlike the protagonists at the end of Kincaid's novels, Joebell loses all his money, faces certain incarceration, and yet maintains a sense of balance as well as pride in his individual and cultural identity. Thematically, in terms of the relationship between the individual and the community, Lovelace's text reveals the most developed individuality and the biggest connection to community. In the interview by Jaggi published in the journal *Wasafiri*, Lovelace states, "For the Africans who were brought to the Caribbean, the central theme was the struggle against enslavement. And because slavery was essentially a process that denied personhood, the central struggle after the wars and the marronage was for self-affirmation: they struggled to declare the self" (27). The "characteristics" that Hurston uses to describe "Negro expression" in the southern, rural, 1920s U.S. context ("the will to adorn," "imitation," "dialect," etc.) are all characteristics that develop "personhood" or what could be called a culturally informed individuality rooted in the collective expression of a people. KRS-One remarks, "When the individual is last and culture is first, you have self. You are a part of a collection of people that have learned and strived for years on end. The struggle *is* your culture. This is what fills you up. This is what makes you the African, the Asian, the Japanese: that your culture has taught you to act and think a certain way" ("Can the Teacher Be Taught?" 173). Similarly, Lovelace also sees struggle as at the heart of artistic and cultural expression in the diaspora. He states that cultural resistance was a continuation of the tradition of resistance against enslavement and dehumanization and ultimately the warrior became the artist. In his novel *The Dragon Can't Dance* he describes the text as presenting "indigenous arts—Carnival, calypso, steelbands—not simply as art in the arty sense, but as art which is part of a struggle" (Jaggi, interview, 25).

Césaire's negritudinal conception of coming to terms with the collective racial and cultural condition of African peoples is expressed in the emphasis on both "personhood" and struggle at the heart of diaspora praxis, exemplified here in Lovelace's work and words. At the end of "Joebell and America" the issue shifts from being about whether Joebell wins or loses and becomes about his ability to *transform himself* in the face of oppression. As I noted earlier, Joebell has to devise a strategy of psychological preparedness to face any circumstance. As my analysis of John Roberts's essay in relation to Lovelace's story makes clear, Joebell's investment in having no hard feelings after he is caught functions as a way of realigning his social relationships after loss. This ability to transform oneself in the face of difficulties not only characterizes Lovelace's enterprise but also seems to lay the foundation for a transnational diaspora subjectivity, one that develops and moves beyond negritude into something old yet new. As my quotations of Hurston's work throughout this chapter make apparent, the Black U.S. population is at the heart of this transformational aesthetic and is a constant source of inspiration for Africans around the world.

Clear Word and Third Sight

As the late Toni Cade Bambara said, "The transformation drama is clearly the hallmark of Afro-American literature, of our culture, as it is and must be of *any people under siege*. It is an imperative for survival. . . . The compelling message [is that] people can awake, people can change, and in changing enable each other. . . . A CLASSICAL PEOPLE DEMAND A CLASSICAL ART" (Bambara, keynote address, italics mine).

Ultimately, therefore, what holds a community together, what holds a people together, is not material wealth but the extent to which there is a spirit of generosity or forgiveness that individuals in the community exemplify and express. This spirit introduces a balance that ultimately allows the community to collectively maintain perspective after crises. This spirit of transformation is a result of struggle and has become part of African diaspora culture and artistic expression. *A classical people demand a classical art.*

4

Diaspora Philosophy,
French Caribbean Literature, and
Simone Schwarz-Bart's *Pluie et vent*
sur Télumée Miracle

Marie-Denise Shelton, in her article "Women Writers of the French-Speaking Caribbean," describes Simone Schwarz-Bart's first novel *Pluie et vent sur Télumée Miracle* as "breaking the chain of alienation" that historically characterized a lot of women's writing from the francophone Caribbean (354). In Shelton's article, as well as in the critical essays devoted to Schwarz-Bart's work in Carole Boyce Davies and Elaine Savory Fido's collection *Out of the Kumbla*, Schwarz-Bart's novels are frequently analyzed in relation to other French-speaking Caribbean writers, most of whom are still bound by the so-called chain of alienation.[1] Of the female writers whose work is addressed here, it is the work of Simone Schwarz-Bart that most successfully establishes a precedent for reconciliation between individual and communal African diaspora experience. *Pluie et vent sur Télumée Miracle* shifts the focus from a French Caribbean literary concern with an explicitly middle-class, female experience of self-alienation to an exploration of the experiences of the rural poor. In her texts, migration away from the island home is not presented as a solution to the crises being experienced.[2] When travel beyond the island is portrayed, as it is in her second novel *Ti Jean L'Horizon*, it is a mythic, surreal portrayal in which the travel out is a means of procuring the survival of the entire island community rather than the solution to one individual's problems.[3]

I maintain, therefore, that despite the centering of female experience in her first novel, Schwarz-Bart's work is not a reification of femininity and explicitly female experiences of survival. Instead, the substance of her writing lies in the systematic reconciliation of *Black* female experience with the experiences of the larger community, male and female. She achieves this through her conscientious representation of an oral legacy of proverbs and creole sayings passed down from generation to generation. These are psychocultural tools with the metaphorical power to wage philosophical warfare against the white colonial assault on Black cultural identity. When Schwarz-Bart stated that with her first novel she wanted to create "tout un univers créole," her statement would be incomprehensible if "un univers créole" were reductively and exclusively interpreted to mean a novel written in the creole tongue.[4] Although creole words are used in her first novel, it is written in French predominantly to and for an audience who reads French. I maintain, however, that the *créolité* of Schwarz-Bart's work is primarily functional in terms of how the proverbs and creole sayings mediate the realities of the characters and help to portray a world that is the countercultural reality of the official colonial culture. This is a world in which the notion of individuality is constantly under siege, and it is Schwarz-Bart's portrait of characters who both cannot and do not desire separation from the larger communal context that constitutes the significance of her literary achievement. At the other end of the spectrum from the flight of the protagonists in Kincaid's novels, Schwarz-Bart's work portrays Caribbean community with a depth of diaspora practices that in many ways seems unparalleled.

Schwarz-Bart's *Pluie et vent sur Télumée Miracle* is a text that implicitly celebrates a diaspora version of African philosophical reality. The Africanity of her novel is apparent in the power of the word and the centrality of a spiritual worldview in which the natural environment and the human and the divine realms are interconnected. In this world, words have the power to affect one's fate; spiritual life and spiritual death are functional concepts that can apply to any individual; and the ability to control spiritual power and transform from human to animal shape is not treated as impossible. In this world, proverbs have a long life and are at the heart of this diaspora-philosophical praxis. The proverbs speak to self-affirmation and survival as well as self-doubt. This dual legacy, rather than having a clear relationship to good and evil, speaks instead to the forces that plague each individual in the text. The extent to which one falls victim to self-doubt is the extent to which one is susceptible to colonial versions of truth. In *Pluie et vent* names are significant, and characters receive names that relate to their identity or their ability to overcome adversity. In Kemetic Egyptian philosophy, symbolic systems were constructed to effect transformation of the individual. This transformation, however, depended on "the inner wisdom of the interpreter." As one scholar states, "Gradually, through an intuitive understanding that involves relating the symbols to your own life, you begin to put the symbols together" (T'Shaka, *Return to the African Mother Principle,* 94). As I will demonstrate, Télumée's transformation through her lifelong journey of interpreting symbols and creole proverbs parallels this philosophical trajectory of knowledge that can be traced back to Kemetic philosophy.

It seems important, therefore, to analyze Schwarz-Bart's work, not just within the confines of a separate female tradition of Caribbean writing but also for its commonality to and difference from representations of Caribbean identity depicted by male writers from the French-speaking tradition. While the uniqueness of Schwarz-Bart's treatment of the issue of cultural alienation has been explored by critics in relation to the French Caribbean female writers, the similarities and differences between her portrayal of this issue and those of other male writers has gone largely untreated. I propose therefore to explore how the issue of self-alienation and communal survival is treated in *Pluie et vent sur Télumée Miracle* as well as in selections from Edouard Glissant's *Caribbean Discourse* and Léon-Gontran Damas's *Pigments.*

The writings of Edouard Glissant are concerned with a specifically Martinican experience of cultural and psychic alienation, one that finds its strongest substantiation in the Martinican as opposed to the Guadeloupean historical experience.[5] Glissant's conceptions of "reversion" and "diversion," addressed in his *Caribbean Discourse,* are the premise for his theory of creolization. This theory appears to be both a result of and a response to white colonial domination. Yet the particular trajectory of alienation he depicts is based on the experiences of the French Antillean educated elite. While this is the point of departure for many French Caribbean writers, the way in which this alienation is depicted and the solutions proposed differ from writer to writer. Glissant's notion of creolization is premised on the idea of African cultural survivals existing at best in "dim traces" and "spontaneous impulses." By contrast, in Schwarz-Bart's novels, these legacies are

Clear Word and Third Sight

represented as ever present and are exemplified by references to the drum, humans who take animal form, the community's collective renaming of individual members, and the representation of a continuity between the life of the living and the life of "the dead." At the same time, Schwarz-Bart's work vividly portrays material and psychospiritual impoverishment as part of the colonial legacy.

Born in French Guiana, and seen by many as writing the precursor to Césaire's *Cahier d'un retour au pays natal* with his collection of poetry *Pigments* (1937), Léon-Gontran Damas is most frequently situated as the "enfant terrible" of the 1930s negritude poets. The sparse, direct, and bitingly cynical tone of his verse is linked most specifically with his relentless criticism of French colonialism and the related mimicry of the class that Frantz Fanon refers to as the native bourgeoisie. *Pigments* indicts the native bourgeoisie's obsession with "good manners" and metropolitan values. Damas links this obsession with colonial violence and social control. At the same time the poems in this collection (produced out of his own experience of alienation from his cultural roots as a student in Paris in the 1930s) systematically lament a perceived cultural vacuum. Of particular interest here are his poems "Hoquet" (Hiccup) and "Limbé" (Blues).

It is my contention that when alienation is depicted as an individual issue, bourgeois middle-class identity is foregrounded and the explicit or implicit critique of colonial violence is framed in terms of the outsider seeking inclusion within the dominant culture, rather than the community seeking a rebalance of power and legitimization for its collective identity. In chapter 3, these issues were demonstrated through analyses of Jamaica Kincaid's novel *Lucy* and Earl Lovelace's story "Joebell and America." How these French Caribbean authors depict colonial violence, and in their depictions negotiate the alienation resulting from it, differs from text to text and writer to writer. This chapter, therefore, will focus on these various negotiations and their implications.

In 1937 the first edition of Léon Damas's *Pigments* was published in Paris with a preface by surrealist poet Robert Desnos. As Lilyan Kesteloot observes, "Apart from the ideas it contained, the originality of *Pigments* lay in the fact that for the first time a Caribbean poet was calling attention to the color of his skin" (123). Many of the poems are critiques of the European values imbibed by a particular class of colonial subjects. In the poem "Hoquet," for example, a son has unsettling recollections of his upbringing—his cultural education in the home space. While the son's voice frames the poem, it is the relationship between this son and his mother that is under scrutiny. Often viewed as embarrassing within the context of "polite" society, a hiccup —like the poem—calls attention to the gaps and disjunctions that disrupt this order of *politesse*. A hiccup is an involuntary, spasmodic, cutting-off of indrawn breath. Associated as it is with the stereotype of the drunkard, the hiccup is also linked to consumption, specifically to overconsumption. The metaphor is typical of Damas's frequent use of poetic imagery suggesting nausea and indigestion. In the context of this poem, the hiccup represents cultural values that have been forcibly consumed:

> Et j'ai beau avaler sept gorgées d'eau
> trois à quatre fois par vingt-quatre heures
> me revient mon enfance dans un hoquet secouant mon
> instinct
> tel le flic le voyou
> Désastre
> parlez-moi du désastre
> parlez-m'en
> (35)
> [I have gulped down seven mouthfuls of water
> three to four times every twenty-four hours
> yet my childhood returns to me in a convulsive hiccup my
> instinct
> like the cop to the thug
> Disaster
> speak to me about disaster
> tell me about it][6]

In this first stanza, the narrating subject (the mature son) regularly and compulsively drinks water, but to no avail. He is unable to rid his body of hiccups. Symbolically, what the hiccup brings to the surface are the son's memories of his childhood. But the water swallowed can neither quell the hiccup nor keep the childhood memories at bay. In this stanza the word "instinct" is given a line to itself, thereby making its interpretation ambiguous. In terms of placement within the poem, "hiccup" mediates the relationship between "childhood memories" and "instinct." The sentence-line "instinct" is immediately followed by the line, "like the cop [to the] thug." Like the policeman who restrains the lawbreaker, the son's childhood memories are of a cultural upbringing that policed his more instinctual behavior. If "hiccup" as

Clear Word and Third Sight

metaphor mediates between "childhood memories" and "instinct," then the cultural upbringing that is the son's memory of his childhood functions as a literal cutting-off of what he views as his more instinctual behavior. The breath being cut off by the "hiccup" is symbolized by the "instinct."

The stanza ends with the lines "Disaster / speak to me about disaster / tell me about it." The son's remembrance of his childhood and his interpretation of the dynamics that informed his upbringing are characterized by a struggle between so-called nature and culture, which he views as a disaster. But why? The answer comes in the next stanza:

> Ma mère voulant d'un fils très bonnes manières à table
> les mains sur la table
> le pain ne se coupe pas
> le pain se rompt
> le pain ne se gaspille pas le pain de Dieu
> le pain de la sueur du front de votre Père
> le pain du pain
> Un os se mange avec mesure et discrétion
> un estomac doit être sociable
> et tout estomac sociable se passe de rots
> une fourchette n'est pas un cure-dents
> défense de se moucher
> au su
> au vu de tout le monde
> et puis tenez-vous droit
> un nez bien élevé
> ne balaye pas l'assiette
> Et puis et puis
> et puis au nom du Père
> du Fils
> du Saint Esprit
> à la fin de chaque repas
> Et puis et puis
> et puis désastre
> parlez-moi du désastre
> parlez-m'en
> (36)
> [My mother wanted a son with good table manners
> hands on the table
> don't cut the bread like that
> the bread is breaking

we don't waste bread God's bread
the bread your Father sweats his brow for
our daily bread.
Eat a bone with moderation and discretion
a stomach has to have good manners too
and a well-bred stomach never burps
a fork is not a toothpick
don't blow your nose in front of the whole world
and then sit up straight
a well-bred nose does not scrape the plate
And then, and then
and then in the name of the Father
the Son
and Holy Ghost
at the end of each meal
And then, and then
and then disaster
speak to me about disaster
tell me about it]

Here and throughout the rest of the poem a pattern is established. A
declarative sentence in the son's voice introduces both a new stanza
and another childhood memory. Each memory is thematically structured around a different aspect of his cultural education at home, and
in the context of the poem, the memories come to life through the
relentless, imaginary voice of the mother. In this stanza we see the
beginnings of what will be a litany of instructions from the mother to
the son on "good manners" and propriety. These rules are meant to
structure the son's physical behavior, as well as indoctrinate him into a
notion of what is "proper," according to French upper class mores. He
must be aware of his hands and stomach, eat discreetly, sit up straight,
and be prudent when blowing his nose. He must break his bread into
appropriately edible pieces and use his fork in what his mother says is
the "right" way, and he must always say grace at the end of each meal.
As in Tee's experiences in *Crick Crack Monkey* once she moves to the
middle-class environment of Aunt Beatrice's household, everything
in this stanza emphasizes "table manners" and outward appearances.
Although the voice of the narrator is ostensibly the son, the text con-
sists largely of the mother's instructions, as recollected and mimicked
by the son. The effect is one in which the son's own voice is marginalized within the text, except when he articulates his exasperation ("Et

Clear Word and Third Sight

puis, et puis, et puis . . . désastre / parlez-moi du désastre"). As readers
we begin to see not only the consuming nature of the mother's role in
the son's life but, more important, the anxious imperative structuring
what the mother wants the son to become. The anxiety is apparent
because the instructions are so inflexible. But other than to portray
this anxiety, the poem does not explicitly account for it. It is accounted
for instead by the implicit struggle between "nature" and "culture" in
the poem: the representation of the dichotomy between what the son
should become according to the mother, versus what he might become if she doesn't police his behavior from an early age.

> Ma mère voulant d'un fils mémorandum
> si votre leçon d'histoire n'est pas sue
> vous n'irez pas à la messe
> dimanche
> avec vos effets du dimanche
> Cet enfant sera la honte de notre nom
> cet enfant sera notre nom de Dieu
> Taisez-vous
> vous ai-je ou non dit qu'il vous fallait parler français
> le français de France
> le français du français
> le français français
> Désastre
> parlez-moi du désastre
> parlez-m'en
> (37)
> [My mother wanted a noteworthy son
> if you don't know your history lesson
> you won't go to mass
> Sunday
> in your Sunday best
> This child will bring shame on our name
> this child will be our disgrace
> Be quiet
> haven't I told you that you must speak French
> the French of France
> the French of the French
> French French
> Disaster
> speak to me about disaster
> tell me about it]

The mother is speaking in this section of the poem, and she uses the *vous* form to address her son. The *vous* introduces formality into their relationship, a formality associated with the respectability the mother wants her son to achieve. She has invested in his ability to "pass" in a certain class/cultural context. In this stanza, the mother's commands refer explicitly to the son's self-presentation (performing well in school, going to church in his Sunday best, speaking "proper" French), but despite these orders what we have is more of a lamentation on the part of the mother about what will happen if her moral/cultural education of her son fails. The worst fear is that the son will be a disgrace to his family and his "name" if he becomes the thing/persona that she is trying to prevent him from becoming: the one that speaks creole instead of French, who doesn't do well in school, and who overall has "bad manners." Yet this stanza makes it clear that it is not a question of becoming but a question of already being; hence the role of "instinct" or "nature" in the poem. Here, what functions as "nature" is actually another set of cultural behaviors that are reinforced within the larger community, but outside of the context of the mother's house. The mother's worst fears have already come true in some form. What she is trying to do therefore is remake the son that she has. She wants to turn him from the "vagabond" that he is more inclined to be (due to outside influences) into a gentleman. These are the two identities that she, like the hiccup, wants to mediate between. The vagabond and the gentleman, *"tel le flic le voyou"*: "like the cop to the thug," the gentleman will not only police the vagabond, he will inhabit him. A possession of sorts.

> Ma mère voulant d'un fils
> fils de sa mère
> vous n'avez pas salué voisine
> encore vos chaussures de sales
> et que je vous y reprenne dans la rue
> sur l'herbe ou sur la Savane
> a l'ombre du monument aux morts
> à jouer
> à vous ébattre avec Untel
> avec Untel qui n'a pas reçu le baptême
> Désastre
> parlez-moi du désastre
> parlez-m'en
> (37)

[My mother wanted her son
to be a mother's boy
you did not greet the neighbor
once again your shoes are dirty
and yet again I find you in the street
on the grass or in the park
under the war memorial
playing
fighting with So-and-so
So-and-so who was not even baptized
Disaster
speak to me about disaster
tell me about it]

In this stanza, the fears hinted at previously in the son's contact with the outside world are made explicit. ("Untel qui n'a pas reçu le baptême" is representative of the outside "culture" constituted as "nature" that the mother is vehemently struggling against.) Of increasing significance is the rhythmic nature of the mother's scoldings. In this stanza, as in the next, the orality of the mother's language, as mimicked by the son, is poignantly captured by Damas. Her scoldings all flow together in one breathy sentence. Lilyan Kesteloot observes that Damas frequently achieves this in his poetry by "beginning each new line with the words of the preceding one" or by repeating "a single phrase or a few words several times." She states that this achievement of rhythm is what Léopold Senghor views as the main defining characteristic of a poetics of negritude (*Black Writers in French*, 154).

The final stanza contains more of the son's commentary than any stanza since the first:

Ma mère voulant d'un fils très do
très ré
très mi
très fa
très sol
très la
très si
très do
ré-mi-fa
sol-la-si
do
Il m'est revenu que vous n'étiez encore pas

à votre leçon de vi-o-lon
Un banjo
vous dites un banjo
comment dites-vous
un banjo
vous dites bien
un banjo
Non monsieur
vous saurez qu'on ne souffre chez nous
ni ban
ni jo
ni gui
ni tare
les *mulâtres* ne font pas ça
laissez donc ça aux *nègres*.
(37–38)
[My mother wanted a son so do
so re
so mi
so fa
so sol
so la
so ti
so do
re-mi-fa
sol-la-ti
do
It has come to my attention that once again you did not go
to your vi-o-lin lesson
A banjo
did you say a banjo
how could you say
a banjo
you really did say
a banjo
No sir
you know in our house we won't tolerate
ban
or jo
or gui
or tar

> *mulattoes* don't do that
> leave that to *niggers*.

The first portion of the stanza indicates the son's opinions about the mother's investment in his classical music training: the completion of his moral/class/cultural home education. The son's do-re-mi riff is a creolizing of the musical scale that is both a literal reconfiguration of form as well as a resignification of meaning. The formal reconfiguration is the son's deconstruction of the scale: "Ma mère voulant d'un fils très do / très ré / très mi." The resignification of meaning occurs by the son's emphasizing to the point of ridiculousness each musical note and tying it to the mother's desires. Furthermore, the repetition of the scale a second time suggests that it is being sung an octave higher. This is in addition to the fact that the rearticulation of the scale is not the same for the reader after its deconstruction by the son. If the average unaccomplished singer attempts to sing two consecutive scales, one an octave higher than the other, there is a high probability that the second octave will sound like screeching. It seems that this is yet another way for the son to draw a parallel between himself and the "vi-o-lon." Like all the values forced on him by his mother, this too does not come "naturally." The exaggerated reconstruction of the word "violin" by the use of hyphens ("vi-o-lon") puts it in the same category as the son's deconstruction of the do-re-mi scale. That is to say, a caricatured emphasis is placed on the importance of the object. But whereas the word "vi-o-lon" is reconstructed for emphasis and not only remains whole but is reified (thus appearing to be more than it is), the deconstruction that occurs with the do-re-mi scale and the word "banjo" is a ridiculing and dismantling of the aura of power surrounding these objects.

After observing that her son has not gone to his violin lesson, the mother's four-time repetition of the word "banjo," before her deconstruction of it, registers her outrage and disbelief. There is a rhythm to the refusal ("un banjo vous dites bien un banjo"), and the way in which these emotions are registered, in a coming together of anger and humor ("ni *ban*, ni *jo*, ni *gui*, ni *tare*"), seems implicated in the very creole logic she wants to militate against. Creole logic in this sense is not so much the choice of non-French words as it is a resignification of the meaning attributable to whatever words are used, as, for example, the son's rearticulation of the do-re-mi scale. After repeating the word "banjo" in the classic fashion of the outraged West Indian mother, she proceeds to resignify by personification both "banjo" and his/its counterpart "guitar." Therefore, by the time she states that "ni *ban*, ni *jo*, ni *gui*, ni *tare*" will be allowed in this house, it is as if she is referring to people rather than inanimate instruments. The personification makes the refusal and outrage funny, at the same time that the mother's adamance is made clear by her willingness to fight against these instruments as if they were alive. Whatever humor is at stake in the mother's vehemence is quickly brought back to very somber divisions when she states, "les *mulâtres* ne font pas ça / laissez donc ça aux *nègres*."

The separation made between the violin, on the one hand, and the banjo and guitar, on the other, is paradigmatic of the divisions enforced throughout the entire poem with the mother's voice as vehicle. What the first stanza suggested was that the struggle between "nature" and "culture" proved to be a class struggle between "Culture" and "culture," compounded in the final instance by the racial distinction "les *mulâtres* ne font pas ça / laissez donc ça aux *nègres*." Yet with the exception of the references to the banjo and the guitar, what the poem definitively posits as the "Culture" of the "gentleman" is constituted by the mores and values of an invisible French aristocracy that the native bourgeoisie of French Guiana strives to emulate. The other "culture," that of the "vagabond," is symbolized by the nonelite Black masses. This "culture," the Black "popular culture," is represented solely as the negation of white, elite French culture. It is the "culture" of the vulgar, unbaptized, non-French speaker, the Joebells of the world. There is no definitive interiority assigned it within the context of the poem.

The division between the violin and the banjo, as well as "Culture" and its perceived negation "culture," has its parallel in the way the mother's and son's voices are represented. Ultimately, despite the poem's critical representation of the mother's voice, there is no ambiguity regarding its dominance. Her voice concludes the poem, and nothing is presented to replace it. It occupies the text in much the same way as the values articulated appear to inhabit the son's body. On the other hand, the son's voice remains peripheral. Repeated four times and becoming the poem's constant refrain is the son's statement "Désastre / parlez-moi du désastre / parlez-m'en." Yet this refrain is of significance, and the audience imagined is worth considering. It is clear that the son is not speaking to his mother, since frequently the mother is referenced in the third person. But the poem appears to have multiple audiences. It is a private musing on the part of the son, one that would appeal to those who had similar upbringings. It is a bitter indictment addressed toward the French colonial class and its imitating colored elite. It is a rhythmic "rap" of solidarity, with the Black masses as audience, on the part of a "brother" seeking commonality and reinclusion.

If we interpret the poem's title, "Hoquet," as representative of an overconsumption that temporarily and repeatedly cuts off the breath, and if the breath being cut off is the "instinct" that is more precisely the cultural values of an outside community, then this, one could argue, is the disaster spoken of: the forced acquisition of values that are at odds with those of the community from which one originates. Alioune Diop's definition of the type of assimilation inspired by (French) colonialism finds an uncanny parallel in the poetic metaphor of the hiccup. He states, "Its aim is to make the individual (it is never concerned with anything but individuals), torn from the background natural to him, which brought out his personality, agree to replace his habits of thinking, feeling and acting by others which he could only share with an alien community" ("Opening Address," 14). In this quotation from Diop, as in Damas's poem, the "natural background" is in actuality the cultural background, since "habits of thinking, feeling and acting" are tied to the values of a community, and collective communal values are an integral aspect of any definition of culture. Ultimately, therefore, the "désastre" spoken of is both forced assimilation and an unspecified and irretrievable loss of communal culture.

In his poem "Limbé" (creole for "blues") the phrase "mon instinct" returns, and Damas explicitly links it to a loss of culture while delineating what he imagines this cultural loss to be:

> Rendez-les-moi mes poupées noires
> que je joue avec elles
> les jeux naifs de mon instinct
> rester à l'ombre de ses lois
> recouvrer mon courage
> mon audace
> me sentir moi-même
> nouveau moi-même de ce que hier j'étais
> hier

sans complexité
hier
quand est venue l'heure du déracinement
Le sauront-ils jamais cette rancune de mon coeur

A l'oeil de ma méfiance ouvert trop tard
ils ont cambriolé l'espace qui était mien
la coutume les jours la vie
la chanson le rythme l'effort
le sentier l'eau la case
la terre enfumée grise
la sagesse les mots les palabres
les vieux
la cadence les mains la mesure les mains
les piétinements le sol

Rendez-les-moi mes poupées noires
mes poupées noires
poupées noires
noires
noires (43–45)

[Give me back my Black dolls
so that I can play with them
the naive games of my instinct
stay in the shade of their laws
recover my courage
my audacity
feel like myself again
once more myself like I was before
once upon a time
without complexity
once upon a time
when the hour of uprooting came

Will they never know the bitterness of my heart
to which the eye of my mistrust opened too late
they stole the space that was mine
customs days life
song rhythm effort
footpath water hut
the smoky gray earth
wisdom words discussions

Clear Word and Third Sight

elders
rhythm hands tempo hands
footstamping
soil

Give me back my Black dolls
my Black dolls
Black dolls
Black
Black]

The last three stanzas of the poem "Limbé" are an explicit lament; there is a loss of culture that is openly being mourned. How is this lost culture imagined by Damas? While "Hoquet" had the feeling of a traumatic memory, the mood of "Limbé" is nostalgic: sentimental recollections of a period of imagined tranquility. Curiously, in each of the poems, childhood is the setting for the reminiscence. In "Hoquet" instinct stood in for cultural ways of being that the mother was determined to militate against. But in "Limbé" "mon instinct" is explicitly seen as a recovery of courage, of spirit, of cultural ways of being that predate the traumatic uprooting from Africa that was slavery ("les jeux naifs de mon instinct"). "Poupées noires" stands in for the loss of all cultural resources, the theft of land and spirit. The lost culture is imagined, on one hand, as a loss of internal resources, coping strategies used to defend oneself and make sense of the world. On the other hand, there is also a loss of a material way of life: "la coutume . . . / la chanson le rythme . . . / le sentier l'eau la case." Despite the move to specify the nature of the cultural loss, it is still hard in "Limbé" to escape the idealization of the past and the seemingly childish demand that toys that were taken away be returned. Here the narrator seems to be explicitly desiring a return to a state of blissful infancy. More explicitly than in "Hoquet," childhood and instincts are associated with psychic and cultural wholeness. Yet while in "Hoquet" cultural ways of being not tied to white colonial dominance are articulated simply in terms of negation, in "Limbé," despite the narrator's idealization of what "he" might have been like if "he" hadn't experienced colonial violence, there is still no getting beyond the loss of both psychic and material resources.[7]

The poem ends with the refrain that has dominated throughout: "Rendez-les moi mes poupées noires / mes poupées noires / poupées noires / noires." This refrain is significant for two reasons. First, it functions as a response to "Hoquet"'s "Désastre / parlez-moi du désastre." While both refrains lament a loss, the refrain in "Limbé" states what has been lost and demands its return. The refrain in "Hoquet" registers horror and shock but leaves the "désastre" spoken of up to the imagination of the reader. The second noteworthy aspect of this last stanza is the way in which the phrase "mes poupées noires" fades out rhythmically like a softly beating drum. These last two stanzas, which use the formal rhythm of the poetry to register the speaker's despair over cultural losses ("la coutume les jours la vie / la chanson le rythme l'effort"), use the written word to emphasize an oral tradition. This attempt to textually represent orality cannot but be seen as a strategy of recuperation on Damas's part. In other words, while the poems themselves at the level of thematics simply articulate and constantly reiterate the fact of loss, it is at the level of the form that a poetics of recuperation exists. Yet it must be emphasized that this is a recuperative poetics tied to a particular class experience. As "Hoquet" demonstrates, it is the colored elite that experiences this alienation most severely.

Published while Damas was a student in Paris experiencing a very individual isolation, and written while he was encountering French Antilleans and Africans in similar situations, _Pigments_ (first published in the periodicals _Esprit_ and _L'Étudiant Noir_) is a response to an alienation characterized by "le Nègre [qui] reste l'éternel démuni, l'Autre, le parasite, qui ne sait que recevoir et spoiler" (Arnold, 13). This is the Black subject who will forever function as the impoverished "other" of whiteness, always striving for recognition and inclusion within what Caribbean scholar Sylvia Wynter refers to as "the word of man" ("Beyond the Word of Man," 637). For Wynter the writings of Glissant, Césaire, and Fanon, in particular, were an uprising specifically directed at this old order of things.[8] J. Michael Dash sees Damas also as resisting the word of man: in his article "The World and the Word: French Caribbean Writing in the Twentieth Century" Dash argues that Damas's anxiety about colonialism is made manifest through an antagonism toward the French language and high literary form in general. He writes, "The fierce asceticism, the use of startlingly unpoetic language, the exploitation of a creole register, the subversion of high literary and political diction are some of the strategies deployed by Damas against a language he saw as oppressively elitist" (117). While Dash views Damas's attack on written language and literary form as an "aesthetics of transgression," he takes issue with what he perceives of as a link between the aesthetic and ethical impulse, one that "is based on a view of language as transparent and utilitarian" (117). Whether or not the connection between the aesthetic and ethical impulses can always be linked to a view of language as transparent will be challenged by the writings of Simone Schwarz-Bart.

The alienation Damas theorizes is not exclusive to but is most harshly experienced by a particular class of colonial subjects. In Damas's homeland of French Guiana, one could argue that he and writers who had been educated like himself wrote from an ambiguous middle position. They were situated between white French colonials, the Black masses, and active and living populations of Amerindians, as well as descendants of maroons (referred to as bush negroes).[9] The existence of real maroons was frequently a source of controversy in this context, and the writers from the region aggressively attempted to assert their "civility" against this backdrop of "savagery" ("French Guiana," 394).[10] Since the Amerindians and former maroons had been at times portrayed as cannibals, the literature written by the educated elite was characterized by an anxiety about not successfully "passing" as "civilized." Texts such as René Maran's *Un homme pareil aux autre* (A Man Like Any Other, 1947) and A. E. Whily-Tell's *Je suis un civilisé* (I Am Civilized, 1953) were representative of this phenomenon. In the work of writers like the Guianese Bertène Juminer, author of the novels *Les bâtards* and *Au seuil d'un nouveau cri,* there is a consistent depiction of extremely alienated characters whose Blackness is a source of shame and suicidal depression rather than pride.

In "Hoquet" the struggle between the son's cultural upbringing, represented as social control, and his "instincts" (the cultural behavior considered to be inappropriate by his mother) is essentially the site of the personal alienation that the poem describes as a "désastre." In Damas's poems, this personal alienation is represented as being without communal recourse. The impulse to respectability militates against participation in the nonelite Black "culture," recognizable mostly as a culture of rebellion. As both Dash and Senghor observe with regard to Damas's poetry, his whole poetic idiom is a war against respectability. This is waged through his attempt to capture an orality in written form. The oral tradition he draws from is part of the disavowed cultural reality portrayed. Ultimately, within these two poems the culture of the narrator's upbringing is represented as violence and collective communal culture is not recognizable in the culture of the everyday folk. It is viewed as absent and lost.

> The theory behind our tactics: "The white man is always trying to
> know into somebody else's business. All right, I'll set something
> outside the door of my mind for him to play with and handle. He can
> read my writing but he sho' can't read my mind. I'll put this toy in his
> hand, and he will seize it and go away. Then I'll say my say and sing
> my song."—ZORA NEALE HURSTON, *Mules*

> Alors grand-mère poussa un profond soupir, signifiant que notre visite
> s'achevait, et, se tournant vers l'enfant que j'étais, man Cia déclara . . .
> sois une vaillante petite négresse, un vrai tambour à deux faces, laisse
> la vie frapper, cogner, mais conserve toujours intact la face de dessous.
> [Then grandmother heaved a deep sigh that signified our visit was
> almost over, and Ma Cia, turning to me, child that I was, said, "Be a fine
> little négresse, a real drum with two sides. Let life bang and thump but
> keep the underside always intact."]—SIMONE SCHWARZ-BART,
> *Pluie et vent sur Télumée Miracle* (*The Bridge of Beyond*)

In her 1935 introduction to *Mules and Men,* Zora Neale Hurston describes her relationship to her research material (the porchside "lies"
of Blacks in south Florida referred to as folklore) as "fitting [her] like a
tight chemise. I couldn't see it for wearing it" (3). With this deceptively
simple metaphor, Hurston articulates the predicament facing the "native intellectual" (anthropologist, writer, or literary critic) when one's
subject is one's own people: how does one approach what is already
known experientially but not consciously—what Rupert Lewis refers
to as "the unfamiliarity of the familiar"?[11] Predictably, this dynamic is
one in which the critical orientation of the scholar is ideally informed
by a process of interpretive recognition that has as its prerequisite
communal immersion in the culture under scrutiny, or what Vévé
Clark refers to as "diaspora literacy."[12] Further along in her introduction, Hurston describes her methodological approach to collecting
this folklore, as an approach informed by her comprehension of the
mode of communication of her subjects. In the passage quoted as one

of the epigraphs to this section, she describes the tactic that she otherwise characterizes as "feather-bed resistance": "The probe [enters] but
it never comes out. It gets smothered under a lot of laughter and
pleasanteries" (4). As *Mules and Men* progresses, one sees moments
where Hurston herself is given this "feather-bed" treatment. In communities where, despite racial commonality she is still perceived as
unfamiliar, the community suspects her of being a tool of the state,
sent to ferret out those hiding from the law. In such circumstances she
has to disprove these assumptions by establishing, not so much her
credibility as anthropologist, but rather her credibility as a member of
the group.

When Hurston describes the "feather-bed" tactic, several points are
made clear. First her use of the pronoun "our" reveals where she
positions herself vis-à-vis her "subjects" in the statement "the theory
behind *our* tactics." Second, the thrust of the tactic (which is to keep
the outsider, in this instance the white man, from gaining any mean-
ingful knowledge of the person or group) both revolves around the
categorical lack of knowledge of the outsider and militates against him
or her in such a deceptively quiet way that the aggression and utter
disdain on the part of the supposed "subject" is disguised. "Set[ting]
something outside the door of [one's] mind for him to play with and
handle" gives the impression of feeding a dog who is too simple to
understand or want more. If this is the case, then this "tactic," far
from being passive and apolitical (as this text by Hurston has sometimes been described), is actually a sophisticated defense strategy that
protects the insider while deceiving the outsider. Herein lies the resistant aspect of the apparently benign cultural text.[13]

The second epigraph to this section, which uses the drum as its
metaphor, is the proverbial saying thematically at the heart of Simone
Schwarz-Bart's novel *Pluie et vent sur Télumée Miracle* (translated as
The Bridge of Beyond). The idea of thinking of oneself as a drum with
two faces (with the topside being the side "set outside the door of
[one's] mind" and the underside being the mind itself, enclosed within the protected interior) bears a striking resemblance to the "tactic"
described by Hurston. The underside of the drum represents the
interior life, the space of psychic recuperation. The topside is the
protective layer that establishes a boundary between this interior life
and inhabiting what Sylvia Wynter describes as the zone of "Ontological Lack" or "symbolic death."[14] For Wynter, being the "embodied
bearers of Ontological Lack" is a way of describing the alienation that

is the assigned and enforced role of the African diaspora subject in a hegemonic colonial order. In this context, the "feather-bed tactic" and the two-sided drum as metaphors for negotiating public and private identities are necessarily strategies of political resistance and cultural self-preservation within the symbolic order of colonial and neo-colonial space.

Pluie et vent sur Télumée Miracle, Simone Schwarz-Bart's first novel, is based on her knowledge of rural Guadeloupe. In an interview she states that she wrote the novel to restore a certain kind of memory: "C'est une espèce de mémoire que j'ai voulu restituer" (185). She describes the process and impetus for writing the novel in communal terms. Plagued by a publisher who wanted her to omit the novel's first section, "Présentation des miens" (My people), she argues that without that section there was no novel: "C'est *notre* mémoire" ("It is *our* memory"; italics mine). In explaining her intentions, she says that she wants to "give back to French West Indians their patrimony": "Il fallait que nous nous retrouvions" ("It is imperative that we rediscover ourselves"; 186). She wants to create "tout un univers créole" ("a creole universe") and responding to critiques of the work as apolitical, she maintains, "Pour moi c'est un acte politique. Mais pas avec un sceau, une marque politique" ("For me it is a political act but not with a political seal or badge on it"; 186).[15]

I will examine how the creole sayings function within the text of Schwarz-Bart's novel, paying specific attention to two incidents. The first is an encounter between Télumée and her employer, the wealthy Madame Desaragne, and the second is a conflict involving a village drifter, Angel Médard. These two encounters are markedly different from the encounters between Kincaid's Lucy and her white female employer and Black maid. In both struggles in Schwarz-Bart's text, the metaphor of the drum operates and there is a negotiation between the topside and the underside that seems to parallel struggles with white colonial domination, on the one hand, and legacies of cultural alienation, on the other. The two-sided drum is also a metaphor for life, with a symbolic topside and underside indicating the differences between the mothering practices of the mother in "Hoquet" and the "mothers" in *Pluie et vent sur Télumée Miracle*. These distinctions involve a cultural education aimed at the exterior rather than interior life of the child.[16]

Schwarz-Bart depicts the trials and tribulations of the main character Télumée in relation to the peasant community she comes from. Set in the rural regions of Guadeloupe; symbolically naming the villages in the story L'Abandonée (deserted), Fond-Zombi (valley bottom peopled by spirits of ghosts), and La Folie (madness); and focused primarily on the lives of three generations of Black women, Schwarz-Bart's text immediately establishes as its subject the lives of the darker masses that the French Caribbean colored bourgeoisie defines itself against. The names of the villages bespeak the physical and spiritual desolation of many of the inhabitants.

> Le pays dépend bien souvent du coeur de l'homme: il est minuscule si le coeur est petit, et immense si le coeur est grand. Je n'ai jamais souffert de l'exiguité de mon pays, sans pour autant prétendre que j'aie un grand coeur. Si on m'en donnait le pouvoir, c'est ici même, en Guadeloupe, que je choisirais de renaître, souffrir et mourir. Pourtant, il n'y a guère, mes ancêtres furent esclaves en cette île à volcans, à cyclones et moustiques, à mauvaise mentalité. Mais je ne suis pas venue sur terre pour soupeser toute la tristesse du monde. (*Pluie et vent*, 11)
>
> [A man's country may be cramped or vast according to the size of his heart. I've never found my country too small, though that isn't to say my heart is great. And if I could choose it's here in Guadeloupe that I'd be born again, suffer and die. Yet not long back my ancestors were slaves on this volcanic, hurricane-swept, mosquito-ridden, nasty-minded island. But I didn't come into the world to weigh the world's woe. (*Bridge of Beyond*, 2)]

In these opening lines of the novel, the narrator, Télumée, says that the size of a country varies according to the size of the person's heart. It may appear that a correlation is being made between the wealth of the country and the generosity of the heart. But on closer examination, "heart" can be seen as synonymous with one's attitude and perspective. Later in the novel, the country's relation to the heart becomes an allegory for the individual's relationship to the community. As with Joebell's relationship to his own community at the end of Lovelace's "Joebell and America," in Schwarz-Bart's opening allegory the individual's attitude and perspective reflect the quality of the dynamic with the community. When Télumée states, "Je n'ai jamais souffert de l'exiguité de mon pays, sans pour autaunt prétendre que j'aie un grand coeur" (11; "I have never suffered from the smallness of my country without also pretending I have a big heart"; 2), there is an embracing of the community despite its weaknesses: "Si on m'en donnait le pouvoir, c'est ici même en Guadeloupe, que je choisirais de renaître, souffrir et mourir" (11; "If given the choice it is here in Guadeloupe that I would choose to be reborn, suffer and die"; 2). She would choose Guadeloupe again in spite of the slavery of her ancestors, the natural disasters it is prone to, and the oppressive mentality of the population. From the outset, therefore, there is an embracing of her circumstance and a determination to survive the difficulties while remaining part of the community. There is an impetus to conceive of the positive and negative, the good and bad experiences as all part of a larger communal experience. An African philosophical worldview, in which the collective is at the center and a balance between positive and negative energy within the forces of nature is desirable, is immediately established as the psychic terrain on which the events of the novel will unfold.

The structure of the text also supports this attempt to tell the story of the individual and the community always simultaneously. The novel is divided into two parts, "Présentation des miens" (My people) and "Histoire de ma vie" (The story of my life). As Abena Busia argues, "Télumée begins her account with *her people;* she first tells the story of the generations immediately preceding hers, so that when she reaches her own, she is already firmly a part of a people and a place" (290).[17] In her 1990 article on *Pluie et vent* Elisabeth Mudimbe-Boyi argues that Schwarz-Bart achieves a communal motif through the narrative strategy she deploys. Although the text as a whole is a first-person narrrative, Mudimbe-Boyi argues that in the first section, since Télumée is telling the story of her ancestors without reference to herself, one is temporarily given the impression of reading a third-person narrative. By now it should be apparent that this mingling of the first- and third-person narrative within African diaspora texts parallels the dialectical relationship between the individual and the community in these texts. Moreover, the novel ends with Télumée speaking in the first-person plural, creating, within her narration, a sense of collective history and experience: "Nous avons lutté pour naître, et nous avons lutté pour renaître . . . et nous avons appelé 'Résolu' le plus bel arbre de nos forêts" (*Pluie et vent,* 251; "We have struggled to be born and we have struggled to be born again, and we have called the finest tree in our forests 'resolute,'" (*Bridge of Beyond,* 169).[18]

The first section begins with Télumée's great-grandmother, Minerve, a slave who lived through abolition and gave birth to Toussine, the grandmother who eventually raises Télumée. The story weaves through Toussine's upbringing, marriage, the birth and death of one of her twin

Clear Word and Third Sight

daughters, her depression, and eventual recovery; the recovery results in the community collectively renaming Toussine "Reine Sans Nom" (queen without a name). The novel's second part begins after the death of Angebert, the father who raised Télumée and her sister Regina through their childhood years. Interestingly enough, there is never any mention of Télumée's biological father, and seeking him out is not a desire that is ever articulated. This reinforces from the outset that "family" within the novel is not reducible to the biological nuclear unit of mother, father, and children. Part 2 ("Histoire de ma vie") begins with the rearticulation of the family structure. Angebert dies; Télumée's mother, Victoire, moves to Dominica with her lover, Haut-Colbi; Regina goes to live with her biological father in Basse-Terre and becomes an "elegant city lady"; and Télumée goes to live with her grandmother, Reine Sans Nom, in Fond-Zombi. This second section doesn't begin with Télumée's birth and a recounting of the story of her biological parents and childhood. Rather, it starts with her cultural upbringing in her grandmother's house. The emphasis is therefore placed from the outset on the production of Télumée's interior life or "insight." Unlike *Crick Crack Monkey*, which is a story about "the colonial production of young Tee's sight," inaugurated by her British education, *Pluie et vent sur Télumée Miracle* is a story about the development of Télumée's interior life; her wisdom and cultural insight is symbolized by the underside of her drum. Télumée's insight parallels her immersion in rural Black culture, and it is ideologically at the other end of the spectrum from Tee's British education.

Throughout the text the community names and renames its members symbolically. As Busia says, "This communal naming, an honour bestowed in many African communities, is an accolade of acceptance. And the very names they chose to give, and the reasons and manner of bestowal, underscore the fact of this being a community keenly sensitive to the metaphoric or signifying power of words as elemental forces which can affect life itself" (293).[19] Functioning in continuum with the significance of naming in the text is the role of language within the structure of the community. There are many examples of language being something physical with the power to create or protect, destroy or curse. This is exemplified most concisely by Télumée's mother Victoire's relationship to speech. "Elle tenait la parole humaine pour un fusil chargé, et ressentait parfois comme une hémmoragie à converser, selon ses propres termes" (32; "She looked on human speech as a loaded gun, and, to use her own expression, talking often felt to her like an issue of blood," 16).

As a child living with Victoire and Angebert, Télumée witnesses the cursing of the village thief Germain in front of the entire village. Télumée recounts, "La malheureuse prophétie ne pénétrait ni la terre ni le ciel, ni le tronc des arbres, elle ne se confondait pas avec le crépuscule tombant, elle restait sur votre coeur et l'on sentait qu'une abomination se préparait quelque part" (38; "The unhappy prophecy did not enter into earth or sky or the trunks of the trees, nor did it mingle with the falling dusk; it stayed there weighing on the heart, and there was a feeling that something terrible was impending somewhere," 21). The curse stays in the very atmosphere, and from that day, Germain is a changed man. He believes his life is over and grumbles that with a word thrown around carelessly, "la folie frappe et elle assaille" (38; "madness strikes, and men kill and are killed," 21). On the other hand, Reine Sans Nom tells Télumée "avec un parole, on empêche un homme de se briser" (79; "With a word a man can be stopped from destroying himself," 48). There follows her advice to Télumée:

> Télumée, mon petit verre en cristal, disait-elle pensivement, trois sentiers sont mauvais pour l'homme: voir la beauté du monde, et dire qu'il est laid, se lever de grand matin pour faire ce dont on est incapable, et donner libre cours à ses songes, sans se surveiller, car qui songe devient victime de son propre songe. . . . Puie elle se remettait en route, susurrant déjà une chanson, quelque biguine des temps anciens qu'elle modulait de façon très particulière, avec une sorte d'ironie voilée, destinée à me faire comprendre, précisément, que certain paroles étaient nulles et non avenues, toujours bonnes à entendre et meilleures à oublier. (51)
> [Télumée, my little crystal glass, she would say thoughtfully, there are three paths that are bad for a man to take: to see the beauty of the world and call it ugly, to get up early to do what is impossible, and to let oneself get carried away by dreams—for whoever dreams becomes the victim of his own dream. Then [Queen Without a Name] would set off again, already murmuring a song, some beguine from the old days to which she would give a special inflection a sort of veiled irony, the object of which was to convey to me that certain words were null and void, all very well to listen to but better forgotten. (30)]

What Reine Sans Nom does here are two things. First she tells Télumée her philosophy about the things one should avoid in life. Second, she resignifies the meaning of an old song, *not by changing the words* but rather by changing *the meaning* that Télumée can attribute to the words. This is similar to the son's resignification of the do-re-mi scale in Damas's poem "Hoquet" and what Abena Busia refers to as the "gift of metaphor."[20]

This kind of relationship to the manipulable spiritual power of the word, as addressed in Schwarz-Bart's text and commented on by Busia, seems to be a significant characteristic of Afro-Caribbean societies. In their article "Forms of African Spirituality in Trinidad and Tobago," Rudolph Eastman and Maureen Warner-Lewis state, "*Obeah* is a pan-Caribbean belief in the power of a spiritually endowed individual, on behalf of the self or another, to manipulate spiritual forces to procure good or to activate evil or to counter evil" (404). While Eastman and Warner-Lewis do not specifically link the manipulation of spiritual power associated with obeah to the power of the word, Schwarz-Bart's text effectively makes this connection. In Caribbean societies there is a deeply rooted orally passed-down belief that obeah is only as powerful as an individual allows it to be. In other words one's mental power, or more precisely, one's positive or negative belief systems profoundly influence how susceptible one is to "spirit works." In the novel, Reine Sans Nom is trying to teach Télumée how to strengthen her positive belief system (which is, at base, her relationship to the things people say and do) in order to be spiritually strong and not at the mercy of any and every negative force she encounters.

Télumée lives by two precepts: the first we have already encountered, that she should be a drum with two faces; the second is to survive "the sorrow that is a wave without end" (51). Both precepts are given to her by Reine Sans Nom and Ma Cia, her grandmother's close friend. Considered a witch and healer within the context of the community, Ma Cia inhabits a world on the border between the real and the spiritual. The education that Ma Cia and Reine Sans Nom jointly give Télumée is aimed at preparing her to cope with the complexities of the world she inhabits and come to terms with the contradictions in the African diaspora experience. At the heart of this training is an attempt to respond to the questions raised by the legacy of slavery. On some level, this is the existential query around which the text is structured. It is articulated through Télumée's internal and external ponderings about what it means to be "un nègre" or "une négresse." Télumée asks Ma Cia what a slave is and what a master is. Ma Cia answers by telling her to go and look at the terror in the eyes of the poultry trapped in cages in the marketplace in order to understand slavery, and to go to the Desaragne family at the Belle-Feuille estate in

order to comprehend masters. What Ma Cia's directs Télumée to become is a witness. She uses referents within the arena of Télumée's
imagination that allow her to comprehend not so much the *technical
definitions* of "slave" and "master" but rather the power, terror, and
drama of *the experience* associated with both terms. This "education"
makes Télumée realize that slavery was not "un pays étranger" (65; "a
strange country," 39) but something that happened right there on the
land, in the place she calls home.

What follows is a philosophical exchange between Reine Sans Nom
and Ma Cia. Reine Sans Nom challenges Ma Cia on exactly what
Télumée will see now if she goes to Belle-Feuille to find an example of
a master. Although this conversation functions as a continuation of
the response to Télumée's question about slaves and masters, Ma Cia
is no longer directly answering Télumée. She speaks more specifically
to Reine Sans Nom, and her responses, when they happen, are not
transparent, straightforward answers to questions posed. The exchange has a proverbial and riddle-like quality to it. It is as if they want
Télumée to listen and learn, absorbing information that she will be
able to come to terms with as her own wisdom grows. It is after this
long discourse between these two women about history, circumstance, and oppression that Ma Cia tells Télumée to be like a drum,
"un vrai tambour à deux faces." Later, Reine Sans Nom tells her:
"Derrière une peine il y a une autre peine, la misère est une vague
sans fin, mais le cheval ne doit pas te conduire, c'est toi qui dois
conduire le cheval" (82; "Behind one pain there is another. Sorrow is a
wave without end. But the horse mustn't ride you, you must ride it,"
51).

When Ma Cia instructs Télumée to be like a drum, she creates a
picture in Télumée's mind that is meant to direct her with its imagery,
just as she did when she explained about slaves and masters and
spoke with Reine Sans Nom about slavery. This is similar to what
Hurston says about "action words" in Black expressive contexts, in
which the "interpretation of the English language is in terms of pictures" (*Hurston*, 830). Further, however, there is a charge given to
Télumée by her "mothers" to interpret the image in such a way that
she will have the tools to negotiate both external and internal challenges. This "gift of metaphor" is the centerpiece of Télumée's cultural education in the home space.

As money gets tight for Télumée and her grandmother, she is forced
to leave the odd jobs she has at Fond-Zombi and hire herself out as a

Clear Word and Third Sight

servant to the Desaragne family. At the Belle-Feuille estate she has an acidic first interview with Madame Desaragne. In asking her if she can cook and iron clothes and if so, how she learned, and whether she has a husband or man (because this is a respectable household), Madame sets up the rules of behavior that Télumée must follow. This initial exchange exposes Madame's assumption that Télumée's "difference" is constituted by an absence of values. She constructs a power relationship with guidelines that establish very clearly the limits of the freedom Télumée can feel in her house. These are rules that, ironically, Télumée won't allow her to forget later.

At Belle-Feuille, Télumée's travails within the environment of the household requires her to put into practice the advice in the two proverbs she learned from Ma Cia and Reine Sans Nom. She must successfully negotiotiate a public persona (represented by the topside of her drum) while being selective about the emotions she allows herself to respond to. She makes no friends, and she attempts neither to engage with the emotional climate in the house nor to assimilate the thinly disguised attacks made on her by her mistress. Setting her mind to her tasks, her sole aim is to be "un caillou dans une rivière," a pebble at the bottom of the river, which stays firmly planted through strong currents (95). While she is working, when she feels sad and misses her grandmother, she sings: "Je coupais ma peine, je hachais ma peine, et ma peine tombait dans la chanson, et je conduisais mon cheval" (95; "I diluted my pain, chopped it in pieces, and it flowed into the song, and I rode my horse," 60). In this way, she rides her horse through the wave of sorrow. She is also selective about the language she allows herself to absorb. She describes early on her strategy for dealing with the tone of her mistress's voice: "Ma maîtresse avait la voix un peu sèche, mais qu'est-ce qu'une voix un peu sèche, si on ne l'écoute pas?" (95; "My mistress's voice was rather curt, but what is a rather curt voice if you don't listen to it?" 60) At another point she imagines using the weight of her body to suppress the mindless chatter: "les paroles de Blanc, rien que ça" (96; "white man's words, that's all," 61).

At Belle-Feuille, Télumée protects herself from the verbal attacks of the mistress and the physical attacks of the master. While she starches the master's shirts under the watchful eye of the mistress, Madame Desaragne inquires: "Mais savez-vous seulement à quoi vous avez échappé? . . . sauvages et barbares que vous seriez en ce moment, à courir dans la brousse, à danser nus et à déguster les individus en potée . . . on vous emmène ici, et comment vivez-vous? . . . dans la boue, le vice, les bacchanales. . . . Combien de coups de bâton ton homme te donne-t-il?" (96–97; "But do you even know what you've escaped? You might be wild savages now, running through the bush, dancing naked, and eating people stewed in pots. But you're brought here, and how do you live? In squalor and vice and orgies. How often does your husband hit you?" 61).

Télumée responds by saying: "Madame, on dit que certain aiment la lumière, d'autres la fange, c'est ainsi que le monde tourne . . . moi je ne sais rien de tout ça, je suis une petite négresse si noire que bleue et je lave, je repasse, je fais des béchamels, et voilà tout" (97–98; "Madame, they say some people love light and others love filth, and that's the way of the world. I know nothing about all that, I'm a little blue-black Negress, I wash and iron and make béchamel sauce, and that's all," 62).

Madame Desaragne's attack is a form of psychological warfare that is part and parcel of the colonial violence that functions on both a symbolic and material level. The language used by Madame to describe the condition of the Black subject before and after the arrival of the colonizers aggressively racializes Télumée's body, lumping her with all those of her race and class into an imaginary brute state trapped in time, while "civilization" (represented by the ability to appreciate béchamel sauce) progresses without them.

In her afterword to *Out of the Kumbla,* Wynter maintains that Western Europe's justification for its expansion into the new world, and before that, Africa, was based on the supposed " 'non-rational' inferior 'nature' of the peoples to be expropriated and governed" (357). She argues that with this shift, the male-female gender divide (previously occupying a space of exclusive historic primacy) came to play a secondary "if none the less powerful reinforcing role," with the "primary code of difference [becoming] one between "men" and "natives" (357). Wynter claims that this shift from an *"anatomical* model of sexual difference as the referential model of *mimetic* ordering to that of the *physiognomic* model of racial/*cultural* difference "is most dramatically enacted in Shakespeare's *Tempest* (358). This difference is depicted in the relationship of enforced dominance and subordination between Miranda (though female) and Caliban (though male). So Caliban, the now " 'irrational' and 'savage' *native* is constituted as the lack of the 'rational' Prospero, and the now capable-of-rationality-Miranda by the Otherness of his/its *physiognomic* 'monster' difference" (358).

A paradigm similar to the one Wynter describes between Miranda and Caliban operates between Madame and Télumée: any presumed commonality of experience based on gender between Madame and Télumée is disrupted, and the dynamic is rearticulated as one of dominance in which gendered commonalities are secondary if not nonexistent.

Domestic relationships between white women and Black women based on dominance and subordination—implicitly theorized by Wynter and commented on by Schwarz-Bart and Kincaid—are also the subject of the book *Thursdays and Every Other Sunday Off*, by the Black woman author Verta Mae Smart-Grosvenor. Toni Cade Bambara cites the book as indicating that "[Black female] domestics are in a better position than most workers to demystify white supremacy" (*Deep Sightings and Rescue Missions*, 105). Télumée serves exactly this function in *Pluie et vent*. While Madame Desaragne both controls Télumée and perpetrates violence against her, the mistress occupies a subordinate position with respect to her husband. As Abena Busia observes, "We can read this work as a story told for black women" (289).

Although there are moments within the text that represent the breakdown of sisterhood among Black women, the violence that Télumée experiences at Belle-Feuille is explicitly represented as *white* colonial violence. We see this in Télumée's struggles with both Madame and Monsieur Desaragne, as well as her dismissal, in two separate contexts, of their mindless chatter as "les paroles de Blanc" ("white people's words").[21] When Télumée speaks she engages in what Wynter refers to as "un/silencing the demonic ground of Caliban's woman," this standing-in for the metaphorical coming-to-voice of the Black Caribbean woman (359–61). In so doing, "speaking," Télumée goes "beyond Miranda's meanings" by using the tools of her communal education to center herself. Her identity is something that exists relationally as opposed to individually.[22]

While Madame speaks, Télumée describes herself as weaving in and out of the words allowing the mistress to hit away at the topside of her drum while the underside stays intact.

> Je me faufilais à travers ces paroles comme si je nageais dans l'eau la plus claire qui soit . . . me félicitant d'être sur terre une petite négresse irréductible, un vrai tambour à deux peaux, selon l'expression de ma Cia, je lui abandonnais la première face afin qu'elle s'amuse, la patronne, qu'elle cogne dessus, et moi-même par en dessous je restais intact, et plus intacte il n'y a pas. (97)

[I glided in and out between the words as if I were swimming in the clearest water. . . . And, thankful to be a little Negress that was irreducible, a real drum with two sides, as Ma Cia put it, I left one side to her, the mistress, for her to amuse herself, for her to thump on, and I, underneath, I remained intact, nothing ever more so. (61–62)]

But when Télumée actually speaks, similar to the "featherbed tactic" described by Zora Neale Hurston, her response functions as a defensive block. It tells Madame nothing while reestablishing the boundaries of their relationship. When Télumée states, " Madame, they say some people love light and others love filth. . . . I wash and iron and make béchamel sauce, and that's all" (62), she effectively places the top side of her drum "outside the door of her mind for [Madame Desaragne] to play with," like the community Hurston speaks from and about.

After her confrontation with Madame, Télumée has a fleeting encounter with Monsieur Desaragne, when he comes to her room late one night and attempts to assault her. Ironically, despite its nature, this episode is assigned a minor role within the text, giving the impression that it requires even less of Télumée's energy than her encounters with Madame. While the master touches her, Télumée is doggedly silent, then quietly whispers, "J'ai un petit couteau ici et si je n'en avais pas, mes ongles y suffiraient" (113; "I've got a little knife here. And even if I hadn't, my nails would be enough," 72). Horrified, Monsieur Desaragne withdraws while Télumée tells him that despite the similarities between chickens and ducks, they don't both go into the water together. This last statement, like Télumée's response to Madame Desaragne's verbal assault, establishes a boundary with the master of the house. What both situations exemplify is a Télumée who has no illusions about the *categorical difference* between herself and her employers, and she makes it clear that she has choices despite her socioeconomic location.

The Underside of the Drum

Levé de grand matin, il appliquait son reste de cervelle à faire germer des pensées subtiles, des manigances destinées à me faire regretter la vie.

Clear Word and Third Sight

[An early riser, he would use what was left of his brain to hatch tricks that would make me wish I'd never been born.]

—SIMONE SCHWARZ-BART, *Pluie et vent sur Télumée Miracle* (*The Bridge of Beyond*)

If Télumée's struggles at Belle-Feuille represent resistance to white colonial domination, then her struggles with L'Ange Médard could be characterized as a battle with the other side of colonial violence, the legacy of cultural alienation on a personal level. After surviving the death of one husband and the departure of another, the death of Reine Sans Nom and the departure of Ma Cia, Télumée, while living in La Folie—a place whose name signals what is to come—adopts a little girl, Sonore, and meets L'Ange Medard, "l'Homme à la cervelle qui danse." This latter name, given him by the people of his village, implies "one born to evil" (160). Télumée's relationship with Médard mirrors that of her father, Angebert, with the village thief Germain, who after the humiliation of being publicly cursed turns on his only friend and murders him. Both Médard and Germain personify the state that Busia describes as "internal, metaphysical enslavement," self-alienation incarnate, described by the villagers as pure evil (293).

Having acquired some of the supernatural powers of Ma Cia, Télumée is perceived as a witch and therefore feared and revered. Angel Médard profits from Télumée's estrangement within the community. He turns Sonore against her by currying her favor and planting seeds of suspicion in the child's mind. At the same time, Télumée is unable to catch Médard in the act ("la main dans la sac de sa vilenie," 241) since his strategy is one of pitting his will against hers, undermining her at every turn, yet comporting himself as one who lives humbly and at the mercy of fate, when confronted with her anger. The contestations between Médard and Télumée escalate into a struggle, as it were, for the "underside of her drum." Médard wants to break her of her ability to survive life's devastations, to prove that it is not possible to have anything good in life and be a "negro," since this runs counter to slavery's legacy as Médard and his predecessor, Germain, have experienced it. Indeed, this legacy of slavery, and the internalization of the belief that one deserves nothing good—"si le pays est miniscule le coeur est petit" (11; "if the country is small the heart is small," 2)—explain Germain's and Médard's spitefulness, as well as the anger that Télumée's first husband, Élie, feels at her calm when he beats her and the constant struggle in the text between the creole sayings of doom and those of hope. In a final stroke of vengeance, Médard kidnaps Sonore and then hurries back to La Folie to witness Télumée's devastation. But Télumée states:

> Cependant, ma case était plus nette que jamais, la poussière de ma cour brillait comme un sou neuf et j'étais en vêtements du dimanche, coiffée, sanglée, caparaçonnée de la tête aux pieds, allant et venant à mes affaires avec un air de dire qu'elle peut bien se dresser sur ses ergots, la vie, elle ne me déplumera pas. (243)
>
> [But my house was more spotless than ever, the sand in the yard shone like a new sou, and I was in my Sunday best with my hair properly done and decked out from head to foot, going about my business as if to say however fiercely life used its spurs it would never pluck out my feathers. (164)]

Médard's subsequent attempt to murder Télumée ends in his accidentally killing himself. In the moments that follow, he acquires a brief sense of calm before his death and Télumée says to him, "Nous voyons les corbeaux et nous disons: ils parlent une langue étrangère, les corbeaux parlent leur propre langue et nous ne la comprenons pas" (245; "We see the crows and we say, They speak a foreign language. But no, the crows do not speak a foreign language, they speak their own language, and we do not understand it," 165). The villagers claim that Médard lived like a dog but died like a man because of Télumée. Because of this they rename her Télumée Miracle.

Télumée's struggles with Médard are ultimately quite different from her battles at Belle-Feuille. One forces her to skillfully use the "topside of her drum," while the other is a struggle for the underside. The topside represents struggles with those who are outside the community; the underside represents struggles with those who are part of one's community and part of oneself. Both fights are aggressive attempts to break her spirit, but the way in which she positions herself vis-à-vis both sets of opponents differs substantially. L'Ange Médard, despite his menacing qualities, is still a member of the community that Télumée comes from. Because of this, there is a need on Télumée's part to reconcile her ordeal with him within the larger context of her life. She describes Médard as a being without a soul, a poisonous tree that hoped others would touch him and die, but one who was ultimately felled by his own poison. She compares her lot to his, describing them both as two beings struggling to survive. The proverbial saying that she uses to communicate with him at his life's end is very different from the one she used to communicate with Monsieur Desaragne. When she tells Monsieur that chickens and ducks may look similar but don't go into the water together, she enforces the divide between herself and the master. Her statement to Médard, on the other hand, can be seen as the opposite of her statement to Monsieur: "the crows . . . speak their own language, and we do not understand it" (165). Here, there is an attempt made to reconcile alienation rather than assert difference. Télumée uses the first person plural when speaking to Médard, thus invoking a sense of community. She then tells him that what many perceive as alien (crows speaking a foreign language) is in fact part of a natural order. In this sense she resignifies both her and Médard's self-alienation by indicating that even if they are unable to make sense of their experiences, these experiences are not without meaning.

Pluie et vent sur Télumée Miracle depicts cultural alienation as part of the collective experience of the community: a state of being portrayed as resulting from white colonial domination. There is a constant struggle between self-affirmation and self-doubt that many of the characters face. Schwarz-Bart addresses both states by focusing on Télumée's individual crises and questions and connecting them through proverbs to the collective situation of the community. Télumée states at one point, "And I understood at last what a Negro is: wind and sail at the same time, at once drummer and dancer, a first-class sham, trying to collect by the basketful the sweetness that falls scattered from above, and inventing sweetness when it doesn't fall on him" (137).

The relationships among oppression, colonial domination, and survival are addressed within the narrative in several ways. First, there is always continuity established between Télumée's story and that of her ancestors. She is never an isolated individual without a past but always someone who is descended from a strong ancestral line. Second, Télumée's individual crises are always resignified in terms of a larger experience. Her oppression is tied to the community's oppression. When Madame Desaragne insults her at Belle-Feuille, it is not so much an attack on Télumée personally as it is on the Black condition in general. When Monsieur Desaragne attempts to assault her, Télumée is portrayed as finally experiencing the same aggression that the rest of the maids at Belle-Feuille have to face on a daily basis. When

Télumée is betrayed by her husband and reduced to working in the canefields, she is depicted, once again, as having to face experiences that are common among her people. Finally, her encounter with Médard mirrors her father's experiences with Germain; here, once again, Télumée's experiences are part of a communal cycle as opposed to unique, individual, and isolated.

Télumée copes with each of these crises by drawing on resources that the community she comes from has given her. She maneuvers through Belle-Feuille by relying on the advice given to her by Reine Sans Nom and Ma Cia. When Élie leaves her for Letitia and Télumée falls into a depression, she is brought out of it, like her grandmother before her, by the women's purposeful singing and talking in front of her house and by their many visits. When she struggles with Médard, it is her faith in the fact that she has survived many trials as well as her staunch enactment of the proverbial advice she was raised on that saves her. After recovering from her long depression when Élie leaves her, she tells us, "La folie est une maladie contagieuse, aussi ma guérrison était celle de tous et ma victoire, la preuve que le nègre a sept fiels et ne désarme pas comme ça, à la première alerte" (173; "Madness is contagious, and so my cure was everyone's, and my victory the proof that a Negro has seven spleens and doesn't give up just like that at the first sign of trouble," 115). So, in both her experiences of crises and her responses to them, Télumée's story is always that of her community. Unlike the son in Damas's "Hoquet," whose cultural education passed on through his mother is geared toward mimicry and the outside appearance, Télumée's cultural education, coming from both her grandmother and the women within the community, is geared toward the preservation of the inside. She passes this gift on to others:

> La Reine, la Reine, qui dit qu'il n'y a rien pour moi sur la terre, qui dit pareille bêtise? . . . [E]n ce moment même j'ai lâché mon chagrin au fond de la rivière et il est en train de descendre le courant, il enveloppera un autre coeur que le mien. . . . [P]arle-moi de la vie, grand-mère, parle-moi de ça. (172)
>
> [Queen, Queen, who says there is nothing for me in the world, who says such foolishness? At this very moment I have left my grief at the bottom of the river. It is going downstream, and will enshroud another heart than mine. Talk to me about life, Grandmother. Talk to me about that. (114)]

Clear Word and Third Sight

Yet it is out of the experiences of the most oppression that the most transformational impulses emerge. It is surviving the very worst experiences (violent spousal abuse, madness, the brutality of the canefields) that equips Télumée with the spiritual self-knowledge necessary to help the community maintain its collective center and balance. When Télumée goes into the canefields, she temporarily loses sight of the underside of her drum. It is not restored until she leaves the fields and marries Amboise, the marriage celebration doubling in the text as the moment of liberation. This is an interesting move on Schwarz-Bart's part since, among other things, it resignifies marriage in this context as a partnership and space of liberation, distinct from the ownership and subordination historically linked with the institution in the Western context. Télumée's first marriage to Élie functioned in the Western way. Significantly, Élie is described in the narrative as hankering after a formal French education and subsequently giving in to a debilitating self-alienation when this doesn't materialize. Amboise, on the other hand, is the man who goes to France and returns with no illusions about European civilization. He says, "Télumée we have been beaten for a hundred years but I tell you girl, we have courage for a thousand" (151). During her description of her marriage ceremony to Amboise, Télumée states:

> Amboise uttered one summons after another throughout the night, and people came and went in and out of the circle. . . . Early in the morning, Olympia pushed me silently into the middle of the circle. . . . Amboise's fingers tapped the goatskin lightly, as if looking for a sign, for the rhythm of my pulse. Seizing my skirt in either hand, I started to whirl like a top out of control, back hunched, elbows raised above my shoulders, trying in vain to parry invisible blows. Suddenly I felt the waters of the drum flow over my heart and give it life again, at first in little damp notes, then in great falls that sprinkled and baptized me as I whirled in the middle of the circle. And the river flowed over me and . . . I was Adriana, down and up, and I was Ismene of the great pensive eyes, I was Olympia and the rest. . . . I was the drum and Amboise's helping hands, I his little hunted watchful dove's eyes. And now my hands were opening on all sides, taking lives and refashioning them as I pleased, giving the world and being nothing . . . the drumbeats issuing from beneath Amboise's hands, and yet existing with all my strength, from the roots of my hair right down to my little toes. (145–46)

The Africanity of Schwarz-Bart's text is brought to the fore by this description. The circle and the drum are highly symbolic. Télumée's account of her experience while dancing is like the description of spirit possession in traditional African-influenced spiritual contexts. For a moment she gives up her "head," her conscious rational self, and in that moment she is a vessel that experiences the identities of some of those in her community. The experience is also like spirit possession in the African traditional context in that it functions as an initiation and Télumée describes herself as "baptized by the drum." The profundity of the way in which everyday proverbs function in Schwarz-Bart's text speaks to the complexity of the Africanity that she reveals. Far from being quaint and simple phrases, the proverbs are deeply philosophical in character. The drum metaphor functions for Télumée as a seemingly simple folk saying which in actuality endows her with a strategy for surviving life and influencing destiny. The African philosophical principle of balance, sometimes called "Nommo," is demonstrated through the proverbs as one of the highest cosmic values. Toni Cade Bambara describes Nommo as the "harmonizing energy that connects body/mind/spirit/self/community with the universe" (*Deep Sightings and Rescue Missions,* 113). When Télumée dances at her wedding, the fusion described is conceptually similar to Nommo.

"Metaphor of Blocking" or "Gift of Metaphor"

> Diversion is the ultimate resort of a population whose domination by an Other is concealed: it then must search elsewhere for the principle of domination, which is not evident in the country itself: because the system of domination (which is not only exploitation, which is not only misery, which is not only underdevelopment, but actually the complete eradication of an economic entity) is not directly tangible. Diversion is the parallactic displacement of this strategy.
>
> —EDOUARD GLISSANT, *Caribbean Discourse*

In her article "A Politics of Location in Simone Schwarz-Bart's *The Bridge of Beyond,*" Jeanne Garane draws on the critical work of Maryse Condé and the theories of Edouard Glissant to analyze Schwarz-Bart's novel. Citing Fanon in order to argue that a split between a "maternal Africa" and a "tutelary France" has characterized much of the work on the Antilles, she attempts to situate Schwarz-Bart's text within an exclusively Guadeloupean framework that refuses recourse to either external location. In order to make Glissant's Antillanité work as a frame for Schwarz-Bart's text, Garane has to subsume the Africanized distinction that some scholars make between the situation of Martinique and that of Guadeloupe. While I maintain that Schwarz-Bart's novel theorizes culture and identity in a distinctly different way than *Caribbean Discourse,* Jeanne Garane treats Glissant's text as the theoretically superior one and reads Schwarz-Bart's novel as a demonstration of Glissant's theories.[23]

Edouard Glissant's *Caribbean Discourse* is a collection of poetic essays that attempt to wrestle with various components of the francophone Antillean experience. Existing at the intersection of theoretical, prosaic, and poetic genres of writing, Glissant's text is a critical analysis of the thematics of alienation that are a foundational aspect of the Martinican experience. In the essay "Reversion and Diversion" Glissant's style is more prosaic and analytical than poetic. Still, the poetic nuance is maintained by the repetitive yet elusive definitions of the essay's key concepts. "Reversion" and "diversion" are terms that describe, not so much the experience of psychic alienation specific to the "transplanted" Antillean (ex-slave) population, but rather their responses to this experience. "Reversion" is partially characterized as a response to a loss of an "old order of [cultural] values," while "diversion" is partially characterized as a frequently subconscious reaction to "domination by an Other"—a domination that is concealed from the Antillean subject (16, 20). Following from this, "creolization" describes the "transplanted" population's transformation into something "new." This change is the result of the experience of "transplantation" itself (which for Glissant is tantamount to a fundamental loss of previous cultural ways of being) as well as "contact" with other cultures. The stakes, therefore, of Glissant's notion of creolization are ultimately determined by how he reconciles the tension between "transplantation" and "contact" as descriptions of slavery and colonial violence.

Reversion is "the obsession with a single origin. . . . To revert is to consecrate permanence, to negate contact" (16). For Glissant reversion is most concretely symbolized by "back to Africa" movements. He describes this particular desire for return as "a compensatory impulse" resulting from the loss of an "old order of values" (16). He maintains that this specific distinction can be seen as generally constituting the difference between the African and Jewish diasporas, based on what he argues is the latter's maintenance of cultural collectivity despite displacement. On the other hand, Glissant states, "The return of the Palestinians to their country is not a strategic maneuver; it is an immediate struggle. Expulsion and return are totally contemporary. This is not a compensatory impulse but vital urgency" (16–17). The distinctions that he makes between perceivedly legitimate and illegitimate desires for return are premised explicitly on the notion of slavery as having abolished certain cultural ways of being, and implicitly on the notion that slavery bequeathed no immediate legacy of present-day violence—violence that would require hardcore resistance and constitute "an immediate and contemporary struggle of vital urgency." "Reversion," therefore, not only refers to the illegitimate desire for return, but makes creolization impossible, since there is a refusal to "come to terms with the new land." Glissant argues that white American financing of Black migration to Liberia was a loss for the forces of creolization. Creolization here would appear to be "positive" interaction between Black ex-slaves and the white population that was free of cultural imperialism and one-directional colonial violence.[24] What for the Black supporters of nineteenth-century return to Africa has historically been theorized as the only sane choice in a situation in which "Blacks had no rights that whites were bound to respect," is for Glissant a loss of transformative potential.[25]

Glissant states that "diversion is the ultimate resort of a population whose domination by an Other is concealed" from itself. For Glissant, diversion is, in this instance, unconscious subversion of the dominant order. On one hand, it is a reaction to oppression that lacks both collectivity and productivity, and, on the other hand, it is exemplified by political movements that begin in the Caribbean but take root elsewhere. To make this latter point, Glissant refers to Césaire, Fanon, and Garvey, arguing that they each had more significant political impact outside the Caribbean than in the countries of their birth. But the creole language is Glissant's primary example of diversion as a tactic of unconscious subversiveness. He maintains that creole is incapable of "transcending its French origins" (20). He describes Martinican creole as reactive speech that appears to imitate the speech of a child ("*pretty pretty baby* for *very pretty child*," 20) while systematically engaging in a "strategy of trickery" originally aimed at deceiving the slave master. He argues that it is a language without subtlety, which, unlike Haitian creole, has never become a "productive and responsible language" (20–21). Yet what is of interest here is Glissant's confession that "the controversy over the origin and composition of the [creole] language bores [him]" (20). This is significant precisely because of his claims that creole never transcends its French origins. In other words, his lack of interest in the language's origin and composition, far from making his analysis impartial, displays a partiality toward French as the interpretive lens for analyzing Creole. This is at odds with analyses of creole that view it as formally complex, with a construction that surpasses mere imitation.

Amon Saba Saakana, for example, analyzes the relationship between Yoruba and the oral structure of vernacular speech in the anglophone, francophone, and Dutch-speaking Caribbean diaspora. In both the Caribbean and Yoruba context he finds an almost identical grammatical order to similar expressions. Saakana states:

> In European languages the problem of grammatical transfer exists, and [linguist Robert] Lado gives an example of a German asking a question in English: *Know you where the church is?* as opposed to *Do you know where the church is?* This is a direct result of the grammatical formation of German *Wissen sie wo die krche ist?* If we transfer this problem to African languages, we will arrive at the same conclusion as the German-English example. Yoruba *Mo'n bo* is literally equivalent to English *Me coming.* This is equivalent to the Trinidadian *Ah coming* and to the Jamaican *Me a come.* In all three examples there is the absence of a verb, as in the English equivalent *I am coming.* Another example is Yoruba *Mo wa* which is equivalent, literally to English *I exist* or *I am* in relation to the question *How are you?* The Trinidadian response would be *Ah dey,* the Jamaican *Me dey ya* or the Creole (of Guadeloupe, Dominica, St. Lucia and Martinique) *Mwen la.* The important shared constant in the examples is the philosophical response: all stating a state of existence or being, as opposed to the English *I am well* or *I am fine* or *I am not too bad,* which all relate to a state of health. (46)

This deeply philosophical approach to the question of one's existence is apparent in Schwarz-Bart's novel in the existential content of the proverbs. What this proves is that the continuity of an African philosophical worldview is alive and well and shaping cultural identity in the diaspora context despite the loss of actual words and languages. With Saakana's analysis what we have is a complexifying of the notion of creole as mere imitation of French speech. From the outset, Glissant juxtaposes a "fascination with imitation" in the francophone Lesser Antilles with the "denigration of original values" (16). This is not the mimicry "for the sheer love of it" that Hurston describes but rather what she calls the "slavish imitation" of a certain class. Glissant is quick to qualify the notion of original values by stating that abandoning them is not just a loss but also "an unprecedented potential for contact" (16). He views moments of African diaspora "loss" as simultaneously opportunities for perpetually deferred "contact" between cultures. However, the presumption of possibility for positive "contact" when there are actually relationships of domination in place would seem to be a foray into the realm of fantasy. Throughout Glissant's essay—in fact, through his entire book—imitation is akin to cultural death: "the insidious promise of being remade in the Other's image, the illusion of successful mimesis" (15). Time and again, throughout "Reversion and Diversion," Glissant maintains that while creolization is premised on the loss of "methods of existence and survival, both material and spiritual, which [the transplanted population] practiced before being uprooted" he is nevertheless staunchly opposed to the creativity of creolization being premised on imitation (15).

Glissant attempts to theorize the psychological alienation of the collective in Martinique. His theoretical point of departure and the root metaphor for his entire oeuvre is what Sylvia Wynter describes as psychocultural blockade.[26] If Glissant's text is analyzed in terms of its poetics, it can be seen as an enactment of the kind of psychological alienation it seeks to critique and come to terms with. This is the case specifically in terms of how the notion of "contact" is theorized with regard to the concept of creolization. What Glissant calls "contact," Césaire theorizes as "colonization." Césaire's argues that the illusion of colonization is the notion that it is contact with civilization like any other, rather than being "a phenomenon that, among other disastrous psychological consequences, involves the following: it raises doubts regarding the concepts on which the colonized could build or rebuild their world" (205). While maintaining the option of a "creolization" that is not rooted in African cultural survivals, the poetics of Glissant's text is characterized by a vehement opposition to mimicry. Ultimately, his text is plagued by the very ambivalence and self-doubt about the possibilities for the dominated to "transcend their French origins" that he attributes to creole speech. Unlike Zora Neale Hurston's dual notions of mimicry, with Glissant, only one culturally deadening form of imitation is described. He is therefore trapped in a philosophical paradox. Imitation of whites equals cultural death, and original culture is lost. But mutual contact between cultures resulting in something new (creolization) is desirable. What will be the foundation for these creolized identities if both imitation and recourse to origins are impossible or deeply flawed? Fortunately, Schwarz-Bart's text charts a different set of alternatives for African diaspora subjectivity.

This metaphor of "blocking" that is the foundation for Glissant's notions of "creolization" and "Antilleanity" is an enterprise in which psychic recuperation necessarily remains a fiction if the colonial situation (void of a critique of violence) is the source for the creative impulse. At the 1956 First International Conference of Negro Writers and Artists, Haitian writer Jacques Stephen Alexis took issue with Senghor's notion of an "African Negro Culture," arguing instead for a *"New Humanism*, which comes just as much from the West as it does from Asia. It is specifically the fruit of a selection, of a conscious choice by all men of culture of all nations on earth of what is to be the human culture of the future" (Présence Africaine Conference Committee, 75). Senghor responded by asking what civilizational legacy the African diaspora subject was heir to (218). Thirty years later, Sylvia Wynter asked, "Which 'order of discourse' (the *ordo verborum*) is to provide the system of meanings through whose mechanism our collective behaviors are to be regulated? . . . [W]hich behavior-regulating order of discourse . . . one which continues to impose a situationally blocked destiny upon the people of the Antilles, or a new one to be consciously put in place capable of enabling the liberation of the majority of peoples of the Antilles from their enforced role of Other to the Self [?]" (640).

Léon Damas's *Pigments* is a solid analysis of the mimicry and psychocultural blockade that is at the heart of Glissant's critique of the Martinican situation. But whereas Glissant's critique is also characterized by an ambivalence toward the relationship to a hegemonic order, Damas's negritude poetics are not. For Damas it is not possible to criticize the "native bourgeoisie," yet maintain a notion of European culture that is uncontaminated by its involvement in colonial violence. In the context of *Pigments*, the cultural specificity of an African diaspora is suggested by what Dash refers to as Damas's "transgressive poetics," his textual representation of orality through his use of colloquial speech and rhythm. Yet a "recuperative poetics" is implicitly conceivable in the early poetry of Damas. While Glissant's creolization remains a utopian desire, firmly rooted in the metaphorical space of psychocultural blockade, Damas's early poetics both critique violence and represent African diaspora cultural reality with recourse to the very creole speech that Glissant characterizes as simply reactive. I wish to argue that Simone Schwarz-Bart's oeuvre, on the other hand, is both a response to Glissant's representation of psychocultural blockade and an explicit expansion of the representation of African diaspora cultural reality delineated by Damas.

The metaphorical blocking described by Glissant, in which "domination by an Other is [always] concealed," is at odds with the primary metaphor of Schwarz-Bart's work which could be described as *restitution:* "Il fallait que nous nous retrouvions" ("It is imperative that we rediscover ourselves"; 186).[27] "Restitution" in this sense would refer to a reconstruction premised on communal decolonization and psychospiritual renewal. In *Pluie et vent sur Télumée Miracle,* Angel Médard and Germaine are representative of "blocked," self-alienated subjectivity. They are not ostracized, but they are seen as the weakest links in the communal chain, the ones who have most thoroughly internalized the abjection projected onto the colonized by the colonial order. The notion of restitution chez Simone Schwarz-Bart responds to the idea of blocked subjectivity, since self-alienation is addressed vis-à-vis the representation of a communal regeneration.

Since it is continuous with Damas's work in terms of its representation of colonial violence, Schwarz-Bart's first novel makes no attempt at a utopian representation of the culture of the colonizer. Madame and Monsieur Desaragne are both seen as perpetrating violence against Télumée, and they are represented as culturally alien. On the other hand, Angel Médard, and by implication Germaine, Black subjects who direct violence against members of their own community, are not seen as alien by Télumée, and they are ultimately reconciled to the communal spirit. This is an interesting and significant move on Schwarz-Bart's part because it portrays both colonial violence and resistance to that violence simultaneously, while gender identification *based on sex alone* is radically disrupted by the refusal of a representation of sisterhood and friendship between the Madame and Télumée. Instead, despite the alienation and internal communal violence found in the story, Schwarz-Bart's text reconciles the "shadow of the whip" roles that Black men and women inherited from slavery and restores the possibility of "we."[28] On the other hand, Schwarz-Bart gives an interiority to Black cultural life by her representation of a community premised on a tradition of storytelling. In this context, the stories, their meanings, and their uses are part of an alternative philosophical vision and metaphysical order, one that endows the participants in this process with the skills to struggle against psychic violence while representing a world that is still, after all is said and done, more derived from an African cultural order than a European one: *Fashion me a people*.[29] Schwarz-Bart's metaphor of the two-sided drum for African diaspora psychic survival goes beyond Damas's deconstruction of French and his textual representation of orality. In the final instance, the metaphorical point of departure for Schwarz-Bart's theorizing appears to be rooted in that different "order of discourse" hinted at by Caribbean scholar Sylvia Wynter.

5

The Spoken Word
and Spirit Consciousness

AUDRE LORDE AND PAULE MARSHALL'S

DIASPORIC VOICE

Without community there is no liberation, only the most vulnerable and temporary armistice between an individual and her oppression.—AUDRE LORDE

Later that night, when the fire was roaring in the chimney and the cold came slicing through the cabin's wall, Old Jack taught me another lesson: if you would bend a man, abandon the usual means. . . . [I]f you would bend a man, not just influence him or sway him or even convince him but *bend* him, do it with ritual. For even if he claims to have no belief, no religion, no adherence to any formal or informal order of service, there is, somewhere within him, a hidden agenda.—DAVID BRADLEY

My study would be incomplete without examining the work of two writers who straddle both U.S. and Caribbean literary traditions and who are themselves first-generation Caribbean diaspora writers. The literary oeuvres of Paule Marshall and Audre Lorde have been of substantial significance to both U.S. and Caribbean traditions of literature. This chapter will address the relationship between vision and voice in their writing, with an eye to showing how these issues work together as a continuation of the notion of the empowered word, addressed in the writings of Simone Schwarz-Bart.

In Audre Lorde's early prose and poetry, there is a symbolic relationship between words without power and an absence of vision. The disempowered voice and lack of sight are compounded by an ambivalent Black cultural identity. This threefold relationship among vision, voice, and cultural identity emerges again and again in Lorde's early collections of poetry, *First Cities, Cables to Rage,* and *Coal.* Her later books, the "biomythography" *Zami: A New Spelling of My Name* and the poetry collection *The Black Unicorn,* however, function as transitional utterances in the context of her lifelong shift from a poetics of loss toward one of recuperation. Research into African continental spiritual systems informs both *The Black Unicorn* and *Our Dead behind Us.* The fact that the former collection is dedicated to her mother and father implies a reclamation of the culture of the home space renounced in both the early poetry and the early sections of *Zami. Zami,* Lorde's only long, semifictional prose work, can be interpreted as an autobiography of her racial identity, one that documents her production as an "individual." This text shows the relationship between a dominant white culture outside the home space and young Audre's transformation into a "subject" who renounces her Black Caribbean home environment in search of a new and separate identity. As with Tee in *Crick Crack Monkey,* young Audre's gaze and vision are gradually replaced by her Western education. But unlike Tee, by the end of *Zami* Audre is transformed again: the symbol in the title of the text is beginning to take effect and the power of the word is altering adult Audre's identity. There is some connection, therefore, between the embrace of a Western individualism and the rejection of a more local ethnic, cultural identity. This is a connection that Lorde as a writer, poet, and activist exhaustively examines and appears to repudiate in her later life. Her later collection of poetry, *Our Dead behind Us,* cements the movement toward empowered word and inspired vision.

Lorde's literary movement away from a poetics of loss toward a more empowered utterance has its parallel in the movement she made away from a culture of individualism toward a notion of both local and Pan-African community. After a fourteen-year struggle with cancer, she spent her final days revising old poems and writing new ones. The last poem in her final volume *Undersong,* entitled "Need: A Chorale for Black Woman Voices," is a tribute to Black women who have been violently killed. In the title of this last poem, Lorde joins the grammatically singular "Black Woman" to the plural "Voices," signifying once again an integration between individual and community that approaches the inseparable. The writings of Paule Marshall maintain a prominent place within the Caribbean and African American literary traditions. Of interest here is her fourth and most significant novel, *Praisesong for the Widow,* in which disempowered voice and vision, as in the final poem "Call" in Lorde's *Our Dead behind Us,* are transformed into a powerful relationship between the spoken word and spirit consciousness.

The notion of "spirit consciousness" is defined for the purposes of this study as the ability to know beyond the point that the rational self can comprehend. In their essay, "Forms of African Spirituality in Trinidad and Tobago," Rudolph Eastman and Maureen Warner-Lewis give us the political and cultural context of this mode of apprehension as they outline the structures of African-based spiritual practices in Trinidad and Tobago: "African mindsets and forms of cultural behavior were disparaged and outlawed, while European religions and worldview were promoted. . . . [D]espite ethnic links, Caribbean societies have been historically colored by hostility toward and ignorance of Africa and its cultures. All the same, some African cultural traits have continued a vibrant existence. But their expression has assumed a correlation with class and educational status" (403). Eastman and Warner-Lewis address their topic under the subheadings "Individual Acts of Spirituality," "Orisha Religion," "Voduun," and "The Spiritual Baptist Faith." In the section "Orisha Religion," Eastman and Warner-Lewis explain that "the Orisha" are deities that are sometimes referred to as "powers," "the old people," and "saints" in Trinidad and Tobago. "Membership in the Orisha faith is attained . . . through possession by an Orisha, or mediated dreams, visions, and divination," far from attending service every Sunday and giving collection. They further state that "the initiation process covers nine to fourteen days and involves a symbolic death and rebirth, expressing the neophyte's break with the past. Initiation marks the surrender of one's 'head' and formally continues with seclusion within an inner sanctum" (406).

This concept of surrendering the "head" seems to be a process in which a divine spirit center combines with ancestral knowledge to replace rational consciousness. The connection between this kind of spirit consciousness and the spoken word is conscientiously developed in the later poetry of Audre Lorde and in Paule Marshall's *Praise-*

song for the Widow. The emphasis these two writers place on this concept makes it clear that African cultural and spiritual traditions are alive in the diaspora and are not reducible to continental and national boundaries.

Individuality and the Poetics of Loss

The poetics of loss that functions in Lorde's early work is characterized by words having no power, community that is nonexistent, and a symbolic focus on sight and vision in which blindness is prevalent. I maintain that the loss characterized is the departure/separation from a Black community and familial context, one that occurs as "individuality" is pursued. This "individuality" is experienced as loss because of the impossibility of Black assimilation into the imperial societal context, the sign of which is white racism.

In Lorde's *The First Cities,* published in 1968, the poem "Pirouette" opens with the lines

> I saw
> Your hands on my lips like blind needles
> Blunted
> From sewing up stone
> And
> Where are you from
> you said. . . .
> A land where all lovers are mute.
> (16)

The imagery here is of needles without eyes, "blunted" from sewing up lips that won't speak. There is no vision and no voice. Communication of any sort is paralyzed.

In the second stanza of the poem "Generation," the poet states:

> In a careless season of power
> We wept out our terrible promise. . . .
> Warning—the road to Nowhere is slippery with our blood. . . .
> We are more than kin who come to share
> Not blood, but the bloodiness of failure.
> (17)

"Generation" talks about a generation without a future that paid a dangerously high price for their indulgences. The poem is dominated by images of stagnancy, "the road to Nowhere," and "the bloodiness of failure."

Another poem in the collection, "A Family Resemblance," explicitly addresses the absence of familial community:

> My sister has my hair my mouth my eyes
> And I presume her trustless . . .
> My sister has my tongue
> And all my flesh unanswered
> And I presume her trustless as a stone.
> (5)

In this poem, lack of trust and "family resemblance" are bedfellows, indicating not just a breakdown in the communal integrity of the family structure, but also implying that anyone with features too similar to one's own will be automatically suspect.

One loss that permeates Lorde's early work is the suicide of her high school friend Gennie. At least three poems in her first two collections of poetry, as well as a substantial portion of the first part of *Zami,* are devoted to this loss. One of these poems, "Memorial II" (originally the first poem in *The First Cities*), is worth considering in full:

> Genevieve
> What are you seeing
> In my mirror this morning
> Peering out like a hungry bird
> From behind my eyes
> Are you seeking the shape of a girl
> I have grown less and less to resemble
> Or do you remember
> I could never accept your face dying
> I do not know you now
>
> Surely your vision stayed stronger than mine
> Genevieve tell me where dead girls
> Wander after their summer.
>
> I wish I could see you again
> Far from me—even
> Birdlike flying into the sun.
> Your eyes are blinding me Genevieve.
> (3)

In this poem, the narrator constructs herself as sightless, and, as is apparent from the last two lines of the first stanza and the poem's title, her friend Genevieve is dead. Yet strangely, in the opening lines the narrator endows Genevieve with more sight than herself. The image that the reader has is one of Genevieve's seeing through the narrator's eyes and having a better perspective on the narrator than the narrator has on herself ("Surely your vision stayed stronger than mine"). On the other hand, we have no sense of what the narrator herself is capable of seeing. At the poem's end she states, "Your eyes are blinding me Genevieve," implying that she has no sight of her own. What we have then is a narrator who is *alienated from herself,* since the "vision" of her dead friend is presented as stronger than her own. This representation of alienation is significant since it functions as a sign of the poetic subject's lack of identification with her own psychic and physiological self. While internalized white identification is not explicitly flagged as the cause of the narrator's alienation from self, what we are told is that Genevieve's vision is stronger than her own. What can this possibly mean, since Genevieve is dead? It is as if Genevieve is the only person capable of understanding the predicament the narrator finds herself in; her only community is another Black girl, like herself alienated from both family and white society.

"Suspension," the final poem in *The First Cities,* ends on the same ambiguous note that permeates the collection. The term "suspension" implies that something is hanging in the balance. In this poem, the narrator describes a tense silence between two people, with the narrator waiting for the other party (the "you" in the poem) to speak. The poem's first stanza creates the impression that the unnamed and unspeaking party controls the physical atmosphere in the room by his or her silence. The last stanza states:

> I remember now, with the filled crystal
> Shattered, the wind-whipped curtains
> Bound, and the cold storm
> Finally broken,
> How the room felt
> When your word was spoken—
> Warm
> As the center of your palms
> And as unfree.
> (26)

While the first stanza creates the impression of a chilly room filled with tension and silence, the last stanza describes the room after the silence is broken. Yet the spoken word, at least in this context, brings with it no sense of liberation. Instead, the terms used to describe the atmosphere after the silence is broken ("Warm . . . And . . . unfree") invoke images of suffocation.

The title poem of Lorde's first book, *Coal*, takes a different direction:

> I
> is the total black, being spoken
> from the earth's inside.
> There are many kinds of open
> how a diamond comes into a knot of flame
> how a sound comes into a word, coloured
> by who pays what for speaking.
> (6)

These opening lines contain more optimistic imagery than most of the other earlier work, although "Coal" is among her earlier poems. After this opening, the narrator goes on to say that the power attributable to words is not separate from the forces controlling the speaker:

> Some words are open like a diamond
> on glass windows
> singing out within the passing crash of sun
> Then there are words like stapled wagers
> in perforated book,—buy and sign and tear apart,—
> and come whatever wills all chances
> the stub remains
> and ill-pulled tooth with a ragged edge.
> Some words live in my throat
> breeding like adders. Others know sun
> seeking like gypsies over my tongue
> to explode through my lips
> like young sparrows bursting from shell
> Some words
> bedevil me.
> (6)

Here the narrator describes many different kinds of speech, most of which are characterized by the speaker's holding onto the power of "her" words in a calculating way ("words like stapled wagers") or being suffocated by "her" words ("Some words live in my throat

Clear Word and Third Sight

breeding like adders"). The poem ends with the narrator returning to the original diamond imagery, thereby expressing an interest in having her words be interpreted in the best possible light:

> Love is a word, another kind of open.
> As the diamond comes into a knot of flame
> I am Black because I come from the earth's inside
> now take my word for jewel in the open light.
> (6)

Lorde published the collection *Coal* in 1976, combining new poetry (including the poem "Coal") with poems previously published in *The First Cities* (1968) and *Cables to Rage* (1970). *Coal* the anthology and "Coal" the title poem therefore come a little later in her poetic career than those first books, and later in the process of transformation of her poetic voice.

Of some significance in *Coal* is "Story Books on a Kitchen Table," an early poem dealing with her feelings for her mother. Like the daughter's relationship to the mother in Jamaica Kincaid's work, Lorde's ambivalent relationship to her mother is a tension she struggled to negotiate throughout her life. This struggle is at least symbolically at the center of *Zami: A New Spelling of My Name*. In fact the term "zami" is in part Lorde's attempt to reclaim this conflicted legacy. As she tells us in the book's epilogue, zami is "a Carriacou name for women who work together as friends and lovers," where it is said "the desire to lie with other women is a drive from the mother's blood" (*Zami*, 255–56). Yet this conflicted relationship is far from being remythologized in "Story Books on a Kitchen Table." The narrator states:

> Out of her womb of pain my mother spat me
> into her ill-fitting harness of despair
> into her deceits
> where anger re-conceived me
> piercing my eyes like arrows
> pointed by her nightmare
> of who I was not
> becoming.
> (*Coal*, 27)

Interestingly enough, the imagery in this stanza is of the narrator being blinded by her own anger at her mother's disappointment in her. She loses her sight in the glare of her mother's vision of who she should be. In this poem there is an identity forged out of anger, yet this is not an identity that is able to guide her, since the last stanza of the poem describes a girl wandering without direction once her mother is gone. These recurring images of blindness, voicelessness, and isolation thematize loss in Lorde's early writing.

In a 1979 interview with Adrienne Rich, Audre Lorde said, "I wrote a lot of those poems you first knew me by, those poems in *The First Cities*, way back in high school" (*Sister Outsider*, 88). The implication is that her early poetry, the texts in which her poetic voice is permeated by the most extreme alienation, cannot be entirely separated from the exterior forces structuring her life at the time.

Zami documents young Audre's exploration of a sexual identity that explicitly requires a deculturalization and individuation from her family and Black community in general. Black communal life and her participation within it are in evidence thrice within the text, twice within familial contexts. Those two instances are more revealing of the character of Audre's alienation than is the rest of the "novel."

Zami begins not with the story of Audre's separation from her family but with the story of her parents immigrating to New York City. As in Simone Schwarz-Bart's *Pluie et vent sur Télumée Miracle*, which opens with a section entitled "My People" and begins with the life of Télumée's great-grandmother Minerva, Audre's "story of her life" begins before her life, with her parents. By beginning the book in this way, Lorde establishes her family and the "Black island women" her mother is descended from as inseparable from her own identity:

> Grenadians and Barbadians walk like African peoples. Trinidadians do not.
>
> When I visited Grenada I saw the root of my mother's powers walking through the streets. I thought, this is the country of my fore-mothers, my forebearing mothers, those Black island women who defined themselves by what they did. "Island women make good wives; whatever happens, they've seen worse." There is a softer edge of African sharpness upon these women, and they swing through the rain-warm streets with an arrogant gentleness that I remember in strength and vulnerability. (9)

While there is little direct focus on Audre's father, the text opens with a generous envisioning of the mother's ancestry. This representation is at odds with the mother portrayed in the poem "Story Books on a Kitchen Table," as well as with the actual mother presented throughout the rest of the text. Lorde's descriptions of her mother Linda portray her as a private, shy woman with an "imposing, no-nonsense exterior," a woman who shares all the decision-making with her husband (17). She is a large, powerful woman who is lighter in complexion than her husband and her three daughters. Amidst all these descriptions, Linda is also established as a woman of few words who has an island consciousness.

> She knew about bundling up against the wicked cold. . . . She knew about mixing oils for bruises and rashes, and about disposing of all toenail clippings and hair from the comb. About burning candles before All Souls Day to keep the soucoyants away, lest they suck the blood of her babies. . . . *She knew how to look into people's faces and tell what they were going to do before they did it.* . . . She knew how to prevent infection in an open cut or wound by heating the black-elm leaf over a wood-fire until it wilted in the hand, rubbing the juice into the cut, and then laying the soft green now flabby fibers over the wound for a bandage. . . . She told us stories about Carriacou, where she had been born, amid the heavy smell of limes. She told us about plants that healed and about plants that drove you crazy, and none of it made much sense to us children because we had never seen any of them. (10–13, italics mine)

Linda is a woman who leaves nothing to chance. She is invested in seeing her daughters achieve upward mobility in this new land. Yet this desire is mitigated by her investment in maintaining some cultural autonomy and imparting different types of cultural knowledge even within the confines of "America." This means that as girls growing up they must never leave the house alone, and any act indicating a desire for privacy in the home space is regarded as a direct affront to the mother's authority. This also means that although her daughters are sent to the "best" schools (Catholic schools in which they are the only Black students), they are still advised not to trust white people. This focus on the mistrust of whites as an aspect of the maternal advice young Audre receives from her mother has an equivalent in the practice of mothering and the psychocultural skills that Télumée is exposed to by Ma Cia and Reine Sans Nom in *Pluie et vent sur Télumée Miracle*. Being like a drum with two faces, the metaphor that Télumée aggressively enacts when she works for Madame Desaragne, is what allows her to disempower the negative discourse she is subject to in her work environment and disregard it as "les paroles de Blanc, rien que ça" (96; "white man's words, that's all," *Bridge of Beyond,* 61). Linda is a woman whose ways of mothering are substantially informed by the place she came from. In the passage just quoted she is presented as someone with a significant amount of "outside" knowledge. She understands the powers of various plants and herbs, and she has an awareness of non-Western rituals of protection (disposing of toenail clippings and hair). She tells her daughters stories about Carriacou, stories that Audre confesses didn't make much sense to her as a child (*Zami,* 13). She is also described as being able to foretell what people were going to do. With these descriptions of Linda, Lorde unwittingly establishes her mother as having a kind of insight not accessible to those operating solely by the official cultural norms. This is significant, since the Audre who narrates the story throughout the majority of the text appears to be an aggressively rational subject without this kind of "third sight." One could argue that while young Audre misses the significance of some of the mother's lessons during the mother's physical life, she comes into her mother's power and the fullness of her mother's legacy of internal strength later in life.

Most significant, however, is the early portrait of Audre's home as an environment in which individuality is inconceivable. Linda and Bee make their decisions as a unit. When her older sisters go to buy comics, the price their mother exacts for this pleasure is taking Audre along. Audre as narrator tells us, "Being the youngest in a West Indian family had many privileges but no rights" (35).

> Both of my parents gave us to believe that they had the whole world in the palms of their hands for the most part, and if we three girls acted correctly—meaning working hard and doing as we were told—we could have the whole world in the palms of our hands also. It was a very confusing way to grow up, enhanced by the insularity of our family. Whatever went wrong in our lives was because our parents had decided that was best. Whatever went right was because our parents had decided that was the way it was going to be. Any doubts as to the reality of that situation were rapidly and summarily put down as small but intolerable rebellions against divine authority. (18)

It is made clear that acting and thinking alone are unforgivable acts of individuation. There is no question of being an "individual" with "rights" within the context of the family. Parental rules and wisdom structure both the appropriate use of space *and* ideas within the home environment. As a child, however, Audre has no desires for privacy.

She sleeps in her parents' bedroom and is jealous of the fact that her sisters, Phylis and Helen, "led a magical and charmed existence down the hall in their room" (43). When her family goes on vacation, the high point of the trip for Audre is being allowed to sleep between her sisters. "I was so enchanted with the idea of sharing a bed with them" (45). While sleeping between them during the vacation, Audre discovers their secret. They tell each other stories at night. Even young Audre recognizes this for the covert transgression that it is: the right to individual voice. "And too besides, I'm goin' to tell [Mommy] what among-you doing in bed every night!" (46).

Predictably, therefore, when Audre seeks separation from her family it takes the form of an increased desire for privacy and periodic verbal outbursts. She is the exceptional Black student (in predominantly white school contexts) who believes she is just like everyone else. She begins to acquire a language of individual rights. She is surprised when her family is denied ice cream in an all-white ice cream parlor in Washington, D.C. She thinks it is unfair when she loses the election for class president. Her mother's response to this is to beat her for her foolish belief that she would be treated fairly within a racist school system: "If I told you once I have told you a hundred times, don't chase yourself behind these people, haven't I? What kind of ninny raise up here to think those good-for-nothing white piss-jets would pass over some little jacabat girl to elect you anything?" (64–65).

As far as her mother is concerned, Audre is supposed to take the formal education her school offers but not seek self-affirmation within this context. This is like the advice that Tantie gives Tee in *Crick Crack Monkey* when, being forced to enroll her in the elementary school of the condescending Mrs. Hinds, she tell Tee, "Remember you going to learn *book* do' let them put no blasted shit in yu head" (23). By sophomore year of high school, however, Audre is seeking affirmation entirely within her school environment, while her relations with her family resemble "a West Indian version of the Second World War" (82). She desperately desires privacy and discovers that she can be alone after midnight when everyone is asleep: "I had discovered a new world called voluntary aloneness. After midnight was the only time it was possible in my family's house. At any other time, a closed door was still considered an insult. My mother viewed any act of separation from her as an indictment of her authority. . . . A request for privacy was treated like an outright act of insolence for which the punishment was swift and painful" (83).

Audre Lorde and Paule Marshall

Here we see an Audre who is now feeling "entitled" and is enraged by her parents' infringement on her "rights." She also begins to fault her parents for not displaying affection toward her in a more traditional manner. She believes that their disciplinarian household is an indication of their lack of love. She claims that her "heart ached and ached for something [she] could not name" (85). It is interesting that her acquisition of this unspeakable pain parallels her movement into individuation and her separation from her family. Audre leaves home after her best friend commits suicide and her father refuses to let her white boyfriend into the house. Determined to prove her individuality, she spends Christmas alone and suffers through an illegal abortion in isolation rather than return. From this point on, the narrative shifts substantially and there is next to no mention of Audre's family throughout the rest of the work. Instead we are immersed in the world of predominantly white lesbian relationships that Audre explores.

Audre's second experience of Black community is in the family of her first female lover Ginger, as well as at the factory she works at in Connecticut. Ginger, who is Black, demonstrates a knowledge of Black history that Audre does not share. Audre's ignorance functions as a reminder to the reader of the predominantly white social and cultural world Audre occupied in high school and in the period immediately after she left her parents' house. In Ginger's Black home space, where Audre temporarily lives, Audre is still exercising her individualism. It takes the form here of selfishness, as when she greedily eats three servings of mashed potatoes in a house with many mouths to feed. She also uses hot water prodigally while bathing and is reprimanded for it by Ginger's mother, Cora. On the other hand, Cora is well aware of Ginger and Audre's passionate, nightly activities. Interestingly enough, while Cora makes it clear that she expects Ginger, who is divorced, to remarry, she seems rather unperturbed by Ginger's relationship with Audre. At the same time, it is abundantly clear that Cora's investment in procuring Ginger a husband is bound up in issues of financial security rather than emotional happiness: " 'Friends are nice, but marriage is marriage,' she said to me one night as she helped me make a skirt on her machine, and I wondered why Ginger had asked me over and then gone to the movies with a friend of Cora's from American Cyanimid. 'And when she gets home don't be thumping that bed all night, neither, because it's late already and you girls have to work tomorrow' " (142). This passage is important since it indicates, at least within the context of the Black space of Ginger's home, that any objections to her sexual relations with Audre are not premised on moral outrage and disgust.

In the factory, Audre continues with her individual commitments to no-one but herself. She cheats to earn quick bonus money to go to Mexico, alienating her coworkers since she risks increasing the pace of the assembly line. After she leaves for Mexico, she fills the narrative with exhaustive descriptions of her lovers and her feelings for them. This contrasts sharply with the absence of any substantial reference to her family, a discrepancy that becomes especially noticeable after the sudden and brief mention of the death of her father after the end of her relationship with Ginger. The narrative voice becomes increasingly unreliable as the story progresses, making it apparent that Audre's alienation from her family and alienation from self are connected.

Erin G. Carlston comments on these issues of identity in her article "*Zami* and the Politics of Plural Identity":

> Audre Lorde's *Zami: A New Spelling of My Name* . . . is an early, important attempt to articulate a politics of location in a work of fiction. Though similar in many of its premises to Bernice Johnson Reagon's groundbreaking "Coalition Politics: Turning the Century," *Zami* seems rather more complicated and subtle than Reagon's piece, particularly in its treatment of "identity." To the idea of coalition between individuals Lorde adds the concept of "positionality," or individual identity as an unstable construct, constantly (re)produced both by and within the social matrix, and by the subject's conscious creation of her self. In this regard Lorde prefigures more recent theoretical work by writers like Chandra Mohanty, Gayatri Spivak, and Trinh Minh-ha, while presenting a unique vision of the construction and uses of subjectivity. (226)

It is the posture of racial identity in Lorde's text that Carlston isolates as indicative of a "revolutionary" identity politics. She says, "I will try to show [how Lorde] describes her relation to her racial identity in such a way as to problematize blackness as a wholly natural or self-evident category" (227). Reducing racial identity to skin color, Carlston argues, "Skin color may be given, but race is constructed, both by a racist society and by the individual reacting to that society. If Audre's racial identity seems self-evident . . . her light-skinned mother's is not" (227). When Carlston states that race is a construction, her proof seems to be in the contrast between Audre's mother's light-skinned complexion and Audre's somewhat darker skin tones. This instability, at the level of skin color, is viewed by Carlston as a factor that positively destabilizes racial categories and exposes the constructedness of race within the text. In absence of a framework for articulating "race" as part and parcel of cultural identity, Carlston is boxed into a two-dimensional construct of race and how it functions within the text. In fact, in *Zami*, as in all the texts discussed, race is intimately bound up with the cultural. After Audre leaves home, her Black "cultural" identity is replaced by a self-deceptive "get mine" individualism, despite the fact that her skin color remains the same. As her white socialization increases during her time in high school and after, she experiences her Black family as a burden not worth dealing with. In pursuit of her newfound freedom and lesbian identity, she jeopardizes the jobs of her coworkers as well as her own health. She disregards safety measures and exposes herself to radiation in order to increase her productivity and profit, so that she can get to Mexico quickly. While Blackness *is* problematized in Lorde's text, contrary to Carlston's analysis, what is revealed is the problematic nature of young adult Audre's cultural politics, rather than the reader being provided with a progressive cultural praxis worth emulating.

On the other hand, ironically, Carlston is critical of the text's representation of lesbian community. She states, "Lesbianism is made to seem self-evident, and manifested in some of her earliest childhood experiences. That this is an artifice, however, part of Lorde's mythologizing of her own life, is suggested by the fact that there is neither an awareness on young Audre's part of the significance of those experiences, nor a narrator's intervention to explain it to us" (229). Carlston substantiates what Anna Wilson argues in "Lorde and the African-American Tradition: When the Family Is Not Enough" when Wilson states:

> In the absence of a Black tradition, then, Lorde's biomythography *Zami* initially constructs a lesbian existence that has needs and features in common with the lesbian myth produced by white Anglo-American novelists. Her sexual coming out is described within a series of metaphors for recognition familiar from that tradition: making love is "like coming home to a joy I was meant for"; the act of lesbian sex is naturalised through being presented as a return to an original knowledge that the protagonist has temporarily forgotten. . . . This is a

country of body rather than people. Audre's community as a young lesbian in New York is defined as sexuality, and it is a community that attempts the utopian separation and newness of lesbian nation: "We were reinventing the world together"; "we had no patterns to follow, except our own needs and our own unthought-out dreams." (81)

Wilson characterizes Lorde's depiction of the character Audre's lesbianism as self-evident and as an unself-conscious continuation of a culturally white, Anglo-American genealogy of lesbian identity. But Wilson goes further. She maintains that Audre's membership within the (white) lesbian community "is purchased at the price of non-recognition of Blackness; Lorde repeatedly describes Audre's 'invisibility' to the white lesbian community as Black; she is admitted *only* under the assumption of sameness" (81, italics mine). As *Zami* progresses, the text is replete with examples of this:

> Pauli turned to me. "Hey, that's a great tan you have there. I didn't know Negroes got tans." Her broad smile was intended to announce the remark as a joke.
>
> My usual defense in such situations was to *ignore the overtones, to let it go.* But Dottie Daws, probably out of her own nervousness at Pauli's reference to the unmentionable, would not let the matter drop. Raved on and on about my great tan. . . . I grew tired and then shakingly furious. . . . "How come you never make so much over my natural tan most days, Dottie Daws; how come?" (223, italics mine)

Training herself to "ignore the overtones" of these situations (situations that are indicative of the white lesbian community's complicity, despite its marginalization, in the larger racial/imperial structures organizing the nation) as the text draws to a close, Audre grows tired of responding in this way and her self-deception become less effective as the incidents of racism increase.

Carlston argues that the proof that Audre has a positively disruptive identity in *Zami* lies in the fact that this identity is not reducible to any one difference. To substantiate this point, she cites the famous "house of difference" passage from the text: "Being women together was not enough. We were different. Being gay-girls together was not enough. We were different. Being Black together was not enough. We were different. Being Black women together was not enough. We were different. Being Black dykes together was not enough. We were different. . . . we could not afford to settle for one easy definition, one narrow individuation of self" (226).

Carlston then states, "And so her constant, uncomfortable aware-ness of her ineradicable difference within any given situation or group becomes, eventually, a consciously articulated loyalty to difference itself" (232). Carlston closes her article by maintaining that Audre's loyalties are with no one particular group or identity and that it is this investment in an "internal coalition" that, in the final instance, is constitutive of Lorde's "most radical, insightful contribution to the whole notion of identity politics" (233). Strangely, what Carlston ul-timately identifies as the radical nature of the identity imagined bears a stunning resemblance to the basic tenets of an individualism that need not be accountable for too long to anything or anyone. This debunks the notion of radical coalition politics entirely. By contrast Wilson draws opposing conclusions with regard to Lorde's "house of difference" when she states:

> The "uncharted territory" that she finds in trying to discover new ways of relating in "a new world of women" is not just uncharted but inaccessible: there is no pathway for the Black lesbian nation. It is from this experience that Lorde constructs the "house of difference" that she finally articulates as "our place"; it is a refusal of the aspira-tions to unity that lesbian nation encodes. The "house of difference," then, is a movement away from otherworldliness. It accepts the inev-itability of a material world where class, race, gender all continue to exist. It is therefore, a step back towards acknowledging the necessity of reasserting ties of identity with the Black community. (82)

What Carlston views as a positive escape into an identity that has no hard and fast obligations to any one group, Wilson reads as Audre's slow recognition that "hierarchised differences" exist and with that recognition comes not just responsibility, but an interest and invest-ment in reestablishing ties with the Black community (82). Ulti-mately, while Carlston views Lorde's *Zami* as a more sophisticated version of the coalition politics of Bernice Johnson Reagon, Wilson's reading of *Zami* shows that as the text progresses Audre moves away from a sort of "internal coalition" without definite commitments to any one thing toward the more concrete coalition-based politics repre-sented by Reagon. The way that Lorde ends *Zami* appears to give more credence to Wilson's conclusions about the novel than to Carlston's.

The last few pages of the novel and its epilogue can be interpreted as a repudiation of the "self" that occupies the majority of the narrative. When Audre's relationship with her white girlfriend Muriel ends, at

Clear Word and Third Sight

the moment that she finally accepts this as a reality, she has a transformational experience as she boards a bus. She hears a choir, in her
head, singing "the last chorus of an old spiritual of hope [and she] . . .
suddenly stood upon a hill . . . hearing the sky fill with a new spelling
of [her] own name" (238–39). For the next ten pages until the novel's
close, Audre's world is an exclusively Black lesbian one. The text
closes with the epilogue, significant for its attempt to reconcile her
sexual identity with her mother and her mother's cultural identity.
This latter move, which Carlston maintains is the most problematic
aspect of Lorde's book ("Lorde mythologizes her sexual identity . . .
deliberately ahistoricizing lesbianism to link it with her maternal/
ethnic heritage," 227) is, in actuality, the most radical move in the text.

Afro-Caribbean critic Carole Boyce Davies identifies Lorde's *Zami*
as the work that definitively highlights the Caribbean aspects of her
identity. Lorde, like Paule Marshall, was born of Caribbean parents
and raised in New York City; but unlike Marshall, whose Caribbean
identity was claimed early on with her publication of *Brown Girl,
Brownstones* (1959), Lorde's defining work *Zami* wasn't published until 1982. "This marked her identification as an Afro-Caribbean writer.
Although her explicit lesbian and Black identification had been clear
in her earlier works, this text functions as a re-/clamation (a biomythography as she calls it) of her many selves, living in the 'house of
difference' " (116). Davies further maintains that the term "zami" "is a
bold epigraph to the work," which "allows [Lorde], like Michelle Cliff,
to enter the process of 'Claiming an Identity' she was taught to despise" (120). The reappropriation of the term "zami" can function at
this level since, within the culture of Lorde's matrilineal Carriacou
heritage, the word is frequently an insult "invoked to control women's
power" (120).[1] As Davies, points out, "[T]he recognition of *zami*, love
between women, as a submerged conceptual and physical reality of
Caribbean life, is a critical factor in that reintegration of Caribbean self
and its broader acceptance" (117).

Still, it needs to be pointed out that Lorde's reappropriation of zami
goes much further than Jamaican writer Michelle Cliff's notion of
"claiming an identity they taught [her] to despise" (from the title of her
essay "Claiming an Identity They Taught Me to Despise"). Critic Françoise Lionnet argues instead that "*Zami* constitutes the condition of
possibility of Michelle Cliff's novel *Abeng*" and that "*Zami* is a prominent example of the kind of revisionist mythmaking that a writer
engages in when she does not feel legitimated and validated by a long

tradition of self-conscious self-exploration" (322). While Lionnet's point is well taken with regard to the latent, autobiographical lesbian theme of *Abeng*, the reclaimings at stake in the use of the term "zami" are quite different from those at stake with "abeng." Cliff's appropriation of the abeng (the conch shell used by the maroons to communicate with one another, and by slave owners to call slaves to work) does *not* highlight the intersection of race, sexuality, and gender as does the term "zami." Rather, "abeng" highlights the violence of white oppressor culture as well as the resistance of Black oppressed culture as the two legacies that the main character in *Abeng*, Clare Savage, must acknowledge and choose between. As Cliff herself acknowledges in both an interview and the essay "Claiming an Identity," the identity she was taught to despise was Black and Jamaican. Lorde's reappropriation of "zami" as insult is a reappropriation of a term in which "deviant sexuality," Blackness, and femaleness are inseparable within the Caribbean context.[2] Thus what Lorde appropriates is a term whose degraded origins refer to an already Africanized Caribbean sexual identity. Although Cliff states that in "Claiming an Identity" she was "demanding—to be a whole person" and this wholeness would necessarily include her own lesbian identity, this aspect of her identity is not systematically highlighted. When "lesbian" identity is given voice in Cliff's work, it is not articulated from or situated within an explicitly Afro-Caribbean framework.[3] Even though the reclamation made manifest under the name "zami" occurs at the very last moment in Lorde's text, she still attempts to root it within the linguistic and cultural mores of the people she is from.

Transitional Utterance and Recuperative "Voice"

What happens to a dream deferred?

Does it dry up

like a raisin in the sun?

Or fester like a sore—

And then run?

Does it stink like rotten meat?

Or crust and sugar over—

Clear Word and Third Sight

like a syrupy sweet?

Maybe it just sags

like a heavy load.

Or does it explode?

—LANGSTON HUGHES, "A Dream Deferred"

In his 1980 interview with René Depestre, Césaire's three-point definition of negritude anticipates Audre Lorde's intellectual trajectory
and consciousness. He describes negritude first as a concrete coming-
to-consciousness premised on pride in collective Black identity. Second, it is the result of the psychological repression of a European
colonial order that denies both the humanity and cultural particularity
of Black peoples. Third, it is an affirmation of international Black
solidarity within the context of political struggle.[4] The first two parts of
Césaire's definition apply to Lorde's recognition, in her early poetry
and fiction, of the debilitating effects of racism on the Black subject in
the United States. The poetics of loss that permeate her early work are
a manifest example of the alienation experienced by the U.S. subject
of "double consciousness" desperately invested in claiming, "I too
sing America."[5] The loss, therefore, can be interpreted as the constant
frustration this subject feels at being excluded from full participation
in the "inalienable rights" theoretically accorded all American cit-
izens. As I argue, in *Zami,* the more Audre the narrator is seduced by
a discourse of individual rights, the more alienated she becomes from
her Caribbean family and herself. Audre's movement at the end of
Zami toward an Afro-Caribbean identity is a movement toward the
collective.

This movement fits in with another aspect of Césaire's account of
negritude: his belief that "Black culture is not only a thing of the past"
(Depestre, *Bonjour et adieu,* 78). It moves Blacks away from the individualism produced by miseducation back toward the collective cultural norms of the people they are descended from. The affirmation of
a transnational Black solidarity applies to both Lorde's later work and
her political activism. Her renunciation of an earlier poetics of loss is
accompanied by her renunciation of "America." Never invested in
organizing across differences solely within the context of the United
States, Lorde consistently introduced the struggles of third world
women and people in general into her political agendas. She was one

of the founders of Kitchen Table: Women of Color Press, as well as a founder of Sisterhood in Support of Sisters in South Africa.

Lorde's movement in later life toward an activism mobilized by her poetry is also infused with Senghor's legacy. Her essay "Uses of the Erotic: The Erotic as Power" lays out and encapsulates the paradigm that guides her later work. In this essay she states, "It has become fashionable to separate the spiritual (psychic and emotional) from the political, to see them as contradictory or antithetical. 'What do you mean, a poetic revolutionary a meditating gunrunner?' . . . The dichotomy between the spiritual and the political is also false, resulting from an incomplete attention to our erotic knowledge. For the bridge which connects them is formed by the erotic" (*Sister Outsider,* 56). Lorde's notion of the "erotic" encapsulates the recuperative poetics that dominates her later writings. It is the equivalent of the notion of restitution (communal decolonization and psychospiritual renewal) that permeates the novels of Simone Schwarz-Bart. Further, her notion of the erotic as "an assertion of the lifeforce of women" (*Sister Outsider,* 55) resonates with Senghor's use of the notion of life force to describe an African cultural dynamic.

Although Lorde connects her notion of the erotic to a specifically female sensibility, her articulation of this concept seems like the diaspora permutation of an African cultural legacy. Her book of poetry *The Black Unicorn* systematically splices references from an ancient African spiritual-cultural context into situations related to contemporary diaspora experiences. Originally published in 1978, the same year she underwent a "modified radical mastectomy for breast cancer," *The Black Unicorn,* like *Zami,* functions as a transitional work within Lorde's oeuvre.[6] However, this astounding collection of poems is much more than a movement away from an earlier poetics of loss. Its breakaway engagement with both a "new world" poetics and African cosmology prompted R. B. Stepto, in his analysis of the book, to state:

> While *The Black Unicorn* is unquestionably a personal triumph for Lorde in terms of the development of her canon, it is also an event in contemporary letters. This is a bold claim but one worth making precisely because, as we see in the first nine poems, Lorde appears to be the only North American poet other than Jay Wright who is sufficiently immersed in West African religion, culture and art (and blessed with poetic talent!) to reach beyond a kind of middling poem that merely quantifies "blackness" through offhand reference to Afri-

can gods and traditions. What Lorde and Wright share, beyond their abilities to create a fresh, New World Art out of ancient Old World lore, is a voice or an *idea* of a voice that is essentially African in that it is communal, historiographical, archival, and prophetic *as well as* personal in ways that we commonly associate with the African *griot, dyeli,* and tellers of *nganos* and other oral tales. However, while Wright's voice may be said to embody what is masculine in various West African cultures and cosmologies, Lorde's voice is decidedly and magnificently feminine. ("The Phenomenal Woman," 315–16)

Divided into four sections with a glossary of African cosmological terminology at the end, *The Black Unicorn* is an attempt to link ancient science with the contemporary reality of struggle on the part of the children who were sent away. The attempt to build a new mythology out of something old and "Black" is evidenced by the first and title poem, "The Black Unicorn":

> The black unicorn is greedy.
> The black unicorn is impatient.
> The black was mistaken
> for a shadow
> or symbol
> and taken
> through a cold country
> where mist painted mockeries
> of my fury.
> It is not on her lap where the horn rests
> but deep in her moonpit
> growing.
> The black unicorn is restless
> the black unicorn is unrelenting
> the black unicorn is not
> free.
> (3)

Dislodging readers from a linear Western interpretive perspective and disorienting them by changing the narrative voice constantly, as in many of the poems in the collection, Lorde's title poem opens the book with an ambiguity that is nothing if not complex. The black unicorn seems to be both male and female, at once real and yet larger than life. He/she has been wronged, "mistaken / for a shadow / or symbol / and taken / through a cold country," and is now ready for payback: "The black unicorn is unrelenting / the black unicorn is not / free." The duality associated with an African philosophical worldview is carried forth in the poems from the first section of the book. We see this in "From the House of Yemanjá," for example, in lines such as,

> I am the sun and moon and forever hungry
> . . . I bear two women upon my back
> one dark and rich and hidden
> in the ivory hungers of the other.
> (6)

The words speak to an implicit drive toward balance, both in the forces of nature and within the individual. At the same time, the dark woman hidden in the "ivory hunger of the other" brings to mind the colonial "black skin, white masks" dilemma that haunts the diaspora subject.

The poem "Dahomey" reads like the poetic utterance of an ancient deity, using references to "Abomey," "Seboulisa," and (later in the poem) "Eshu," and "Shango":

> It was in Abomey that I felt
> the full blood of my fathers' wars
> and where I found my mother
> Seboulisa
> standing with outstretched palms hip high
> one breast eaten away by worms of sorrow.
> (10)

Starting with a reference to Abomey, the center of cultural power in Dahomey, the narrator refers to a neglected Seboulisa, who stands in here for "Mawulisa." Mawulisa is "the Dahomean female-male, sky-goddess-god principle, sometimes called the first inseparable twins of the Creator of the Universe" (*Black Unicorn*, 120). The poem ends with richly symbolic and complex imagery:

> Bearing two drums on my head I speak
> whatever language is needed
> to sharpen the knives of my tongue
> the snake is aware although sleeping
> under my blood
> since I am woman whether or not
> you are against me
> I will braid my hair

Clear Word and Third Sight

even / in the seasons of rain.
(11)

These lines imply that she will speak the language of whatever orisa communicates with her through the drums and that she will make herself a warrior whose words are drawn from deep ancestral mother tongues.

In the poem that immediately follows "Dahomey," entitled "125th Street and Abomey," the narrator brings together the old world and the new: "Head bent, walking through snow / I see you Seboulisa / printed inside the back of my head" (12). The snow references the "New World" environment temporally and spatially removed from the continent of Africa. "Seboulisa" is now something deep in the subconscious, not readily accessible, but still a part of the identity. The end of the first stanza of this poem states, "give me the woman strength / of tongue in this cold season." It suggests that this "new world" poet is calling upon this female deity for forgiveness and protection in the harsh diaspora winter. The next stanza reads, in part:

Half earth and time splits us apart . . .
Seboulisa mother goddess with one breast
eaten away by worms of sorrow and loss
see me now
your severed daughter
laughing our name into echo
all the world shall remember.
(13)

The first line is a literal reference to the spatial and temporal separation of this diaspora sister from her ancient ancestral line. The echo from the previous poem in the collection, with its reference to the mother goddess's one breast, and the naming of the poetic speaker in this poem as the goddess's "severed daughter," cannot but resonate for the knowledgeable reader with images of Lorde's mastectomy transforming itself into a powerful legacy of survival.

The first poem in part 2 of the collection, "Harriet," comes back to everyday struggles in the diaspora with its opening lines:

Harriet there was always somebody calling us crazy
or mean or stuck-up or evil or black
or black
and we were nappy girls quick as cuttlefish

scurrying for cover
trying to speak trying to speak
trying to speak.
(21)

Following the richly empowered, almost deified voice of the book's
first section, this section's opening "trying to speak trying to speak/
trying to speak" is difficult not to read as a loss of voice connected to a
loss of culture and ancestry. The poem ends symbolically with the
lines, "Harriet Harriet / what name shall we call our selves now / our
mother is gone."

The poems in the third section end with "Bicentennial Poem
#21,000,000," which is a lamentation concerning the loss of land:

I know/the boundaries of my nation lie within myself
but when I see old movies
of the final liberation of Paris
with french tanks rumbling over land that is their own again.
My eyes fill up with muddy tears
that have no earth to fall upon.
(90)

The fourth and final section of *The Black Unicorn* contains the poem
"Power," one of the most startling poems in the collection. This poem,
like Langston Hughes's "A Dream Deferred," is almost an inversion
of Lorde's notion of the power of the erotic. Or, rather, it is a tribute to
the potential misuses of this kind of erotic power, an example of the
rage that results when previously internalized psychic violence is ex-
ternalized without collective recuperative possibilities:

The difference between poetry and rhetoric
is being
ready to kill
yourself
instead of your children.
(108–9)

In this stark opening to the poem, Lorde establishes the subject:
violence in the context of communal survival. In "Uses of the Erotic"
she states, "The aim of each thing which we do is to make our lives
and the lives of our children richer and more possible" (*Sister Outsider*,
55). For Lorde, survival is always a collective and generational issue. It
is no longer a question of the survival of the individual, as it was for

young Audre working in the factory in *Zami*. The idea in the opening stanza, of killing oneself instead of one's children, implies a decision to sacrifice oneself for the larger good, thereby proving that one is no longer thinking like an individual.

The second stanza of "Power" develops this idea in a dramatic way:

> I am trapped on a desert of raw gunshot wounds
> and a dead child dragging his shattered black
> face off the edge of my sleep
> blood from his punctured cheeks and shoulders
> is the only liquid for miles and my stomach
> churns at the imagined taste while
> my mouth splits into dry lips
> without loyalty or reason
> thirsting for the wetness of his blood
> as it sinks into the whiteness
> of the desert where I am lost
> without imagery or magic
> trying to make power out of hatred and destruction
> trying to heal my dying son with kisses
> only the sun will bleach his bones quicker.

We have here what appears to be a dream-sequence depiction of the problems with violence and resistance in the diaspora. The dead boy is imagined to be the narrator's son and the narrator herself is faced with the choice of drinking the son's blood "without loyalty or reason." The "I" in this stanza, the "mother" of the son, is without recuperative alternatives. Made into a vampire by imperialistic violence, "she" is trying to figure out how to salvage her spirit in a "desert where [she] is lost without imagery or magic," "[t]rying to make power out of hatred and destruction." In the next stanza, the source of this rage is revealed:

> The policeman who shot down a 10-year-old in queens
> stood over the boy with his cop shoes in childish blood
> and a voice said "Die you little motherfucker" and
> there are tapes to prove that. At his trial
> this policeman said in his own defense
> "I didn't notice the size or nothing else
> only the color." and
> there are tapes to prove that, too.
> (108)

Audre Lorde and Paule Marshall

In her interview with Adrienne Rich, Lorde describes this poem as inspired by the murder by police of ten-year-old Clifford Glover and the jury's subsequent acquittal of the officer (Lorde, *Sister Outsider*, 107). The jury contained one Black woman. Moving back and forth between the facts of the actual case and Lorde's fictive attempt to imagine what it would be like to be that one woman, the poem is carried along by the force of this imagery. The narrator adopts a journalistic tone, describing in straightforward terms the injustice that has transpired. But by this stanza there is no ambiguity about the child and the mother's being any woman and any child. The stanza makes the politics of the situation historically specific and very clear to the reader: this is a poem about white police brutality and violence against the Black community in the United States:

> Today that 37-year-old white man with 13 years of police forcing
> has been set free
> by 11 white men who said they were satisfied
> justice had been done
> and one black woman who said
> "They convinced me" meaning
> they had dragged her 4' 10" black woman's frame
> over the hot coals of four centuries of white male approval
> until she let go the first real power she ever had
> and lined her own womb with cement
> to make a graveyard for our children.
> (109)

The narrator moves between a rhetorical and poetic voice, making it clear that the police murder of the boy is part of centuries of violence. This is the case whether it takes the form of police forcing, or white intimidation, or coercing individual Blacks to sanction violence that perpetuates communal genocide, or the killing of one's children. The description of the Black female juror as "lin[ing] her own womb with cement to make a graveyard for our children" links state-sanctioned white violence to individual "Black" acts of complicity.

> I have not been able to touch the destruction within me.
> But unless I learn to use
> the difference between poetry and rhetoric
> my power too will run corrupt as poisonous mold
> or lie limp and useless as an unconnected wire
> and one day I will take my teenaged plug

Clear Word and Third Sight

and connect it to the nearest socket
raping an 85-year-old white woman
who is somebody's mother
and as I beat her senseless and set a torch to her bed
a greek chorus will be singing in 3/4 time
"Poor thing. She never hurt a soul. What beasts they are"
(108–9)

In the final stanza of "Power," the poetic "I" of the first stanza resurfaces. Here, the difference between poetry and rhetoric is the difference between the productive uses of the "erotic" (a cause calling the "meditating gunrunner" into action) and what happens to a "dream deferred" ("Maybe it just sags like a heavy load / Or does it explode?"). The message of the final stanza is to not simply demonize violence but to highlight the problem of misdirected rage and speculate about what historical forces create it. Two competing notions of power emerge from this poem, notions that ironically have a kind of parallel in African versus European cultural legacies. One notion of power is related to dominance, violence, and the survival of the (fittest) individual, while the other notion is connected to communal survival, justice, and individual self-sacrifice. In the tradition of the African griot, Lorde equates poetry with the internal "power" to be true to one's deepest ethical and spiritual impulses and values. Rhetoric, on the other hand, is equated with external hierarchical power, the manipulation of historical truth, unaccountability, and the perpetuation of violence.

Lorde ends this poetic collection with the poem "Solstice," the last lines of which read:

may I never lose
that terror/that keeps me brave
May I owe nothing
that I cannot repay.
(118)

In a companion piece to this statement, Lorde tell us: "As women we were raised to fear. If I cannot banish fear completely, I can learn to count with it less. For then fear becomes not a tyrant against which I waste my energy fighting, but a companion, not particularly desirable, yet one whose knowledge can be useful" (*Cancer Journals,* 15).

Paule Marshall's *Praisesong for the Widow* charts the transformation of consciousness of Avey "Avatara" Johnson from a contrite older woman who has become materialistic, self-contained, and spiritually numb into a woman born anew after a series of unsettling and enlightening experiences. In a symbolic and significant way, Marshall's *Praisesong* continues the process opened up at the end of Lorde's *Zami*. The new "spelling of the name" articulated at the end of Lorde's text is linked to Lorde's mother's homeland on the tiny island of Carriacou off the coast of Grenada. Lorde's text ends with Audre the narrator beginning to focus her energies in the direction of her mother's homeland, and in Marshall's *Praisesong for the Widow*, Avey's transformation is set in motion when she undertakes the physical and spiritual journey to an ancestral ceremony in Carriacou.

Praisesong for the Widow is divided into four sections with a combined total of twenty chapters. The opening section, "Runagate," charts a day in the life of Avey Johnson. It begins with her sudden departure early in the morning from the luxurious cruise ship the *Bianca Pride,* and it ends with her arrival later that evening at a hotel in Grenada where she plans to spend just one night before returning to New York. In linear time, the present-day "action" of the novel takes place over the course of five days; in reality, however the events represented in the story cover a lifetime.

A dream is what instigates Avey's cycle of transformation; a dream makes her leave the cruise ship. The dream serves a multipurpose function within the context of the novel. Marshall uses it as a point of departure to flash back to Avey's childhood and her summers spent with her great-aunt Cuney in the South. Marshall's references to slavery, an oral tale about the Ibo, and the cultural practice known as the Ring Shout make it apparant that it is in the South that the memory of Africa is most strongly retained among the Black U.S. population. At the thematic level, Marshall's use of the dream as catalyst for Avey's awakening privileges African cultural and spiritual practices in yet another way. As Rudolph Eastman and Maureen Warner-Lewis observe, participation in "the Orisha faith [can be] mediated through dreams, visions and divination" ("Forms of African Spirituality," 406). The dream, therefore, is significant within various traditional African contexts as a space in which communication from the other side occurs.

Avey's dream is about her Great-aunt Cuney, a female ancestor who was the most influential presence in her early life. Not only did she visit her aunt every summer from the time she was seven, but "there was the story of how [her aunt] had sent word months before her birth that it would be a girl and she was to be called after her grandmother who had come to [her aunt] in a dream with the news" (*Praisesong*, 42). Yoruba oral tradition speaks of the spirit of an ancestor returning generations later in the form of another child. In *Crick Crack Monkey*, Tee tells the reader, "Ma said that I was her grandmother come back again. . . . She couldn't remember her grandmother's true-true name. But Tee was growing into her grandmother again, her spirit was in me. They'd never bent down her spirit and she would come back and come back and come back" (19). In Julie Dash's film *Daughters of the Dust*, the great-grandmother Nana Peazant tells her son-in-law, Eli, "There ain't no child that wasn't sent to you by the ancestors." She says this in response to his anxiety that his pregnant wife's child is a product of white rape rather than their love. So Marshall, with the use of the dream, participates in the *diasporic* representation of ancestral return, a concept that is traceable back to continental beliefs. The power of the word is also significant here. Avey is named Avatara after this ancestral grandmother figure. She has a destiny that she can tangibly claim, unlike Tee, whose grandmother's true-true name is never remembered. Further, since the dream inaugurates Avey's re-birth and awakening, it harks back to the forms of the Orisha faith: as Eastman and Warner-Lewis observe, initiation into the Orisha faith involves not only "dreams and visions" but also "symbolic death and rebirth" (406).

While aboard the *Bianca Pride*, Avey dreams that her father's great-aunt Cuney came to her one evening while she was dressed in all her finery on her way to a function with her late husband, Jerome John-son, formerly known as Jay. They were living in their house in White Plains, New York, a house that they struggled for some twenty years to attain. In the dream Great-aunt Cuney wants to take Avey back to "Ibo landing," a place she took her frequently as a child in order to tell her the story about the Ibos arriving as slaves and then walking on water back to Africa. In the dream, Avey is appalled that her great-aunt expects her, in all her finery, to go traipsing across the marsh. A physical fight ensues between the two women, and Avey feels literally sore when she awakens the next morning.

The tale of the Ibo within the context of the story is yet another significant diaspora trope that Marshall utilizes. This story of Africans who arrived, enslaved, and then walked on water, drowned, or flew back to Africa has had constant incarnations within African diaspora cultural representation. In the U.S. context, in Toni Morrison's *Song of Solomon*, Milkman discovers that his forefather Solomon is one of the flying Africans. In the Caribbean context, the opening section of Earl Lovelace's *Salt* utilizes both the concept of the flying African and the importance of dreams in the account of "Jo-Jo's great-grandfather, Guinea John [who] . . . put two corn cobs under his armpits and flew away to Africa, taking with him the mysteries of levitation and flight." Guinea John later appears in a dream to his eldest daughter "Titi" to explain his abrupt departure (3–4). In Julie Dash's *Daughters of the Dust*, set on the Gullah islands off the coast of the Carolinas, Dash as filmmaker takes her version of the Ibo tale from Marshall's novel when the character Eula goes to the edge of the water and tells the tale to her unborn child.

Wendy Walters's significant essay, "One of Dese Mornings, Bright and Fair, / Take My Wings and Cleave De Air: The Legend of the Flying Africans and Diasporic Consciousness," amply demonstrates the significance of this tale in the diaspora context. Arguing that the Black female novel has become the realm of folkloric transformation, Walters's essay is also an important compilation of the wide distribution of the flying African trope, citing variations of the tale from the United States, Cuba, and Jamaica. What appears initially to be a "tale" calculated to lift the spirits of an oppressed people takes on a startling "alternate consciousness" reality in Walters's account. Walters tells us that there were twenty-seven variants of the tale in South Carolina, and in many narratives collected from formerly enslaved persons, the informants insisted on having been eye-witnesses to the events described. One of the most interesting informants was a former Cuban slave called Esteban Montejo, who stated that flying Africans came from a particular Congolese tribe who flew so frequently that the Spanish stopped importing them.

In *Praisesong for the Widow* the flying African tale has substantial significance. Avey's great-aunt Cuney is really her father's great-aunt. This means she is Avey's great-great-aunt. The tale she tells Avey was told her by her own grandmother, who may have been Avey's great-great-great-great-grandmother. The significance of this lineage to the context of the story is that it shows Marshall's conscientious attempt, yet again, to connect the diaspora with the continent. Aunt Cuney's grandmother is foregrounded as not just telling a fictional folktale passed down to her through her family, but telling a story about an event that she actually witnessed during the time of slavery. In Great-aunt Cuney's accounting the tale goes as follows:

> It was here that they brought 'em. They taken 'em out of the boats right here where we's standing. . . . And the minute those Ibos was brought on shore they just stopped, my gran' said, and taken a look around. A good long look. Not saying a word. . . . And they seen things that day that you and me don't have the power to see. 'Cause those pure-born Africans was peoples my gran' said could see in more ways than one. The kind can tell you 'bout things happened long before they was born and things to come long after they's dead. Well, they seen everything that was to happen 'round here that day. The slavery time and the war my gran' always talked about, the 'mancipation and everything after that right on up to the hard times today. Those Ibos didn't miss a thing. . . . And when they got through sizing up the place real good and seen what was to come, they turned, my gran' said, and looked at the white folks what brought 'em here. . . . And when they got through studying 'em, when they *knew* just from looking at 'em how those folks was gonna do . . . they just turned, my gran' said, all of 'em . . . and walked on back down to the edge of the river here. . . . Left the white folk standin' back here with they mouth hung open and they taken off down the river on foot. . . . And they was singing by then, so my gran' said. . . . [T]hey sounded like they was having such a good time my gran' declared she just picked herself up and took off after 'em. In her mind. Her body she always usta say might be in Tatem but her mind, her mind was long gone with the Ibo. (37–39)

The way vision, third sight, and spirit consciousness are emphasized in the telling of the tale is important. The significance of how these things function in the Ibo worldview plays a key role in Avey's transformation throughout the rest of the novel. When the Ibo are described as seeing things that "you and me don't have the power to see" and being able to "see in more ways than one," there is a depiction of a visionary knowledge that supersedes Western ways of "seeing" and "knowing," a kind of third sight at odds with a purely rational notion of consciousness. As Marimba Ani notes: "Plato's conception of man, a conception that has become reality in western societies, is a thinking, intellectual, logical human being devoid of intuition and emotion. Man's primary function, according to Plato, is to think, not to intuit or feel. Man becomes separate from the cosmos and nature" (quoted in Oba T'Shaka, *Return to the African Mother Principle*, 77).

When Great-aunt Cuney retells her grandmother's story about the Ibos, she stops briefly to ask Avey what the Ibos did after they looked around and saw the future. Avey tells us that although she answers her question, her great-aunt "wouldn't even have heard it *over the voice that possessed her*" (*Praisesong*, 38, italics mine). The ending of the tale is always the same: the grandmother says that although her body is still in Tatem, her mind is long gone with the Ibos, which is to say that the grandmother had moved from rational to spiritual consciousness. Further, the narration of the tale to Great-aunt Cuney as a young child is a ritual in which the power of the word as proverbial tale is in the repetition that inaugurates a shift in the listener to the register of alternate consciousness. The power of the word is apparent also in the song that the Ibo sing as they leave. Song is here revealed as the site or place in which one can switch registers. It follows that when songs are sung during hard times they can function to inspire the switch from rational to spirit consciousness.

Later on in the novel, when Avey recalls taking her young husband Jay to Ibo Landing and telling him the story, she "half expect[s] him to dismiss the whole apocryphal tale with a joke." But he surprises her by saying, "I'm with your aunt Cuney and the old woman you were named for. I believe it Avey. Every word" (115). Young Avey, on the other hand, is depicted as struggling with her ability to shift to this register. One day she asked her great-aunt Cuney how come the Ibos never drowned. The old woman regards her with such disappointment and sadness she wishes she could withdraw the question. She finally says to Avey, "Did it say Jesus drowned when he went walking on the water in that Sunday School book your momma always sends with you?" "No, ma'am," answers Avey. "I din' think so," responds the great-aunt. "You got any more questions?" (40). The implication here is that in order to grasp the true meaning of the tale, the listener has to *believe*. Belief involves giving up rational consciousness, *giving up the head* in order to be initiated into the realm of this ancestral knowledge.

"Runagate" (the title of the first part of the novel) is a term describing a fugitive or runaway. This amply describes Avey Johnson as she flees the cruise ship for reasons that she cannot even explain to herself. After her dream nothing is the same. In the dream, the fight with her aunt highlights the contradiction between material and spiritual

Clear Word and Third Sight

wealth and it signals that a disentanglement from material reality will have to precede spiritual transformation. Avey begins to feel off-kilter the night that she and two friends dine in the Louis XIV Versailles room on the *Bianca Pride*. In keeping with the idea that excess material wealth signals spiritual stagnation, Avey's "entire midsection [suddenly] felt odd," even though she had not eaten much that evening (50). Prior to this moment, on at least two occasions, Avey had the strange experience of looking in a mirror and for a split second, not recognizing herself. This temporary inability to see is an inversion of the visionary third sight that blesses the Ibo and touches both her great-aunt Cuney and her ancestral namesake, Grandma Avatara. After the dream, however, as evidenced by her reaction to the dessert served that night in the Versailles room, Avey becomes "allergic" to decadence. A series of strange things begin to happen to her on the ship. She has an unsettling sensation of the ship rocking uneasily. She feels as if she is constantly being followed by the same group of people and develops a feeling of paranoia about it. While watching a game being played with cue sticks, the sound that reaches her ears resembles "some blunt instrument repeatedly striking human flesh and bone" (56). She has a flashback at that moment to a night in which she and Jay witnessed the police beat a Black man in the street for a minor traffic violation. She sees an old man sitting on deck and at second glance he appears to be reduced to a skeleton. It is as if Avey has suddenly been given extra perception, an ability to see the past and see into the future. "Something [has] dramatically expanded her vision, offering her a glimpse of things that were beyond her comprehension, and therefore frightening" (59). She has, after the dream, developed a kind of Ibo third sight, though not the spirit consciousness to interpret it. Like a new initiate, she now has powers but no guidance. She has visions that scare her since she is out of touch with the ancestral consciousness that would normally be a guide. The materially centered reality of the West has influenced her into defining herself from the outside rather than the inside.

"Sleeper's Wake," the second part of *Praisesong for the Widow*, depicts an Avey Johnson who is slowly awakening from a numbed state of consciousness. While reflecting back on her early life with Jay, she tries hard to remember when she began to change. In linear time, this five-chapter section of the novel takes place in the few hours between Avey's arrival that evening at the hotel in Grenada and nightfall. She has a vision of her husband chastising her for wasting the cruise money by departing from the ship. She remembers how much he sacrificed physically to move them out of the poor, Black Halsey Street tenement where they lived for over twenty years.

Yet what stays in Avey's mind all these years after is less the joy of having escaped poverty and more the sadness of what they gave up in the process. They sacrificed culture and spirit to escape poverty without realizing it. Avey remembers a Jay who came home and immediately played music by Ida Cox, Ma Rainey, Big Bill Broonzy, and Mamie Smith. The music functioned, once again, as a release from rational consciousness. As the music played, "his head would . . . come up and the tension could almost be seen slipping from him like the coat or jacket he would still have on falling from his shoulders to the floor" (95). Sometimes they would stage dances in their living room, pretending they were out at one of the clubs they could not afford to go to. Then on Sundays Jay would recite poetry for Avey and their oldest daughter, Sis. When they made love, "Jay might have felt himself surrounded by a pantheon of the most ancient deities who had made their temple the tunneled darkness of his wife's flesh. And he held back, trembling a little, not knowing quite how to conduct himself in their presence" (127). Avey describes all these activities as small rituals, and as in the Ibo tale, these small rituals have the power to sustain them on the inside rather than the economic wealth they achieve later, which only sustains them on the outside. As Avey remembers this past she thinks:

> Something in those small rites, an ethos they held in common, had reached back beyond her life and beyond Jay's to join them to the vast unknown lineage that had made their being possible. And this link, these connections, heard in the music in the praisesongs of a Sunday: " . . . *I bathed in the Euphrates when dawns were/young . . . ,*" had both protected them and put them in the possession of a kind of power. (137)

Significantly, Marshall uses the term "praisesong" to describe these restorative rituals whose power they had underestimated.

The third part of the novel, "Lavé Tête," opens with the epigraph "Papa Legba, ouvri barrière pou' mwê" (Papa Legba open the gate for me). The epigraph puts the reader directly in the realm of the African spiritual traditions spoken of by Eastman and Warner-Lewis. They tell us in their article that "Legba [is] the divine messenger between the vodun and humankind" ("Forms of African Spirituality," 409). "Lavé

Tête" literally implies clearing the head of negative spirits in order to ready up for spirit consciousness. Disoriented after her vision of Jay and her reminiscences about the turns her life has taken, Avey stumbles down the beach away from the high-rise hotel she is staying in, realizing that she feels more and more at ease the further she gets away from material excess. In this way she meets Lebert Joseph, an elderly man with a small bar on the beachfront who is an out-islander from Carriacou. He is the oldest living person from his part of the island, and he invites her to come with him on an excursion to experience the "Big Drum" ceremony that is held each year to remember the "Old Parents" or the "Long-time People." Functioning as a thinly disguised "Papa Legba" figure, Lebert talks to Avey about the importance of the Big Drum ceremony in which they remember their ancestors and ask for their forgiveness. He then lists the names of various old-time dances, done in honor of the various "tribes" or "nations," pausing after he names each one to see if she recognizes any of them. The idea that forms of dance in the diaspora are linked to sacred activities is evoked by his litany. If an individual knows what "nation" or group he or she is descended from, then he or she dances at the appropriate time to celebrate this ancestry.

In the shade and protection of his establishment, Avey opens up and begins, much to her own astonishment, to speak of the tribulation she has suffered of late. As she speaks, the narrative describes Lebert as already knowing of "the Gethsemane she had undergone. . . . His penetrating look said as much. It marked him as someone who possessed ways of seeing that went beyond mere sight and ways of knowing that outstripped ordinary intelligence" (172). Here, Lebert is marked as someone with the kind of third sight associated with the Ibos. He gives her some rum and coconut water to drink and tells her, "It have quite a few like you. People who can't call their nation. For one reason or another they just don't know" (175). Lebert connects "being able to call your nation" with not only knowing where you are from but also who you are.

When Lebert invites Avey to come to the Big Drum she reverts to her proper respectable persona and tries to refuse him, only to have the sensation of being in a physical battle with him, like the one she had with her great-aunt Cuney in her dream. When she finally acquiesces, she realizes that "the strange discomfort in her stomach was gone and her head had stopped aching" (184). The boat ride to Carriacou functions as Avey Johnson's reverse middle passage. Not only does she vomit and defecate on herself but, when she is put to lie down in the small deckhouse midship, she has the sensation of being in the hold of a ship with other bodies packed together in their own filth. This final moment in the chapter fulfills the Lavé Tête notion of the section title. It is as if Avey has finally undergone the violent physical and spiritual cleansing of all the psychic stagnation brought into her life by materialistic goals.

The last part of the novel, "The Beg Pardon," represents Avey Johnson's transition—once her head is clear—to spirit consciousness. The first sign of this is that the arrogance and fear that were characteristic of her throughout the text are replaced with humility and respect. The similarities between Lebert Joseph and Papa Legba are abundantly clear as he opens up the "Beg Pardon" portion of the Big Drum ceremony by entering the circle and singing on his knees. He is the crossroads figure representing the crossroads deity, "the divine messenger between the vodun and humankind," and Avey Johnson is at the crossroads of a new identity and consciousness (cf. Eastman and Warner-Lewis, "Forms of African Spirituality," 409). As the ceremony progresses Avey finally allows herself to be pulled into the circle of dancers moving in counterclockwise fashion, calling to mind the Ring Shout that her great-aunt Cuney once attended. Movements that she did not realize she knew or remembered come back to her. As she gets into the rhythm of the dancing, Lebert Joseph pauses and salutes her, and others from the community, old and young, follow suit. Although she does not understand much of the language spoken around her, or the rituals being performed, Avey "surrenders her head," symbolically, and crosses over to this alternate form of consciousness. As the narrative states, "she had finally after all these decades made it across" (248).

At the end of the novel, Avey Johnson, although transformed, is at the beginning of a new spiritual journey. She plans to rebuild the house her great-aunt left to her and bring children down to it in the summer to educate them about the Ibo. She plans to proselytize those selling their souls in the corporate sector. Giving up her "head" to her ancestral line and passing on her great-aunt's legacy inaugurates the cycle of the transfer of spirit consciousness to a new generation. The title of Marshall's book, *Praisesong for the Widow*, conjures up the nexus of continental and diasporic cultural practices. Like the title of Simone Schwarz-Bart's novel *Pluie et vent sur Télumée Miracle*, which translates as "Rain and Wind on Télumée Miracle," Marshall's title suggests tribulation that has been survived. As Oba T'Shaka tells us,

Clear Word and Third Sight

"African philosophy and cosmologies understand that humanity achieves perfection out of imperfection" (*Return to the African Mother Principle*, 91). The "praisesong," therefore, is a literal tribute not only to survival but also to the triumph of a woman overcoming her weaknesses as she attempts to fulfill her destiny.

Calling Diaspora: The Spoken Word, Spirit Consciousness, and Lorde's Prophetic Utterance

> Well did you know the pen
> Is stronger than the knife
> They can kill you once
> But they can't kill you twice
> Did you know destruction of the flesh,
> Is not di ending to life
> Fear not of the anti-christ.
>
> —DAMIAN "JR. GONG" MARLEY, "It Was Written"

Originally published in 1986, six years before Lorde herself "crossed over," her book *Our Dead behind Us* achieves a striking union between the spiritual and the political impulse, the site at which the individual is endowed with the most power to struggle on behalf of the community As Lorde tells us in the poem "Learning to Write" (53), "I am bleak heroism of words / that refuse / to be buried alive / with the liars."

The collection opens with the poem "Sisters in Arms," which interweaves ancient and contemporary accounts of women warriors in South African history. The poem introduces themes that run throughout this collection, of the violence of war and struggle in which rituals of death and proper burial cannot be honored. The poem reads like a divinely inspired utterance made to ancient deities in order to "beg pardon" for these transgressions of appropriate ceremony during times of genocidal strife:

> We were two Black women touching our flame
> and we left our dead behind us
> I hovered . . . you rose . . . the last ritual of healing.
> (4)

Audre Lorde and Paule Marshall

The political theme moves from the continent to New York in the second poem in the collection, "To the Poet Who Happens to Be Black and the Black Poet Who Happens to Be a Woman":

> I was born in the gut of Blackness
> from between my mother's particular thighs. . . .
> No cold spirit ever strolled through my bones
> on the corner of Amsterdam avenue . . .
> but I can recall without counting
> eyes
> canceling me out
> like an unpleasant appointment. . . .
> I cannot recall the words of my first poem
> but I remember a promise
> I made my pen
> never to leave it
> lying
> in somebody else's blood.
> (6–7)

Lorde links continental suffering again with the situation in the diaspora with a poem titled "Diaspora":

> Afraid is a country with no exit visas
> a wire of ants walking the horizon
> embroiders our passports at birth
> Johannesburg Alabama
> (32)

Another poem on the diaspora experience is "Every Traveler Has One Vermont Poem." It has a spoof-like quality, starting out as a poem about the beauty of nature in that hilly northeast state and ending with the racist slur "nigger" as an exposé of the kind of racism found in such parts of the United States, where Black people are infrequent.

The poem "Mawu" (the poem's title refers to the God-Creator figure of the universe) develops a spiritual theme, reminding the reader of the spiritual deities register birthfully resurrected in her 1978 collection *The Black Unicorn*. The lines "flashes of old toughness . . . shine through like stars / teaching me how to die . . . insisting / death is not a disease" (27) tie death to the universal cycle of life in the cosmos: the death of the body is not the death of the spirit, but a new beginning.

Lorde's most striking tribute to the poem as the vehicle of empowered utterance, conjuring up the past and future in a cyclical way, is

Clear Word and Third Sight

the final poem in the collection "Call." In this poem, Lorde's poetic voice, far from being resigned or tentative, bursts powerfully onto the scene with a certainty not evident in some of her earlier work. Here, the power of the poetic voice comes from the interweaving of continental African and African diaspora cultural realities. As Sylvia Washington Bâ states when describing the African philosophical worldview that influenced Senghor's poetry, "The word is both expression and creation and, as such, unites poetic creation and [the] reinforcement of life forces" (*The Concept of Negritude*, 63). This description of the word not only gets to the heart of the practice of the word in the work of writers such as Simone Schwarz-Bart and Audre Lorde; it also perfectly describes what Lorde achieves in the poem "Call." "Call" is like a chant invoking the voices of Black women, dead and alive, from both the continent and the diaspora. Women who are incarcerated, women who are struggling, women whose spirits are broken, as well as women who have found the power of their voice. Black women all of them.

The notion of giving up rational consciousness, "giving up the head" in order to be initiated into the realm of ancestral knowledge, is functional here as well. Like the path Avey Johnson must travel in *Praisesong for the Widow*, giving up the head is the point of departure for access to the spirit consciousness at work in Lorde's "Call." The poem is a testimony of the extent to which this kind of ancestral consciousness is part of the deepest recesses of creativity within Black women's artistic expression:

> Holy ghost woman
> stolen out of your name
> Rainbow Serpent
> whose faces have been forgotten
> Mother . . . loosen my tongue or adorn me
> with a lighter burden
> Aido Hwedo is coming.
> (73)

Like a prayer or a chant, the poem opens with the speaker "calling" on the "holy ghost mother" whose sacred name may have been lost, but who can still be restored to power through the energy of the spoken word. In a footnote to the poem Aido Hwedo is described as "the Rainbow Serpent [who is] also a representation of all ancient divinities who must be worshipped but whose names and faces have been lost in time" (75).

In the second stanza, the "weapons" are "scraps of different histories." Instead of being a liability, as we have been taught to believe, the differing nature of our cultural, spiritual, social, and political experiences, wherever we are in the diaspora, is one of our greatest strengths. The speaker asks the deity to prevent us from "shattering any altar," transgressing any unknown taboo as we prepare for war. Linking the menial labor of the women who clean toilets to the power of the guerrilla warrior's voice, the speaker claims honor for both women through the sacred invocation of the name of the deity:

> On worn kitchen stools and tables
> we are piecing our weapons together
> scraps of different histories
> do not let us shatter
> any altar
> she who scrubs the capital toilets, listening
> is your sister's youngest daughter
> gnarled Harriet's anointed
> you have not been without honor
> even the young guerrilla has chosen
> yells as she fires into the thicket
> Aido Hwedo is coming.
> (73)

Offering up as sacred utterance to the deity the gift of not being forgotten, the speaker in the third stanza moves into a realm beyond and before consciousness, invoking dreams, cheekbone scarification, and the memory of the flesh. Sisters and children are brought into the litany, as those who will pay respect by example:

> I have written your names on my cheekbone
> dreamed your eyes . . . flesh my epiphany
> most ancient goddesses . . . hear me
> enter
> I have not forgotten your worship
> nor my sisters
> nor the sons of my daughters
> my children watch for your print
> in their labors
> and they say Aido Hwedo is coming.
> (73)

The power of the word as something that can protect and heal is directly alluded to in the fourth stanza, when the speaker mentions the deity's name as a "password / through seductions . . . self-slaughter." The concept also of "enduring / warring / sometimes outside your name" asks forgiveness for any profane acts committed more from a lack of freedom than willful disrespect. The linking of Black women in different places continues with the reference to Soweto:

> I am a Black woman turning
> mouthing your name as a password
> through seductions self-slaughter
> and I believe in the holy ghost
> mother
> in your flames beyond our vision
> blown light through the fingers of women
> enduring warring
> sometimes outside your name
> we do not choose all our rituals
> Thandi Modise winged girl of Soweto
> brought fire back home in the snout of a mortar
> and passes the word from her prison cell whispering
> Aido Hwedo is coming.
> (74)

The emphasis on speech as a way to honor the deity is made clear yet again in the fifth stanza. The speaker has "sung the spirals of power"; she has offered up her life as a sacrifice and is ready to cross over:

> Rainbow Serpent who must not go
> unspoken
> I have offered up the safety of separations
> sung the spirals of power
> and what fills the spaces
> before power unfolds or flounders
> in desirable nonessentials
> I am a Black woman stripped down
> and praying
> my whole life has been an altar
> worth its ending
> and I say Aido Hwedo is coming.
> (74)

In the final stanza Lorde's invocation surpasses litany and becomes a "call." The daughters of the diaspora are called upon to receive their names and fulfill their destinies. These destinies, which will require us to "learn by heart / what has never been taught," break new ground. But we cannot do it alone, we have to reach back further than our temporal and spatial memories to ancient forms of knowledge. We have to elevate the forgotten deities by giving them voice, calling them back and uniting them with our heroines across the diaspora:

> I may be a weed in the garden
> of women I have loved
> who are still
> trapped in their season
> but even they shriek
> as they rip burning gold from their skins
> Aido Hwedo is coming.
> We are learning by heart what has never been taught
> you are my given fire-tongued
> Oya Seboulisa Mawu Afrekete
> and now we are mourning our sisters
> lost to the false hush of sorrow
> to hardness and hatchets and childbirth
> and we are shouting
> Rosa Parks and Fannie Lou Hamer
> Assata Shakur and Yaa Asantewa
> my mother and Winnie Mandela are singing
> in my throat
> the holy ghosts' linguist
> one iron silence broken
> Aido Hwedo is calling
> calling
> your daughters are named
> and conceiving
> Mother loosen my tongue
> or adorn me
> with a lighter burden
> Aido Hwedo is coming.
> Aido Hwedo is coming.
> Aido Hwedo is coming.
> ("Our Dead," 73–75)

Aido Hwedo is calling. Calling us to "mourn our sisters" lost to sorrow while simultaneously celebrating our warriors taking us to victory. As Alice Walker states in her poem "Each One, Pull One":

> We who have stood over so many graves
> know
> that no matter what they do
> all of us must live
> or none.
> (*Horses Make a Landscape Look More Beautiful*, 53)

This study began by turning back to examine literary quarrels between writers and artists about the contours of Black cultural
identity. During the process of exploring how these earlier conversations continued to influence later generations of Black writers and
scholars, several issues became apparent. There has systematically
been a cry for traditions of thought that can explain who we are,
collectively, as African and African diaspora peoples at the deepest
level. This desire has coexisted historically with suppression, in the
mainstream academic context, of the intellectual traditions that could
shed light on this alternate philosophical worldview. However, scholar
Greg Thomas's analysis of the politically opposite ideological invest-
ments of E. Franklin Frazier and Carter G. Woodson creates a paradigm for understanding the intellectual production of the Black elite
subject. As Thomas argues, Woodson's text, *The Mis-Education of the
Negro*, rather than being a dated analysis of Black education, in actuality establishes as paradigmatic a Black intellectual trajectory premised on a rejection of folk mores and a flight toward hegemonic discourse.

A further ramification of Woodson's discursive paradigm is the
light implicitly shed on the very system that produces the "highly
educated Negro." Woodson's analyses are a racial-cultural (as opposed
to psychoanalytic) mirror of the psychosis at the heart of Western
knowledge systems. The hypocritical coexistence of so-called rational
and humane theories of culture alongside the violent realities of conquest, imperialist expansion, slavery, and colonialism reveals the
flaws that inhere in the institutions of the dominant society. The deepest criticisms of negritude were rooted in the hegemonic, scholarly

assumption that any totalizing or "essentializing" gestures would result in manifestations of hierarchy and dominance of the same degree and order that rational "enlightenment" discourse appeared unable to avoid. Yet this was a culturally specific fear, masquerading as objective science, concealing its own politics of location. Coming out of the historical realities of conquest, totalizing narratives within Western discourses were rightly viewed as products of this past. In this scenario, power is inseparable from violence and hierarchy necessarily means domination. Western traditions of thought, therefore, projected their own ills onto discursive narratives coming out of other cultural traditions. The relatively new field of "whiteness studies" is of interest here in terms of the extent to which it explores the contradictions and the psychological dimensions of this racial narrative from the white perspective.[1]

The critical analyses done in this study of eastern Caribbean, French Caribbean, and Caribbean diaspora writings demonstrate the extent to which Woodson's theories about the intellectual production of the Black subject are borne out. Eastern Caribbean writer Merle Hodge's *Crick Crack Monkey* is the literary manifestation of the negative transformation theorized by Woodson. Influenced by the work of Léon Gontran Damas, the French Guianan negritude poet, Hodge wrote her master's thesis on Damas's writings. His book *Pigments*, written in the same era as Woodson's study, criticizes the "slavish imitation" of the colored elite in the French West Indies.[2] Woodson's theories are also borne out in Audre Lorde's Caribbean diaspora text, *Zami: A New Spelling of My Name,* which effectively traces the connections between young Audre's flight from her Black Caribbean family and her exposure to the white school system.

Escape and recovery from this purposefully designed program of miseducation is revealed to be a schizophrenic struggle at best. The works of Audre Lorde and Frantz Fanon are stunning examples of the attempt to engage in that struggle nonetheless. In Fanon's work, the decolonializing movement from his first text to his last specifically addresses this issue. In his introduction to *Black Skin, White Masks,* Fanon states, "I propose nothing short of the liberation of the man of color from himself" (8). By the time he writes *The Wretched of the Earth,* on the other hand, frequent references to "l'intellectuel colonisé" appear alongside a desperate plea for the "third world" to develop a "new [notion] of man," one that is not premised on and rooted in European discourse.

The concepts "folk groundings," "diasporic consciousness," and "alternate consciousness" mobilized in this study are continuations of ideas prevalent in the writings about cultural life in various parts of the African diaspora. Here, my focus has been on some of the literature and culture emanating from the Caribbean region, crosscut with influences from the United States and continental West Africa. My aim has been to tap into a widely felt but still understudied aspect of the experience, namely, the idea that an alternate philosophical world-view, negotiating in and through a range of Western discourses, has continuously shaped the consciousness of various peoples in the African diaspora in similar kinds of ways. This diasporic consciousness is grounded in the mores and cultural traditions of the masses of Black people. In this study, the defining characteristic of this consciousness is shown to be the cultivation and development of internal resources that provide a sense of balance for both the individual and the collective. Proverbial sayings, folktales and folksongs, poems, and oral histories are some of the manifestations of this consciousness that have appeared time and again in the literary writings. The literatures that draw on these cultural practices have attempted to translate and transfer into written narrative the power associated with the spoken word within the multiple contexts of the oral tradition.

This "third sight" approach to consciousness represents another intellectual trajectory, or more accurately, another way of knowing. This second cultural praxis, rooted in intergenerational oral narratives, does not isolate and privilege the academically trained intellectual as the supreme philosopher. Instead, the philosopher in this context is frequently the artist, musician, poet, writer, comedian, and priest, revealing a concentric rather than linear approach to systems of knowledge. Negative critiques of negritude successfully suppressed certain key questions that were discursive attempts to understand alternate existing models of philosophical consciousness. At the First International Conference of Negro Writers and Artists, Léopold Senghor's notion of a "cultural stock-taking," had it been seriously engaged, would have entailed a rigorous comparison of the cultural similarities and differences between various continental African and African diaspora peoples and societies. The critical question being raised was whether or not a civilizational legacy existed that the diasporic subject was heir to, one that was equally if not more important in understanding the diaspora than the legacy of Europe. Despite his criticism of negritude in *The Wretched of the Earth*, Frantz Fanon's final statement at the end of the same text declares: "Humanity is waiting for something from us other than such an imitation, which would be almost an obscene caricature. . . . If we want to turn Africa into a new Europe, then let us leave the destiny of our countries to Europeans. They will know how to do it better than the most gifted among us" (315).

In the context of Fanon's statements, the cultural stock-taking that Senghor suggests takes on a new relevance. Both at the 1956 conference and in his work, Senghor describes five characteristics of the society he comes from. He describes its art as functional and not simply created for abstract aesthetic value. He discusses the privileged position of the word in his culture and the expressive and creative power attached to it. He compares the work that certain words do in Wolof and other indigenous African languages to the work that those same words do in Greek, Latin, French, and English. His work on these issues is a precursor to the assessment by the African scholars Oyeronké Oyewumi and Ifi Amadiume of the symbiotic relationship between language and culture, discussed in the second chapter of this book. Senghor's fourth and fifth characteristics deal with the notion of a life force extending beyond the physical divisions of life and death, and time as synchronic and diachronic rather than historical.

This unfinished comparative cultural stock-taking is at the heart of Vévé Clark's concept of diaspora literacy and can be discerned in the cultural characteristics that Zora Neale Hurston identified in the early twentieth century among rural Afro-American folk in the United States. As I demonstrated in chapter 2, Senghor's conception of art as a functional aspect of culture correlates to Hurston's description of the role and function of the original spirituals. Of the twelve characteristics that Hurston identifies in her essay "Characteristics of Negro Expression," three of them ("the will to adorn," "asymmetry," and "drama") are shown to be present in the rural Black subject's use of speech. Hurston's studies support similar statements made by Senghor, Oyewumi, and Amadiume about the way indigenous languages shed light on differing cultural mores. These diaspora cultural characteristics are made manifest, at least in part, in terms of *how* the language is used. This is particularly interesting since the diaspora is frequently discredited as having no connections to the continent precisely because of the substantial deterioration and disappearance of continental languages. What Hurston's research proves is that the cultural patterns and some of the cultural logic of the former African traditions have

Afterword

remained with us and are still enacted in the way the language is patterned and practiced, despite the loss of actual words.

Hurston's notions about the connections between language and culture, Senghor's cultural stock-taking, and Oyewumi's and Amadiume's analyses of language are the manifestations of a trajectory of thought that attempted to respond to Fanon's cry. Carter G. Woodson's financial support of Hurston's research as well as his founding of *The Journal of Negro History* (a journal that Senghor cites as one of his influences), demonstrate the degree to which, despite his skepticism of the Western-trained, "highly educated Negro," he was simultaneously laying the groundwork for an alternate strategy. This diasporic consciousness rooted in folk mores is amply demonstrated in Earl Lovelace's short story "Joebell and America" and is carried forward in his books *The Dragon Can't Dance, Salt,* and *The Wine of Astonishment.* This philosophical ethos is also seen in Simone Schwarz-Bart's two novels, the diaspora poetry of Audre Lorde, and in writings of Paule Marshall.

The competing views of Audre Lorde's *Zami: A New Spelling of My Name,* which I analyze in chapter 5, amply demonstrate current-day manifestations of these two approaches to reading and understanding Black texts. Erin Carlston's analysis of Lorde's "house of difference" passage maintains that the text is at its theoretical best in its description of the unstable and perpetually incomplete identity. This privileging of instability fits in neatly with a deconstructive analysis of culture, one that is continuous with James Clifford's theories in *Predicament of Culture,* as well as the essays from the work of Paul Gilroy and Stuart Hall addressed in the introduction. Carlston accepts the destabilization of notions of universal truth that lie at the heart of the poststructuralist enterprise as an unquestionably good thing that is culturally neutral. Her privileging of cultural instability, however, is implicitly a rejection of "folk mores," since Audre the narrator in *Zami* comes to the "house of difference" position as a result of her cultural flight from her parents' home toward a world of individualism and the white lesbian nation. In contrast, Anna Wilson reads the "house of difference" passage as Lorde's recognition that instability is a completely unacceptable foundation for any "house"; she argues that Audre's route back to both the Black community and a viable notion of activist politics requires that she first know where she is from. Wilson's reading is validated by the turn the text takes from there on, toward Black lesbian community exclusively and the remythologizing of the mother's homeland as the source of Audre's power.

The decision to root oneself firmly in the home culture and accept both its strengths and weaknesses is the point of departure for Simone Schwarz-Bart's narration of *Pluie et vent sur Télumée Miracle,* the title itself indicating a woman who survives great tribulation. The instability privileged in the poststructuralist context is discarded from the outset as a liability to the survival of the spirit. In fact, instability in the form of self-doubt is characterized in the text as the legacy of slavery and colonial violence. Evil is typified as the internalization of these negative legacies, and a firm and positive belief in the cultural and spiritual self is revealed to be the only antidote for this sickness. Senghor's notion of the word as having the power of both creation and expression is actively exemplified in Schwarz-Bart's text by a world in which words can curse and destroy the spirit and life force of persons —or heal and revitalize them.

The simple proverb takes on a deeply philosophical power in Schwarz-Bart's novels. Its power comes from the implicit linking of rational and intuitive systems of knowledge. The man or woman listening to the proverbs only has access to a powerful interpretation after surviving life experiences that endow him or her with the wisdom of insight. Since the spiritual and intuitive legacies have been systematically unlinked from the rational within Western knowledge systems, "diaspora literacy" of this sort has been shrouded in a kind of opacity and incomprehensibility that has been deceptive in appearance and has frequently been mistaken for a kind of "essential" simplicity. This is a struggle over completely different notions of the inside and the outside.

At the end of Earl Lovelace's "Joebell and America," Joebell decides to sing in the midst of disaster. Once his performance as American citizen is revealed as a farce by white immigration officers, he turns inward to seek out culturally grounded psychospiritual resources. In Merle Hodge's *Crick Crack Monkey,* colonization has succeeded in destroying the protagonist Tee when she begins to believe that the world she came from is inferior. The moment that her inside consciousness is destroyed, she starts to root her identity in exterior markings of status, and she begins to suffer from a pervasive and seemingly inexplicable shame. Paule Marshall's *Praisesong for the Widow* reverses this story, recounting a diaspora woman's journey back to the inside. Status and material success had taken precedence in Avey's life, and as her wealth increased her marriage fell apart. But then a dream about the past alters Avey's perception and opens the door to

Afterword

an alternate "self"-consciousness. It is only when she begins to shed the outward trappings of success that she can remember and recall parts of the self she left behind. She has to travel back to a symbolically more advanced place, one in which social relations replace social hierarchies. The text is replete with tropes that Vévé Clark would associate with "diaspora literacy": Papa Legba, the Ring Shout, dreams, Ibo Landing, traditional dances, blues, Nina Simone, and Langston Hughes. Remembering and learning how to interpret these markers is Avey's route to an alternate, diasporic consciousness.

Throughout the literature, the concept of inside consciousness is represented by a character's development of the internal resources necessary to survive the oppression of the body and spirit. These resources have proven to be among the most highly developed African characteristics that diaspora subjects have maintained. When times get hard and external wealth proves fleeting or inaccessible, inside consciousness is waiting to be channeled through the songs, poems, proverbs, folktales, dreams, dances, or rituals. They are the vehicles that carry us to the other side:

> Holy Ghost Woman
> Stolen out of thy name
> Rainbow Serpent
> Whose faces have been forgotten.
> Mother Loosen my tongue
> Or adorn me with a lighter burden.
> Aiedo Hwedo is coming.
> (Lorde, *Our Dead behind Us,* 73)

Notes

1 Paris in 1956

1 The expression "n'était pas tombé de la dernière pluie" has a proverbial creole ring to it. Literally translated as "did not drop from the sky with the last rainfall," this expression is obviously a way of rejecting the systematic denigration of an African civilizational background as the historical backdrop that informs Black cultures, traditions, and experiences.

2 It is worth noting at this point the complexities of Césaire's use of the term "nègre" both in this context as well as in how it resonates within the context of the term negritude itself. For further explication of this point, see Keith Q. Warner's *Critical Perspectives: Léon Gontran Damas* (1988). Among other things, Warner's text shows the degree to which Césaire was influenced by Damas with regard to the use of the term "nègre." Despite the fact that some French dictionaries translate "nègre" as "negro," the ideological complexity of what is at stake does not translate that simply. While the term "Negro" within the Black U.S. context has at times been used to refer to a mass Black populace, by the late 1960s it was discarded as a passive and confining definition when compared with Black or African. What some perceive to be the controversial use of the term "nigga" within contemporary hip-hop rather than the elite and polite "African American" or the now more conventional "Black" comes closer to capturing the controversy of Césaire's use of "nègre" rather than the more polite and conventional "noir." Hence "negritude" as a term that subsumed "nègre" within it was breaking new ground in more ways than one.

3 Césaire states, "Je dirais que la négritude est d'abord à mon avis, une prise de conscience concrète et non abstraite . . . c'était d'avoir conscience concrètement de ce que l'on est, à savoir le fait premier, que l'on est *nègre*, que nous étions des *nègres*, que nous avions un passé, et

que ce passé comportait des éléments culturels qui avaient été très valables, et que les nègres, comme tu dis, n'étaient pas tombés de la dernière pluie. . . . A l'époque où nous étions, où nous écrivions, des gens pouvaient écrire une histoire universelle de la civilisation sans consacrer un chapitre à l'Afrique, comme si l'Afrique n'avait rien apporté au monde. . . . [E]nfin c'était l'idée que ce passé nègre était digne de respect; ce passé nègre n'était pas uniquement du passé; que les valeurs nègres étaient encore des valeurs qui pouvaient apporter des choses important au monde. . . . C'était aussi l'affirmation d'une solidarité. . . . J'ai toujours pensé, considéré, que ce qui se passait en Algérie et chez les Noirs des États-Unis retentissait en moi. J'ai pensé que je ne pouvais pas être indifférent à Haiti, je ne pouvais pas être indifférent à l'Afrique. Alors, si tu veux, nous sommes un peu arrivés à cette idée d'une sorte de civilisation noire répandue dans le monde entier" (quoted in Depestre, *Bonjour et adieu*, 78–79; translation mine).

4   J. Michael Dash argues that the 1955 debate between Depestre and Césaire "has not always received the attention it deserves though it is central to the definition of a French Caribbean literature tradition" ("The World and the Word," 123).

5   Clifford, in his chapter on Césaire, pays specific attention to Césaire's coinage of the word *marronner,* a point that is also of interest to Dash in his article. Both critics wrestle with this notion of "literary marronage," and although coming to different conclusions, both maintain the distinction between Césaire and Depestre, referring to Césaire's radical poetic experimentation and by implication his right to resist the link between poetic expression and political struggle. The term "marronage" is a creative variant on the concept of "the maroons"—enslaved Africans who took their freedom by escaping the plantations and establishing independent societies in the hills. "Literary marronage" suggests a break away from the conventional system of meanings and usually a movement away from social realist approach to the literary, toward surrealist and/or modernist approaches to texts and contexts.

6   Here Césaire states, "Oui. A mon avis, les étudiants martiniquais ou bien s'assimilaient à des Français de droite ou bien s'assimilaient à des Français de gauche; c'était toujours de l'assimilation."

7   The birth and trajectory of negritude is described variously by critics. René Depestre and anglophone critic Selwyn Cudjoe in his book *Resistance and Caribbean Literature* cite works by two nineteenth-century Haitian writers, Antémon Firmin's *De l'égalité des races humaines* and Hannibal Price's *De la réhabilitation de la race noir par le peuple d'Haiti,* as influential early texts. Both cite Jean Price-Mars *Ainsi parla l'oncle* (1928) as foundational, although in the 1980 interview Césaire con-

fesses to having been unaware of Price-Mars's text until much later. Cudjoe also cites René Maran's *Batouala* as another influential text. In an informal interview conducted with the francophone scholar Gerard Pigeon, he located the beginnings of negritude in the nineteenth-century. He links it with the work of Thomas Ishmael Urbain (born 1812), child of a French wine merchant and slave trader and a Guyanese quadroon woman. Urbain traveled to France and became involved with the Saint-Simoniens, a group of visionaries whose mix of spirituality and politics influenced the birth of communism and socialism and is said to have substantially influenced Karl Marx. Urbain was influential in designing French colonialism in Algeria, imagining it (presumably in its ideal form) as a Senghor-like mix of European and North African philosophical values. Pigeon argues that many North Africans view Urbain not as a colonial but as the father of Algerian nationalism. In his poetry he wrote about Black identity and how to reorganize the self in a colonial world. Pigeon sees similarities between his poetry and that of Césaire.

8   Lilyan Kesteloot's book, *Black Writers in French: A Literary History of Negritude*, also describes negritude as a movement formulated by young Black students in Paris.

9   In the original French, Ménil's statement reads, "En politique, la négritude entend ignorer la lutte des classes."

10 Ménil goes on to say, "On sait que la bourgeoisie nationale aux colonies (qui en Afrique et aux Antilles est une petite bourgeoisie) est appelée à se dresser dans une lutte de libération mais cette lutte n'est jamais radicale, n'est jamais menée jusqu'au bout. . . . Cette petite bourgeoisie noire aux dents longues, qui rêve de construire des Versailles africains et qui singe de Gaulle, a été bien décrite par Fanon et René Dumont. . . . Relisons la lettre de démission de Césaire au parti communiste datée de 1956. *Le cas est particulièrement instructif: il montre que les thèses politiques de la négritude ont été élaborées de façon explicite et consciente pour escamoter la lutte des classes, pour condamner le communisme et se concilier l'appui de la bourgeoisie indigène et de l'impérialisme*" (72, original emphasis). ["We know that the national bourgeoisie in the colonies (which in Africa and the Antilles is a petty bourgeoisie) is called to lead a liberation struggle, but this struggle is never successfully completed. This petty Black bourgeoisie with long teeth, who dream of constructing an African Versailles and who ape de Gaulle, have been described well by Fanon and René Dumont. . . . We reread the letter of resignation of Césaire from the communist party dated from 1956. *The case is particularly instructive: it shows that the political thesis of negritude was explicitly and consciously elaborated in order to evade class struggle, con-*

demn communism, and win over the support of the native bourgeoisie and imperialism" (translation mine)].

11 Critic Janice Spleth makes an argument similar to Ménil's and Zahar's in her work on Senghor (*Léopold Sédar Senghor*, 21).

12 The specific question that I am raising here is about the relationship between the experience of alienation on the part of the Black educated elite and the appearance of negritude as a phenomenon. Carter G. Woodson's 1933 book, *The Mis-Education of the Negro*, speaks to the kind of alienation in the U.S. context that would create the need for a movement such as negritude.

13 "Mais cette poésie n'est pas . . . étroitement et uniquement raciale. Exprimant la vie des Noirs colonisés, elle exprime du même coup la condition historique et social des nègres dans la civilisation moderne. Plus concrètement encore, elle tend à décrire toute la richesse de l'âme noire, comme on a dit, c'est-à-dire les haines et les joies, le ressentiment et les espoirs de l'homme colonisé noir. Tel est, par exemple, pour l'essentiel, le contenu du *Cahier du Retour au Pays Natal* de Césaire qui affectera l'allure de manifeste de la nouvelle poésie. . . . *La Négritude* est autre chose."

14 "La culture antillaise passe par cette prise de conscience et le sentiment racial en est un élément nécessaire. . . . J'ai dit *sentiment racial*. . . . C'est plus exactement la fierté racial face au racisme blanc des colons. . . . Je n'ai pas dit *négritude*."

15 "En plus, ma conception de la négritude n'est pas biologique, elle est culturelle et historique" (Césaire). There appears to be a difference between the statements that Césaire makes in his interview with Kesteloot (which Depestre does not date) and his interview with Depestre, published in the 1980 text. His statements in that latter interview are consistent with his speech "What Is Negritude to Me?" given at the First Conference of African Communities in the Americas in Miami in 1987 and organized around the theme "Negritude, Ethnicity, and Afro Cultures in the Americas." In the Kesteloot interview he specifically links negritude as a cultural and historical phenomenon with political struggle, distinguishing his genealogy from that of, say, François Duvalier.

16 See Walter Rodney's *How Europe Underdeveloped Africa*.

17 The proceedings of the First International Conference of Negro Writers and Artists, published in the June–November 1956 issue of *Présence Africaine*, includes the discussions that followed the sessions. The discussions are cited under the name of the Présence Africaine Conference Committee.

18 Fanon makes an almost identical statement in *Wretched of the Earth*, when he states, "But, sooner or later, colonialism sees that it is not with-

in its powers to put into practice a project of economic and social reforms which will satisfy the aspirations of the colonized people. . . . The colonialist state quickly discovers that if it wishes to disarm the nationalist parties on strictly economic questions then it will have to do in the colonies exactly what it has refused to do in its own country" (208).

19   I also argue the importance of native cultural experience guiding anti-imperialist strategies of resistance in my article "Neo-Coloniality, Literary Representation, and the Problem of Disciplinary Solutions."

2   Colonial Legacies, Gender Identity

1   In his literary biography of Hurston, Robert Hemenway states: "If the black folk constituted a class, it was unquestionably a proletariat, but few Renaissance artists—including Locke—had prolonged firsthand contact with it. As critics of the Harlem Renaissance have often argued, the participants' bourgeois backgrounds suggested at least one generation of removal from the 'racy peasant undersoil.' Of them all, however, Zora Hurston was the closest, and her person and her fiction exhibited the knowledge that the Black masses had triumphed over their racist environment, not by becoming white and emulating bourgeois values, not by engaging in a sophisticated program of political propaganda, but by turning inward to create the blues, the folktale, the spiritual, the hyperbolic lie, the ironic joke. These forms of expression revealed a uniqueness of race spirit because they were a code of communication—intraracial propaganda—that would protect the race from the psychological encroachments of racism and the physical oppression of society. Hurston knew that Black folklore did not arise from a psychologically destroyed people, that in fact it was proof of psychic health" (*Zora Neale Hurston*, 51).

2   From the title of Césaire's talk, given at the First Conference of African Communities in the Americas (February 26–28, 1987, Miami), published in Moore, *African Presence in the Americas*.

3   Hodge writes, "The colonial era came to an end and we moved into independence. Theoretically, we could now begin to build up a sense of our cultural identity. But we immediately found ourselves in a new, more vicious era of cultural penetration. Television, which is basically American television, came to Trinidad and Tobago in 1962, the year the British flag was pulled down. The same pattern can be seen all over the Caribbean—withdrawing the most obvious trappings of colonial domination and installing a Trojan horse instead" ("Challenges of the Struggle for Sovereignty," 205).

4   While there are obviously other anthologies and collections of Carib-
    bean writing that I have not cited, my purpose in analyzing the ones I
    do is to show how various critics deal with the question of culture as it
    relates to the issue of gender. I trust that it will become apparent how
    and where the texts that I have not addressed would fit into the critical
    trajectory I am constructing.

5   Jamaica is an interesting example of this phenomenon. Living there in
    the 1970s during the reign of J B C (Jamaica Broadcasting Corporation),
    I remember programming being a mix of locally created news and
    entertainment interspersed with popular overseas serials. The com-
    mercials, however, were exclusively Jamaican creations. Since the late
    1980s, however, the advent of cable and satellite dishes means access to
    thirty-odd U.S. channels that obviously dominate despite the continued
    existence of two local stations, which themselves show a good deal of
    American programming.

6   Esteves and Paravisini-Gebert further note, "In their search for their
    individual voices as Caribbean writers, women have had to address the
    traditional themes and tropes of Caribbean literature—slavery, the
    plantation economy, colonialism, the complexities of class, race, and
    language—from their own particular vantage point, that of women
    from emerging nations where patriarchal/colonial institutions have
    sought to silence women's voices in general—and colored women's
    voices in particular. Therefore, in resisting their double oppression,
    their work both echoes and subverts these themes and tropes, often
    calling into question accepted notions and well-established 'truths,'
    revealing aspects of the Caribbean experience not previously gleaned
    from literary or historical accounts" (*Green Cane and Juicy Flotsam*, xiii).

7   She observes that first-generation Black writers of Caribbean descent
    were more directly affected by regional influences such as calypso,
    Creole, and Caribbean writers such as Edward Brathwaite and Louise
    Bennett.

8   For further explication of this point, see my article "Complicity, Revolu-
    tion and Black Female Writing."

9   Elaine Savory Fido is quoting from Chikwenye Ogunyemi's essay, "The
    Dynamics of the Contemporary Black Female Novel in English."

10 In my article "Complicity Revolution and Black Female Writing," I
    elaborate and expand upon the points made here.

11 Hodge writes, "A large part of male disrespect for the Black woman was
    an expression of his dissatisfaction with her, 'inferior' as she was to the
    accepted white ideal of womanhood" ("Shadow of the Whip," 118).

12 In Hodge's novel, the young protagonist, Tee, goes through a disturb-
    ing transformation, initiated by her miseducation in the colonial school

system. At the novel's end Tee's grandmother dies before she can tell Tee her "true-true name." Within the context of the story the "true-true name" (obviously an African name) is the link to the "tribe" that symbolizes the possibilities for rescue from the psychocultural violence of colonization. See my extended analysis of this text in chapter 3.

13 In her article "Race, Privilege, and the Politics of (Re)-writing History: An Analysis of the Novels of Michelle Cliff," Belinda Edmondson takes issue with this portrait of Cliff. She writes, "Unlike Rhys, whose novels reveal simultaneous attraction to and fear of Afro-Caribbean society and the consequent ambivalence which I have already discussed, Cliff understands that an understanding of black consciousness is crucial to resolving the complexities of being a white colonized subject, and more importantly is empowering not only to black people in the Caribbean, but to white people as well." (180–92). While this may be true, Mordecai and Wilson's critiques of the 'aesthetic authenticity' of the Creole voice in Cliff's texts still has some validity.

14 In the chapter "Of the NAACP and the Integrationists and Garvey and the Separatists: Or the Integrationist Onslaught," from his book *Race First,* Tony Martin notes one scholar's use of the term "scientific lying" to refer to DuBois's misrepresentation of facts concerning Marcus Garvey while using a tone and style that implied objectivity.

15 Oyewumi herself makes this claim in a footnote in her own text: "In her study (*Male Daughters*) of the Igbo society of Nigeria, anthropologist Ifi Amadiume introduced the idea of 'gender flexibility' to capture the real separability of gender and sex in that African society. I, however, think that the 'woman to woman' marriages of Igboland invite a more radical interrogation of the concept of gender, an interrogation that 'gender flexibility' fails to represent" (*The Invention of Women,* 184, n. 45).

16 Cheikh Anta Diop's *The Cultural Unity of Black Africa* (with an introduction by Ifi Amadiume) and Oba T'Shaka's *Return to the African Mother Principle of Male and Female Equality,* vol. I, make similar arguments on the status of motherhood in African cultures as well as on the links among domestic power, agricultural labor, and economic wealth in certain African societies.

17 I elaborate on the ideology and aesthetics of negritude espoused by Senghor in chapter I.

18 A seemingly minor, yet substantial contribution to the discussions of comparative cultural sensibilities is made by Oyewumi when she invokes the term "worldsense" (which I employ here) as opposed to "worldview." "Worldsense" captures the idea of perception using multiple senses, which Oyewumi claims is the mode of perception prevalent

in the African context, in contrast to perception that priveleges sight or vision, which we find in the West or Western-influenced spheres.

19 Carole Boyce Davies talks about "going a piece of the way" with certain theoretical approaches in order to express the complexity of the Black female experience. This conceptual approach is the focus of her chapter "Negotiating Theories or 'Going a Piece of the Way with Them' " from her *Black Women, Writing and Identity: Migrations of the Subject*.

20 Opening verse by T-Mo from "Thought Process" on Goodie Mob's first album, *Soul Food* (1995).

21 Translation: "Jackass says the world is not level." These last two proverbs are taken from *The Jamaica Handbook of Proverbs* by Vivien Morris Brown.

22 This notion of "rap-thetic" in juxtaposition with "aesthetic" is my own formulation. What I am trying to argue here, however, is that in Brathwaite's text rhythm and sound are such a fundamental part of life for diasporic Creoles that it is the movement toward orality, on the part of writers and poets, that comes closest to articulating the cultural expression of African diaspora peoples in the Caribbean region.

3 Negritude and Negativity

1 The phrase "concrete coming-to-consciousness" is Césaire's (from Depestre, *Bonjour et adieu*, 78–79); the passage in which he introduces it is quoted in chapter 1 (French original is given in chap. 1, note 3).

2 Some of this information was passed on to me through conversations with my father, Fitz Allen John, a former resident of Trinidad as well as of St. Vincent and the Grenadines.

3 This biographical information about Kincaid has been gathered from "Through West Indian Eyes" by Leslie Garis and an American Prose Library interview by Kay Bonetti. The particular fact of her getting her break by interviewing Steinem is mentioned in an interview of Kincaid by Selwyn Cudjoe published in the 1990 conference anthology *Caribbean Women Writers*, ed. Cudgoe.

4 This is how Kincaid describes her name change in a 1995 interview with Charlie Rose. The name "Jamaica" seems of significance, given that some of Kincaid's early articles for *The New Yorker* were commentaries on Caribbean life and events.

5 The history of this narrative of West Indian immigration dates back to at least the 1920s but nevertheless applies in the present. Malcolm Gladwell's 1996 article "Black Like Them" is one example of the continuing currency of this issue in the public imaginary.

6 Early coming-of-age Caribbean narratives such as George Lamming's Barbadian 1950s *In the Castle of My Skin*, and Joseph Zobel's Martinican 1950s *Rue Cases-Nègres* came out of a predominantly male tradition. The female coming-of-age narrative proliferates after 1970, although there are some early French Caribbean female narratives and Paule Marshall's 1959 coming-of-age migration story, *Brown Girl, Brownstones*.

7 An example of this is when Tee's father goes to "sea" and Tee thinks he's going to "see whether he could find Mammy and the baby."

8 I make a similar analysis of Hodge's narrative strategy in my article "Neo-Coloniality, Literary Representation, and the Problem of Disciplinary Solutions."

9 I believe that this particular style of narration is not unique to Hodge but is a function of many novels by Black writers that employ oral storytelling devices and Black English or creole within the structure of the narrative.

10 The phrase "diaspora literacy" was first invoked by Vévé Clark in her article "Developing Diaspora Literacy and *Marasa* Consciousness."

11 The term "groundings," which comes out of the Rastafari context in Jamaica, refers to a dialogue, conversation, or "reasoning session" rooted in the African cultural mores of the oppressed in a Black Caribbean context.

12 The Black U.S. vernacular expression "signifyin'" is invoked here to mean "making a mockery of something." In the context of the novel, the "thing" being mocked is the desire to imitate European and American culture and behavior.

13 In her insightful article "This Englishness Will Kill You: Colonialist Education and Female Socialization in Merle Hodge's *Crick Crack Monkey* and Bessie Head's *Maru*," Ketu Katrak also explores the negative effects of the colonial educational system on the psyche of young Black women.

14 Erna Brodber made this statement in a guest lecture in November 2001, in Carolyn Cooper's course "African Diaspora Women Writers" at the University of The West Indies, Mona Campus, Kingston, Jamaica, in the fall semester of 2001.

15 Caribbean scholars Pamela Mordecai and Betty Wilson edited an anthology entitled *Her True-True Name: An Anthology of Women's Writing from the Caribbean*. The editors' choice of title emphasizes the significance of names, naming, and cultural retention through oral expression as a part of African diaspora cultures.

16 In a 1976 article written for the *Village Voice* entitled "Last of the Black White Girls" Jamaica Kincaid reviewed a Diana Ross concert and con-

cluded that Ross's success had come as a result of a "devotion to imitation." Speaking of Ross, Kincaid says, "Not only was she a young woman who conveyed the innocence of a girl, but she was a black person who had mastered without the slightest bit of self-consciousness or embarrassment, being white" (15). Kincaid further adds that Ross's voice had no "trace of anything relatively black" (15). If we do an intertextual reading of Kincaid's earlier essay and this novel, it is hard to think of the artificiality of the three girls singing outside of the context of the 1960s group The Supremes and their devotion to white imitation.

17 Adisa's statement here resonates with Kincaid's statements in interviews in which she speaks about not choosing racial identity terms to describe herself but preferring instead to be identified simply as a human being. She has also said that while she feels deeply sympathetic to those who feel that they have been discriminated against on the basis of race and gender, that has not personally been her experience (March 1996 interview by Charlie Rose).

18 In conversations with me back in 1996, Greg Thomas referred me to this book by John Roberts and drew my attention to the uncanny relationship between Roberts's analysis and the actions of Lovelace's character Joebell.

19 I wrote these observations before the 2001 Modern Language Association Conference, in which this contradiction between the social construction of race and critiques of racism was noted also by Carole Boyce Davies, in her critical analysis of Paul Gilroy's text *Against Race*.

20 "Moreover, the contention that the Negro imitates from a feeling of inferiority is incorrect. He mimics for the love of it. The group of Negroes who slavishly imitate is small" (Hurston, "Characteristics of Negro Expression," in *Hurston*, 838).

4 Diaspora Philosophy, French Caribbean Literature

1 Her work is usually compared to writers such as Mayotte Capecia, Michèle Lacrosil, Suzanne Lacascade, Marie Chauvet, Myriam Warner-Vieyra, Jacqueline Manicom, and Maryse Condé.

2 Shelton addresses this point also in her article "Women Writers of the French-Speaking Caribbean," in *Caribbean Women Writers*, stating, "The island in Schwarz-Bart's fiction is not a place to be fled nor a prison in which one slowly dies; it is the locus of self-discovery and human realization" (355).

3 While the work of many French Caribbean women writers can be interpreted as representing the sociopolitical complexities of the so-

cieties they inhabited, frequently the main concern was with an explicitly individual, female experience of alienation. Mayotte Capecia's *Je Suis Martiniquaise,* Suzanne Lacascade's *Claire Solange, âme africaine,* Michèle Lacrosil's *Sapotille et le serin d'argile* and *Cajou,* Marie Chauvet's *Amour,* Myriam Warner-Vieyra's *Juletane,* and Maryse Condé's *Hérémakhonon* can all be seen as representative of this particular thematic concern.

4 Schwarz-Bart makes this statement in an interview with Roger and Héliane Toumson, in *Textes, études, et documents.*

5 In "Beyond the Word of Man: Edouard Glissant and the New Discourse of the Antilles," Sylvia Wynter states, "The situation of Martinique differed not only in the accidental sense of finding itself subordinated to a collaborationist rather than Resistance France, but also in a structural-existential sense; for the dual processes of intellectual and social assimilation specific to the Catholic French model of colonization were already firmly in place in Martinique as distinct from the antithetical processes of intellectual assimilation but of *social exclusion* and economic marginalization which defined the Protestant British model of dominance and subordination specific to the situation of a British colony such as Jamaica" (637). The differences between the situations of Martinique and Guadeloupe was also argued for by Caribbean scholars Marie-Jose Zenga and Armstrong Alexis (among others) at a panel at the 1997 Caribbean Studies Association Annual Conference, Barranquilla, Colombia, where a version of this chapter was first presented. In arguing thus, these scholars described the substantial difference in both the literature and everyday culture of both islands in terms of questions of assimilation and use of creole language.

6 The translation of this poem is a combination of my own and those of Ellen Conroy Kennedy, translator of Lilyan Kesteloot's *Les écrivains noirs de langue française: naissance d'une littérature.* I was not able to obtain full translations of Damas's *Pigments* and Conroy Kennedy only translates portions of Damas's poetry.

7 "He" is in quotation marks since the gender of the speaker in this poem is unspecified.

8 In "Beyond the Word of Man," Sylvia Wynter states, "I want to propose here that this uprising is directed not only at our present order of discourse and at its founding Word of Man, as the Word of the human conceptualized as a selected being and natural organism, but also at the tradition of discourse to which its specific discourse of man belongs: that is, at the tradition on whose basis, from 1512 onward, Western Europe was to effect the first stage of secularization of human existence in the context of its own global expansion and to lay the basis of the

plantation structure out of which the contemporary societies of Glissant's Antilles, as well as the specificity of their Antilleanity, as he insists and reinsists, was to emerge."

9   See Bridget Jones's "French Guiana" and Oruno D. Lara's "Résistance ou assimilation."

10 Jones states, "Any discussion of black authenticity in French Guiana needs to come to terms both with the prior claims of the Amerindians, and with the often controversial presence of real maroons" ("French Guiana," 394).

11 Caribbean scholar Rupert Lewis used this phrase to describe the eye-opening experience that certain Jamaican students had when they analyzed the everyday proverbs that were used in their families.

12 In the article "Diaspora Literacy and Marasa Consciousness" Vévé Clark tells us, "Diaspora literacy defines the reader's ability to comprehend the literatures of Africa, Afro-America, and the Caribbean from an informed, indigenous perspective. The field is multicultural and multilingual, encompassing writing in European and ethnic languages. In the current textual environment, diaspora literacy suggests that names such as *Popul Vuh*, Legba, Bélain d'Esnambuc, Nanny, José Marti, Bigger Thomas and Marie Chauvet represent mnemonic devices whose recall releases a learned tradition. This type of literacy is more than a purely intellectual exercise. It is a skill for both narrator and reader which demands a knowledge of historical, social, cultural, and political development generated by lived and textual experience. Throughout the twentieth century, diaspora literacy has implied an ease and intimacy with more than one language, with interdisciplinary relations among history, ethnology, and the folklore of regional expression. Only recently has literary theory applied to Afro-Caribbean texts become indispensable" (42).

13 For sources criticizing the purportedly apolitical nature of Hurston's *Mules and Men*, see Robert Hemenway's 1978 introduction to the text.

14 Wynter argues that "we live our lives according to the regulatory representations of that which constitutes symbolic *life* and that which constitutes its Lack, its mode of symbolic *death*. Group categories, [such as] that of the indio/Negro/Mad, who embody the Ontological Lack are therefore the signifier of symbolic 'death.'" Wynter theorizes "Ontological Lack" with regards to the shifts from a Christian to a more secular world order, one in which the unbaptized laity were the "bearers of this universal mode of the Abject" within a Christian world order, but within a more secular context, that burden shifted to those who were perceived as embodying "lower sensory nature" in the binary opposition between "European settlers . . . New World peoples (indios)

. . . and enslaved peoples of Africa (Negroes)" ("Beyond the Word of Man," 641).

15 Elizabeth Betty Wilson, "History and Memory," 185–86. Wilson takes her quotes from the interview with Schwarz-Bart in Toumson and Toumson, *Textes, études, et documents.*

16 Bridget Jones, in her introduction to *The Bridge of Beyond* (her English translation of *Pluie et vent sur Télumée Miracle*), observes that this text is often discussed and situated by scholars as a response to Haitian writer Jacques Roumain's *Masters of the Dew.*

17 Busia's interpretation of the creole sayings is similar to my interpretation of how these sayings function in the text.

18 In "*Pluie et vent sur Télumée Miracle* de Simone Schwarz-Bart: memoire du temps et prise de parole," Elisabeth Mudimbe-Boyi writes, "A la fin du roman personnages et narratrice se trouvent réunis dans un même pronom 'nous,' signe de leur destinée commune, d'une même histoire: celle d'un peuple et d'une race" (155–56; "At the end of the novel, both the narrator and the characters are united under the same pronoun 'we,' indicating their common destiny and that they come from the same history: from the same people and the same race").

19 Busia comments further in her footnote in "The Gift of Metaphor": "Speech has always been significant in cultures primarily sensitive to oral traditions. In the context of the African continent, this still remains true in very many aspects of life" (300).

20 Abena P. A. Busia describes this gift of metaphor as the knowledge that there are words that separate and words that bind. This knowledge is bequeathed to Télumée by her grandmother and revealed in the narrative through storytelling and song ("The Gift of Metaphor," 291–92).

21 The first time this occurs is when Télumée states, "Ma maîtresse avait la voix un peu sèche, mais qu'est-ce qu-une voix un peu sèche, si on ne l'écate pas" (95; "My mistress's voice was rather curt, but what is a rather curt voice if you don't listen to it?" 60).

22 Many critical perspectives on Schwarz-Bart's novel seem gridlocked over interpreting the text as demonstrating some feminine and feminist aesthetic as opposed to emphasizing communal and cultural values and aesthetics. Ironically, the critical perspectives break down by and large along racial lines, with white female scholars emphasizing feminist aesthetic readings and Black female scholars emphasizing communality and cultural values. In her analysis of the narrative, Mudimbe-Boyi says, "A ce niveau, le roman dépasse la simple chronique d'une lignée de femmes [et devient] . . . une manière de 'dire' l'espace culturel antillais" ("*Pluie et vent sur Télumée Miracle*," 156; "At this level, the novel moves beyond being a simple chronicle of female lineage and becomes

a way of talking about the cultural identity of the Antilles"). At the other extreme is Karen Smyley Wallace's "Créolité and the Feminine Text in Simone Schwarz-Bart," in which she argues for the text as exemplary of both a creole aesthetic *and* a feminine writing aesthetic that she links to the Hélène Cixous genre of French feminism: "When Hélène Cixous encourages woman to 'write her body' she focuses on an intense, high powered light on the area of sensuality in the feminine text. . . . In its celebration of the women of Guadeloupe, *Pluie et vent* offers many examples of the text as a sensual craft" (559). Critics such as Abena Busia and Clarisse Zimra appear to negotiate between both poles.

23   While many scholars have chosen to discuss Simone Schwarz-Bart's novel in relation to a predominantly Caribbean rather than African cultural framework, it is of some interest that the writer's later work moved in the direction of continental African research. She published a text entitled *Homage à la femme noire* (translated as *In Praise of Black Women* in 2001), which appears to be an encyclopedia-like compilation of stories about ancient African queens.

24   Glissant further argues that with "relocated" and "transplanted" populations "where technical know-how is maintained or renewed" the impulse to revert "will decline . . . with the need to come to terms with the new land [and] as the memory of the ancestral country fades" (18). Both here and when he mentions nineteenth-century white American support of Black migration to Liberia, Glissant, ironically, is forced to simplify the factual reality to maintain his argument. His reference to white support for Black migration does not account for the difference when there was Black mobilization for migration back to Africa. Similarly, his statement that the "impulse to revert will decline as memory of the ancestral country fades" does not thoroughly account for the Garvey movement, a twentieth-century phenomenon, or contemporary Rastafari movements in the Caribbean. Edward Blyden and others in the nineteenth century, as well as Marcus Garvey and the Rastafari movement in the twentieth century, represented Back-to-Africa movements sponsored by Black people and Black organizations. Although this is not the intention, Glissant's analysis implies that the desire to get Blacks back to Africa was mostly white-inspired.

25   This infamous quotation from the 1857 Dred Scott decision is frequently cited by Black scholars as embodying a truth about the governing logic behind constitutional law and race relations in the United States.

26   Wynter makes an analogy between Martinicans' experience of a literal blockade, by French and U.S. troops during World War II, and "the root

metaphor that is central to Glissant's oeuvre . . . that of *blocking*. Its referent is the series of empirical obstacles impeding the Antilles' realization of the full potential of what Glissant defines as 'Antilleanity.' Glissant sees this blocking at a fundamental level, in the case of both Martinique and the Francophone Caribbean in general, as the effect of the French model of assimilation" ("Beyond the Word of Man," 637–38).

27 *Restitution* could be a way of elaborating on the terminology that Schwarz-Bart herself used to describe her project: "restitution" coming from "restituer," to reconstruct and restore. The quote in the text is taken from Toumson and Toumson, *Textes, études, et documents*.

28 "The Shadow of the Whip" is the title of Merle Hodge's essay on Black male and female relations and the legacy of slavery.

29 *Fashion Me a People* was the title of series of interdenominational Christian education materials designed for the Caribbean. This series was designed, named, and substantially written by Dr. Joyce Bailey.

5 Audre Lorde and Paule Marshall

1 Davies states that *zami* "(literally 'les amies' [the friends] in Caribbean French patois) . . . [is] a word spoken in silence or hurled as abuse, or identified as transgressive sexuality" (117–20).

2 For Cliff's own statements about the identity she was claiming in *Claiming*, see Opal Palmer Adisa, "Journey into Speech—A Writer between Two Worlds."

3 Contrary to Lionnet, I would argue that *Zami* constitutes the condition of possibility for Michelle Cliff's *The Land of Look Behind*, which not only functions as a "biomythography" of sorts, combining prose, poetry, and essays, but is also dedicated to Audre Lorde. Yet here, when lesbian identity is claimed, it is articulated within the context of white gay male identity in England and is disarticulated from Caribbeanness. See Michelle Cliff, "If I Could Write This in Fire, I Would Write This in Fire," in *The Land of Look Behind*, 68–69.

4 For an elaboration of these points and a full citation of the Césaire-Depestre interview, see chapter 1.

5 First line of Langston Hughes's poem, "I Too." The poem is included in the anthology edited by Arna Bontemps, *American Negro Poetry*, 64.

6 In her 1980 book *The Cancer Journals*, Lorde makes reference to her mastectomy.

1 See Anne Cunningham's master's thesis, "The Destructive Imagination: Whiteness as Terrified Consciousness."

2 This phrase is used by Hurston in her essay "Characteristics of Negro Expression" in *The Sanctified Church* to describe the inferiority complex of a colored elite that models its cultural values on the dominant society's norms, as distinct from "Negroes," who imitate for the sheer love of it.

Bibliography

Aas-Rouxparis, Nicole. "Espace antillais au féminin: présence, absence." *French Review* 70, no. 6 (May 1997): 854–64.

Adisa, Opal Palmer. "Island Daughter." *Women's Review of Books* 85 (1991): 56–60.

———. "Journey into Speech—A Writer between Two Worlds: An Interview with Michelle Cliff." *African American Review* 28, no. 2 (1994): 273–81.

Amadiume, Ifi. *African Matriarchal Foundations: The Case of Igbo Societies*. London: Karnak House, 1987.

———. *Daughters of the Goddess, Daughters of Imperialism*. London: Zed Books, 2000.

———. *Male Daughters, Female Husbands*. London: Zed Books, 1987.

———. *Reinventing Africa: Matriarchy, Religion and Culture*. London: Zed Books, 1997.

Anim-Addo, Joan. *Framing the Word: Gender and Genre in Caribbean Women's Writing*. London: Whiting and Birch, 1996.

Arnold, James A. *A History of Literature in the Caribbean*. Vol. 2. Philadelphia: John Benjamins, 1994.

Bâ, Sylvia Washington. *The Concept of Negritude in the Poetry of Léopold Sédar Senghor*. Princeton: Princeton University Press, 1973.

Bambara, Toni Cade. *The Black Woman*. New York: Mentor Books, 1970.

———. *Deep Sightings and Rescue Missions*. New York: Vintage Books, 1996.

———. Keynote address. "Journey across Three Continents Film Festival," Detroit, Mich., March 13, 1987. In *Journey across Three Continents: Film and Lecture Series*, 8–9. New York: Third World Newsreel, 1985.

Barrow, Christine. "Caribbean Masculinity and Family: Revisiting 'Marginality' and 'Reputation.'" In *Caribbean Portraits*, edited by Christine Barrow, 339–58. Kingston, Jamaica: Ian Randle, 1998.

Boggs, James. *Racism and the Class Struggle*. New York: Monthly Review Press, 1970.

Boggs, James, and Grace Lee Boggs. *Revolution and Evolution in the Twentieth Century*. New York: Monthly Review Press, 1974.

Bonetti, Kay. "Interview with Jamaica Kincaid." American Audio Prose Library 338, 339, 341. Columbia, Mo.: Western Historical Manuscript Collection, n.d. Audiocassette.

Bontemps, Arna. *American Negro Poetry*. New York: Hill and Wang, 1963.

Brathwaite, Edward Kamau. *Folk Culture of the Slaves in Jamaica*. London: New Beacon Books, 1971.

——. *History of the Voice: The Development of Nation Language in Anglophone Caribbean Poetry*. London: New Beacon Books, 1984.

Brodber, Erna. "Brief Notes on De Laurence in Jamaica." *ACIJ Research Review*, no. 4 (1999): 91–99.

——. *Jane and Louisa Will Soon Come Home*. London: New Beacon Books, 1980.

——. *Louisiana*. London: New Beacon Books, 1994.

——. *Perceptions of Caribbean Women: Towards a Documentation of Stereotypes*. Cove Hill, Barbados: Institute of Social and Economic Research, 1982.

Brown, Mae Verta. *Thursdays and Every Other Sunday Off*. New York: Doubleday, 1972.

Busia, Abena P. A. "The Gift of Metaphor: Symbolic Strategies and the Triumph of Survival in Simone Schwarz-Bart's *The Bridge of Beyond*." In *Out of the Kumbla: Caribbean Women and Literature*, edited by Carole Boyce Davies and Elaine Savory Fido, 289–301. Trenton, N.J.: Africa World Press, 1990.

Carlston, Erin G. "Zami and the Politics of Plural Identity." In *Sexual Practice, Textual Theory: Lesbian Cultural Criticism*, edited by Susan J. Wolfe and Julia Penelope, 226–236. Cambridge, Mass.: Blackwell, 1993.

Césaire, Aimé. "Culture and Colonisation." In *Présence Africaine*, nos. 8–10, *Proceedings of the First International Conference of Negro Writers and Artists*, part 2 (June–November 1956): 193–229.

——. "The Verb 'Marronner' / For René Depestre, Haitian Poet." In *Aimé Césaire: The Collected Poetry*, translated by Clayton Eshleman and Annette Smith, 369–371. Berkeley: University of California Press, 1983.

Clark, Vévé. "Developing Diaspora Literacy and *Marasa* Consciousness." In *Comparative American Identities: Race, Sex and Nationality in the Modern Text*, edited by Hortense Spillers, 40–61. New York: Routledge, 1991.

Cliff, Michelle. *Abeng*. New York: Obelisk / Dutton, 1984.

——. *Bodies of Water*. London: Minerva Paperback, 1990.

——. *Claiming an Identity They Taught Me to Despise*. Watertown, Mass.: Persephone Press, 1980.

——. *Free Enterprise*. New York: Dutton, 1993.

——. *The Land of Look Behind*. Ithaca: Firebrand Books, 1985.

——. *No Telephone to Heaven*. New York: Vintage Books, 1989.

Clifford, James. *The Predicament of Culture*. Cambridge, Mass.: Harvard University Press, 1988.

Cobham, Rhonda. "Dr. Freud for Visitor." *Women's Review of Books* 8, no. 5 (February 1991): 17–18.

Cobham, Rhonda, and Merle Collins. *Watchers and Seekers: Creative Writing by Black Women in Britain*. London: Women's Press, 1987.

Cruse, Harold. *Rebellion or Revolution?* New York: William Morrow, 1968.

Cudjoe, Selwyn R. *Caribbean Women Writers.* Amherst: University of Massachusetts Press, 1990.

———. *Resistance and Caribbean Literature.* Columbus: Ohio University Press, 1980.

Cunningham, Anne. "The Destructive Imagination: Whiteness as Terrified Consciousness." M.A. thesis, Department of English, University of Olahoma, 2002.

Damas, Léon Gontran. *Pigments/Névralgies.* Paris: Éditions Présence Africaine, 1972.

Dance, Daryl C. *Folklore from Contemporary Jamaicans.* Knoxville: University of Tennessee Press, 1985.

Dash, J. Michael. "The World and the Word: French Caribbean Writing in the Twentieth Century." *Callaloo* (winter 1988): 112–31.

Davies, Carole Boyce. *Black Women, Writing and Identity: Migrations of the Subject.* London: Routledge, 1994.

Davies, Carole Boyce, and Elaine Savory Fido. *Out of the Kumbla: Caribbean Women and Literature.* Trenton, N.J.: Africa World Press, 1990.

Depestre, René. *Bonjour et adieu à la négritude.* Paris: Éditions Robert Laffont, 1980.

Dilger, Gerhard. "Jamaica Kincaid Talks to Gerhard Dilger." *Wasafiri,* no. 16, *Special Caribbean Issue* (autumn 1992): 21–25.

Diop, Alioune. "Opening Address." *Présence Africaine,* no. 8, *Proceedings of the First International Conference of Negro Writers and Artists,* part 1 (June 1956): 9–18.

Diop, Cheikh Anta. *The African Origin of Civilization: Myth or Reality.* New York: Lawrence Hill Books, 1974.

———. *Civilization or Barbarism: An Authentic Anthropology.* New York: Lawrence Hill Books, 1991.

———. "The Cultural Contributions and Prospects of Africa." In *Présence Africaine,* no. 10, *Proceedings of the First International Conference of Negro Writers and Artists,* part 2 (June–November 1956): 347–54.

———. *Pre-Colonial Black Africa.* New York: Lawrence Hill Books, 1987.

Eastman, Rudolph, and Maureen Warner-Lewis. "Forms of African Spirituality in Trinidad and Tobago." In *African Spirituality: Forms, Meanings, Expressions,* edited by Jacob Olupona, 403–15. New York: Crossroad, 2001.

Edmondson, Belinda. "Race, Privilege, and the Politics of (Re)-writing History: An Analysis of the Novels of Michelle Cliff." *Callaloo* 16, no. 1 (winter 1993): 180–91.

Esteves, Carmen C., and Lizabeth Paravisini-Gebert. *Green Cane and Juicy Flotsam: Short Stories by Caribbean Women.* Rutgers: Rutgers University Press, 1991.

Evans, Mari, ed. *Black Women Writers (1950–1980): A Critical Evaluation.* New York: Anchor Press/Doubleday, 1984.

Fanon, Frantz. *Black Skin, White Masks.* Translated by Charles Lam Markmann. New York: Grove Press, 1967.

———. *Toward the African Revolution.* Translated by Haakon Chevalier. New York: Grove Press, 1967.

———. *The Wretched of the Earth.* New York: Grove Weidenfeld, 1963.

Ferguson, Moira. "Lucy and the Mark of the Colonizer." *Modern Fiction Studies* 39, no. 2 (summer 1993): 237–59.

Frazier, Edward Franklin. *Black Bourgeoisie.* New York: Collier Books, 1962.

Gabbin, Joanne V. *The Furious Flowering of African American Poetry.* Charlottesville: University Press of Virginia, 1999.

Garis, Leslie. "Through West Indian Eyes." *New York Times Magazine,* October 7, 1990, 42–91.

Gilroy, Paul. *The Black Atlantic.* Cambridge, Mass.: Harvard University Press, 1993.

———. "Cultural Studies and Ethnic Absolutism." In *Cultural Studies,* edited by Lawrence Grossberg, 187–98. New York: Routledge, 1992.

Gladwell, Malcolm. "Black Like Them." *New Yorker,* April 29 and May 6, 1996, 74–81.

Glissant, Edouard. *Caribbean Discourse.* Translated and with an introduction by J. Michael Dash. Charlottesville: University Press of Virginia, 1989.

Griffith, Glyne A. *Deconstruction, Imperialism and the West Indian Novel.* Kingston, Jamaica: University of the West Indies Press, 1996.

Hall, Stuart. "What Is This "Black" in Black Popular Culture?" In *Black Popular Culture,* edited by Gina Dent, 21–33. Seattle: Bay Press, 1992.

Hemenway, Robert E. *Zora Neale Hurston: A Literary Biography.* Urbana: University of Illinois Press, 1977.

Hodge, Merle. "Challenges of the Struggle for Sovereignty: Changing the World versus Writing Stories." In *Caribbean Women Writers,* edited by Selwyn Cudjoe, 202–8. Wellesley, Mass.: Calaloux Publications, 1990.

———. *Crick Crack Monkey.* London: Heinemann, 1970.

———. *For the Life of Laetitia.* New York: Farrar Straus Giroux, 1993.

———. Introduction to *Perceptions of Caribbean Women: Towards a Documentation of Stereotypes,* by Erna Brodber, vii–xiii. Cove Hill, Barbados: Institute of Social and Economic Research, 1982.

———. "Novels on the French Caribbean Intellectual in France." *Revista/Review Interamericana* 6, no.2 (summer 1976): 211–31.

———. "The Shadow of the Whip: A Comment on Male-Female Relations in the Caribbean." In *I Am Because We Are: Readings in Black Philosophy,* edited by Fred Lee Hord and Jonathan Scott Lee, 189–94. Amherst: University of Massachusetts Press, 1995.

———. "Social Conscience or Exoticism? Two Novels from Guadeloupe." *Revista/Review Interamericana* 4, no. 3 (fall 1974): 391–401.

Holmstrom, David. "Jamaica Kincaid: Writing for Solace, for Herself." *Christian Science Monitor,* January 19, 1996: 14.

Hughes, Langston. "The Negro Artist and the Racial Mountain." In *Norton Anthology of African American Literature,* edited by Henry Louis Gates Jr., 1266–69. New York: Norton, 1997.

Hull, Gloria T., Patricia Bell Scott, and Barbara Smith. *All the Women Are*

White, All the Blacks Are Men, but Some of Us Are Brave: Black Women's Studies. New York: Feminist Press, 1982.

Hurston, Zora Neale. *Hurston: Folklore, Memoirs and Other Writings.* New York: Library of America, 1995.

——. *Mules and Men.* Introduction by Robert E. Hemenway. Bloomington: Indiana University Press, 1978.

——. *The Sanctified Church.* New York: Marlowe, 1981.

——. *Tell My Horse: Voodoo and Life in Haiti and Jamaica.* New York: Harper and Row, 1990.

Hymans, Jacques Louis. *Léopold Sédar Senghor: An Intellectual Biography.* Edinburgh: Edinburgh University Press, 1971.

Jaggi, Maya. "Interview with Earl Lovelace." *Wasafiri,* no. 12 (autumn 1990): 25–27.

John, Catherine A. "Complicity, Revolution and Black Female Writing" *Race and Class* 40, no. 4 (April–June 1999): 33–43.

——. "Neo-Coloniality, Literary Representation, and the Problem of Disciplinary Solutions." In *De-Colonizing the Academy,* edited by Carole Boyce Davies, 235–55. Trenton, N.J.: Africa World Press, 2003.

——. "The Haunting Past and the Production of Racial Subjects: Contemporary Afro-Caribbean Women's Writing." Ph.D. dissertation, University of California, Santa Cruz, 1997.

Jones, Bridget. "French Guiana." In *A History of Literature in the Caribbean,* edited by A. James Arnold, 1:389–98. Philadelphia: John Benjamins, 1994.

Jones, Edward A. *Voices of Négritude: The Expression of Black Experience in the Poetry of Senghor, Césaire, and Damas.* Valley Forge, Pa.: Judson Press, 1971.

Jones, Leroi. *Blues People.* New York: Quill, 1999.

Jordan, June. "On Richard Wright and Zora Neale Hurston: Notes towards a Balancing of Love and Hatred." *Black World,* August 1974, 4–9.

Kesteloot, Lilyan. *Black Writers in French: A Literary History of Negritude.* Translated by Ellen Conroy Kennedy. Washington, D.C.: Howard University Press, 1991.

Katrak, Ketu. "This Englishness Will Kill You: Colonialist Education and Female Socialization in Merle Hodge's *Crick Crack Monkey* and Bessie Head's *Maru.*" *College Literature* 22, no. 1 (Feb. 1995): 62–77.

Kincaid, Jamaica. *Annie John.* New York: Plume, 1986.

——. *At the Bottom of the River.* New York: Plume, 1992.

——. *The Autobiography of My Mother.* New York: Farrar Straus Giroux, 1996.

——. "Flowers of Evil." *New Yorker,* October 5, 1992, 154–59.

——. "Jamaica Kincaid's New York." *Rolling Stone,* October 6, 1977, 71–73.

——. "Last of the Black White Girls." *Village Voice,* 28 June 1976, 152–55.

——. *Lucy.* New York: Farrar Straus Giroux, 1990.

——. "On Seeing England for the First Time." *Transition* 51 (1991): 32–40.

——. *A Small Place.* New York: Plume, 1988.

——. "The Talk of the Town." *New Yorker,* July 19, 1976, 33.

——. "The Talk of the Town." *New Yorker,* October, 17, 1977, 37–39.

——. "The Talk of the Town." *New Yorker,* January 3, 1983, 23–24.

——. "When I Was 17." *Ingenue*, 1973.

Kincaid, Jamaica, and George Trow. "The Talk of the Town." *New Yorker*, September 30, 1974.

KRS-One. "Can the Teacher Be Taught? A Conversation with KRS-One and Michael Lipscomb." *Transition*, no. 57 (1992): 168–89.

Lamming, George. *In The Castle of My Skin*. New York: McGraw-Hill, 1954.

Lara, Oruno D. "Résistance ou assimilation." In *Hommage Posthume à Léon-Gontran Damas*, 327–49. Paris: Éditions Présence Africaine.

Lionnet, Françoise. *Postcolonial Representations: Women, Literature, Identity*. Ithaca: Cornell University Press, 1995.

Lorde, Audre. *The Black Unicorn*. New York: W.W. Norton, 1978.

——. *The Cancer Journals*. San Francisco: Spinsters Ink, 1980.

——. *Coal*. New York: W. W. Norton, 1976.

——. *The First Cities*. New York City: Poet's Press, 1968.

——. *Our Dead behind Us*. New York: W. W. Norton, 1986.

——. *Sister Outsider*. New York: Crossing Press, 1984.

——. *Undersong*. New York: W. W. Norton, 1992.

——. *Zami: A New Spelling of My Name*. Freedom, Calif.: Crossing Press, 1982.

Lovelace, Earl. "Joebell and America." In *A Brief Conversion and Other Stories*, 111–24. London: Heinemann, 1988.

Maja-Pierce, Adewale. "Corruption in the Caribbean." *New Statesman and Society*, October 7, 1988, 40.

Marshall, Paule. *Brown Girl, Brownstones*. Old Westbury, N.Y.: The Feminist Press, 1959.

——. *The Chosen Place, the Timeless People*. New York: Vintage Books, 1992.

——. *Praisesong for the Widow*. New York: Plume, 1983.

Martin, Tony. *Race First: The Ideological and Organizational Struggles of Marcus Garvey and the Universal Negro Improvement Association*. Westport, Conn.: Greenwood Press, 1976.

Ménil, René. *Tracées: identité, négritude, esthétique aux Antilles*. Paris: Éditions Robert Laffont, 1981.

Mokhtar, G., ed. *Ancient Civilizations of Africa*. Vol. 2 of *General History of Africa*. London: Heinemann, 1981.

Moore, Carlos. *African Presence in the Americas*. Trenton, N.J.: Africa World Press, 1995.

Mordecai, Pamela, and Betty Wilson. *Her True-True Name: An Anthology of Women's Writing from the Caribbean*. London: Heinemann Educational, 1989.

Morris-Brown, Vivien. *The Jamaica Handbook of Proverbs*. Mandeville, Jamaica: Island Heart Publishers, 1993.

Mudimbe-Boyi, Elisabeth. "*Pluie et vent sur Télumée Miracle* de Simone Schwarz-Bart: memoire du temps et prise de parole." *Continental, Latin-American and Francophone Women Writers*, edited by Ginnette Adamson and Eunice Myers, 2:155–64. New York: University Press of America, 1991.

Nettleford, Rex. "The Aesthetics of Negritude." In *African Presence in the Americas*, edited by Carlos Moore. Trenton, N.J.: Africa World Press, 1995.

Bibliography

Ogunyemi, Chikwenye. "The Dynamics of the Contemporary Black Female Novel in English." *Signs* (1985): 64–89.

Ormerod, Beverley. *An Introduction to the French Caribbean Novel*. London: Heinemann, 1982.

Oyewumi, Oyeronké. *The Invention of Women: Making an African Sense of Western Gender Discourses*. Minneapolis: University of Minnesota Press, 1997.

Patton, Venetria K. *Women in Chains: The Legacy of Slavery in Black Women's Fiction*. New York: State University of New York Press, 2000.

Pollard, Velma. "Mixing Codes and Mixing Voices—Language in Earl Lovelace's *Salt*." *Changing English* 6, no. 1 (1999): 93–101.

Praeger, Michèle. "Figures de l'antillanité dans les romans de Simone Schwarz-Bart." *Symposium* 46, no. 2 (summer 1992): 119–32.

Présence Africaine Conference Committee. *Présence Africaine*, nos. 8–10: *Proceedings of the First International Conference of Negro Writers and Artists*, parts 1–3 (June–November 1956).

Raiskin, Judith L. *Snow on the Cane Fields: Women's Writing and Creole Subjectivity*. Minneapolis: University of Minnesota Press, 1996.

Ramchand, Kenneth. "Terrified Consciousness." *Journal of Commonwealth Literature*, no. 7 (1969): 8–19.

———. *The West Indian Novel and Its Background*. New York: Barnes and Noble, 1970.

Reddock, Rhoda. *Women, Labor and Politics in Trinidad and Tobago: A History*. London: Zed Books, 1994.

Roberts, John W. *From Trickster to Badman: The Black Folk Hero in Slavery and Freedom*. Philadelphia: University of Pennsylvania Press, 1989.

Rodney, Walter. *The Groundings with My Brothers*. Chicago: Research Associates School Times Publications, 1996.

———. *How Europe Underdeveloped Africa*. Washington, D.C.: Howard University Press, 1982.

———. *Walter Rodney Speaks: The Making of an African Intellectual*. Trenton, N.J.: Africa World Press, 1990.

Rose, Charlie. Interview with Jamaica Kincaid. *Charlie Rose Show*, PBS, March 1, 1996.

Rubin, Merle. "A Daughter Forced to be Her Own Mother." *Christian Science Monitor*, January 17, 1996, 14.

Saakana, Amon Saba. *The Colonial Legacy in Caribbean Literature*. Trenton, N.J.: Africa World Press, 1987.

Sawyerr, Harry. "Spirit Belief in the Cosmology of Africa and the Caribbean." *ACIJ Research Review*, no. 4 (1999): 71–90.

Schwarz-Bart, Simone. *Hommage à la Femme Noire*. Paris: Editions Consulaires, 1988. Translated by Rose-Myriam Réjouis, Stephanie Daval, and Val Vinokurov as *In Praise of Black Women*. Vol. 1, *Ancient African Queens* (Madison: University of Wisconsin Press, 2001).

———. *Pluie et vent sur Télumée Miracle*. Paris: Éditions du Seuil, 1972. Translated by Barbara Bray as *The Bridge of Beyond*, with introduction by Bridget Jones (London: Heinemann, 1982).

———. *Ti Jean L'Horizon*. Paris: Éditions du Seuil, 1979. Translated by Barbara Bray as *Between Two Worlds* (London: Heinemann, 1981).

Senghor, Léopold Sédar. *Anthologie de la nouvelle poésie nègre et malgache de langue française*. Paris: Presses Universitaires de France, 1969.

———. *The Foundations of "Africanité" or "Négritude" and "Arabité."* Translated by Mercer Cook. Paris: Présence Africaine, 1971.

———. "The Spirit of Civilization." Translated by Mercer Cook. Paper presented at the First International Conference of Negro Writers and Artists, Présence Africaine Conference Committee, Paris, 1956.

Shelton, Marie Denise. "Literature Extracted: A Poetic of Daily Life." *Callaloo* 15, no. 1 (1992): 167–78.

———. "A New Cry: From the 1960s to the 1980s." In *A History of Literature in the Caribbean*, edited by A. James Arnold, 1:427–33. Philadelphia: John Benjamins, 1994.

———. "Women Writers of the French-Speaking Caribbean." In *Caribbean Women Writers*, edited by Selwyn Cudjoe. Amherst: University of Massachusetts Press, 1990.

Smith, Barbara. *Home Girls: A Black Feminist Anthology*. New York: Kitchen Table: Women of Color Press, 1983.

Spleth, Janice. *Léopold Sédar Senghor*. Boston: G. K. Hall, 1985.

Steady, Filomina Chioma. *The Black Woman Cross-Culturally*. Rochester, Vt.: Schenkman Books, 1981.

Stepto, R. B. "The Phenomenal Woman and the Severed Daughter." *Parnassus: Poetry in Review* 8, no. 1 (fall–winter 1979): 315–16.

Stuckey, Sterling. *Slave Culture: Nationalist Theory and the Foundations of Black America*. New York: Oxford University Press, 1987.

Sutton, Constance R., and Elsa Chaney, eds. *Caribbean Life in New York City: Sociocultural Dimensions*. New York: Center for Migration Studies, 1987.

T'Shaka, Oba. *Return to the African Mother Principle of Male and Female Equality*. Vol. 1. Oakland, Calif.: Pan Afrikan Publications, 1995.

Thomas, Gregory A. "E. Franklin Frazier, on Sexual Imitation and the 'Lumpen-Bourgeoisie': The Class Conflict of Erotic Liberation before the African Revolution of Fanon." Department of Rhetoric, University of California at Berkeley, 1997. Typescript.

———. "Emancipatory Perversions, or The Sex of Slaves." Department of Rhetoric, University of California at Berkeley, 1995. Typescript.

———. "Jamaica Kincaid and the Painful Production of Pleasure, or Reading *Annie John* as a Writing out of 'Zami.' " Department of Rhetoric, University of California at Berkeley, 1995. Typescript.

———. "Re-Reading Frantz Fanon and E. Franklin Frazier: On the Erotic Politics of Racist Assimilation by Class," *Présence Africaine* 159 (1999).

Toumson, Roger, and Héliane Toumson. "Pluie et vent sur Télumée Miracle." *Textes, études, et documents*, 15. Fort-de-France: Éditions Caribéennes, 1979.

Walker, Alice. *Horses Make a Landscape Look More Beautiful*. San Diego: Harcourt Brace Jovanovich, 1984.

Wall, Cheryl A. *Zora Neale Hurston: Folklore, Memoirs and Other Writings.* New York: Library of America, 1995.

Wallace, Karen Smyley. "Créolité and the Feminine Text in Simone Schwarz-Bart." *French Review* 70, no. 4 (March 1997): 554–61.

Walters, Wendy. "One of Dese Mornings, Bright and Fair, / Take My Wings and Cleave De Air: The Legend of the Flying Africans and Diasporic Consciousness." *Mellus* 22, no. 3 (fall 1997): 3–27.

Warner, Keith Q. *Critical Perspectives on Léon-Gontran Damas.* Washington, D.C.: Three Continents Press, 1988.

Wilson, Anna. "Lorde and the African American Tradition: When the Family Is Not Enough." In *New Lesbian Criticism: Literary and Cultural Readings,* edited by Sally Munt, 80–82. New York: Harvester, 1992.

Wilson, Elizabeth Betty. "History and Memory in *Un plat de porc aux bananes vertes* and *Pluie et vent sur Télumée Miracle,*" *Callaloo* 15, no. 1 (1992): 179–89.

———. "Le voyage et l'espace clos—Island and Journey as Metaphor: Aspects of Woman's Experience in the Works of Francophone Caribbean Women Novelists." In *Out of the Kumbla: Caribbean Women and Literature,* edited by Carole Boyce Davies and Elaine Savory Fido, 45–57. Trenton, N.J.: Africa World Press, 1990.

Woodson, Carter G. *The Mis-Education of the Negro,* Trenton, N.J.: Africa World Press, 1990.

Wynter, Sylvia. "Beyond Miranda's Meanings: Un/silencing the 'Demonic Ground' of Caliban's 'Woman.'" In *Out of the Kumbla: Caribbean Women and Literature,* edited by Carole Boyce Davies and Elaine Savory Fido, 355–72. Trenton, N.J.: Africa World Press, 1990.

———. "Beyond the Word of Man: Glissant and the New Discourse of the Antilles." In *World Literature Today,* 637–47. Norman: University of Oklahoma Press, 1987.

Zahar, Renate. *Frantz Fanon: Colonialism and Alienation.* Translated by Willfried F. Feuser. New York: Monthly Review Press, 1974.

Zimra, Clarisse. "Négritude in the Feminine Mode: The Case of Martinique and Guadeloupe." *Journal of Ethnic Studies* 12, no. 1 (spring 1984): 53–77.

———. "Righting the Calabash: Writing History in the Female Francophone Narrative." In *Out of the Kumbla: Caribbean Women and Literature,* edited by Carole Boyce Davies and Elaine Savory Fido, 143–59. Trenton, N.J.: Africa World Press, 1990.

———. "What's in a Name: Elective Genealogy in Schwarz-Bart's Early Novels." *Studies in 20th Century Literature* 17, no. 1 (winter 1993): 97–118.

Zobel, Joseph. *La Rue Cases-Nègres.* Paris: Présence Africaine, 1974.

Index

Hierarchy, social, 65, 69, 96, 185, 204
Hybridity. *See* Authenticity

Identity politics, 71
Imperialism, 7, 54, 57, 72, 161, 203; critique of, 4, 93–95, 183; cultural, 43, 71, 152, 215 n.3
Individualism, 19, 135, 159, 168–174, 177, 207; culture of, 159; rights, 169; Western, 159
Indo-European languages, 35, 40
Instinct, 122–123; intuition, 189. *See also* Nature
Intellectuals: Black, 24–25, 39, 203; elite, 38; European, 4; native, 132

Kincaid, Jamaica: biographical information, 76–77

Lesbianism, 172–175; Black, 174–175; identity, 172–173, 176; white, 170, 173, 207
Liberation, 23, 149, 155, 204
Life force, 11, 28–30, 34, 37, 178, 208. *See also* African symbolic systems
Literacy: cultural, 71; diaspora, 82, 88, 132, 208–209, 219 n.10, 222 n.12; Western, 82. *See also* Orality
Literary theory: the Enlightenment, 40, 204; literary marronage, 212 n.5; social realism, 24; surrealism, 23

Maroon, 131
Marriage, 149, 170
Marxism, 24; contexts, 23; political theory, 24, 32, 56; Third World, 24, 41. *See also* Communist Party
Masculinity, Caribbean male, 61, 81
Matriarchy, 67–70; matrilineal societies, 27, 175
Migration, 79, 87, 100, 114; Black, 152; emigration, 87–88; immigration, 93
Mimicry, 155; cultural, 2, 84–85,

96, 102, 204; double consciousness, 177
Miseducation, 88, 109, 177, 203; British, 137; French, 27, 149
Mulatto, 125–126
Mystery systems: Dogon, 14–15; Kemetic, 14. *See also* African symbolic systems

Narrative, 4, 79, 110, 136, 147; strategy, 81, 108, 136; voice, 80–84, 179
Nation building, 36; culture building, 106; national culture, 55; postcolonial nation state, 38, 54
Nation language, 72, 85, 95, 100. *See also* Creole
Nature. *See* Instinct
Nègre, 22, 31, 124, 126, 211 n.2; negresse, 144
Negritude, 11, 16, 17, 19, 21–31, 41, 43, 56, 61, 70–71, 74–76, 92, 99, 110–112, 177, 204; critique of, 21, 30–31, 33, 203; definition, 18, 31; origins, 212 n.7; philosophy, 18, 28, 30, 104. *See also* Postnegritude

Obeah, 101, 139
Old World languages. *See* African languages
Oppression, history of, 110
Orality, 84, 130, 155; oral consciousness, 100; oral culture, 91, 115; oral traditions, 2, 131, 205. *See also* Literacy
Origin stories, 4, 9; Western civilization, 66–68
Orisha, 160, 181, 186; Papa Legba, 192–194, 209

Palestine, 152
Pan-Africanism, 7–8, 38, 55, 70, 159; transnational identity, 99, 112
Patriarchy, 66; patriarchal institutions, 56, 68

Index

CATHERINE A. JOHN is Assistant Professor of
African Diaspora Literature in the Department of English
at the University of Oklahoma.